1848 – A European Revolution

Also by Axel Körner

DAS LIED VON EINER ANDEREN WELT: Kulturelle Praxis im französischen und deutschen Arbeitermilieu 1840–90

URBANE ELITEN UND KULTURELLER WANDEL (*with C. Gerbel et al.*)

1848 – A European Revolution?

International Ideas and National Memories of 1848

Edited by

Axel Körner
Lecturer in Modern European History
University College London

First published in hardcover 2000

First published in paperback 2004 by
PALGRAVE MACMILLAN
Houndmills, Basingstoke, Hampshire RG21 6XS and
175 Fifth Avenue, New York, N. Y. 10010
Companies and representatives throughout the world

PALGRAVE MACMILLAN is the global academic imprint of the Palgrave
Macmillan division of St. Martin's Press, LLC and of Palgrave Macmillan Ltd.
Macmillan® is a registered trademark in the United States, United Kingdom
and other countries. Palgrave is a registered trademark in the European
Union and other countries.

ISBN 0–333–74929–4 hardback (*outside North America*)
ISBN 0–312–22614–4 hardback (*in North America*)
ISBN 1–4039–2034–6 paperback (*worldwide*)

This book is printed on paper suitable for recycling and made from fully
managed and sustained forest sources.

A catalogue record for this book is available from the British Library.

Library of Congress Cataloging-in-Publication Data
1848, a European Revolution? : international ideas and national memories
   of 1848 / edited by Axel Körner.
      p. cm.
   Originally published: Macmillan, 2000.
   Includes bibliographical references and index.
   ISBN 1–4039–2034–6 (pbk.)
      1. Europe—History—1848–1849. 2. Revolutions—Europe—History–
   –19th century. I. Körner, Axel, 1967–

   D387.A14 2003
   940.2'85—dc21

                                                         2003056408

10   9   8   7   6   5   4   3   2   1
13 12 11 10 09 08 07 06 05 04

Printed and bound in Great Britain by
Antony Rowe Ltd, Chippenham and Eastbourne

To Reinhart Koselleck on his 80th birthday

Contents

Preface to Paperback Edition

The 150th anniversary of 1848 has provoked a new interest in the mid-nineteenth century revolutions, at least if one takes into account the number of recent publications on the topic, the success of exhibitions, the press coverage during the months of the anniversary, or the titles and contents of recently established University courses. The first edition of this book appeared two years after the anniversary in a hardcover edition with Macmillan. The second edition in paperback intends to respond to the increased interest in 1848, making the book available to a wider readership, in particular to students.

Apart from minor alterations the present edition is identical to the first. The authors of this book come from a variety of national backgrounds and historiographical experiences, allowing them to introduce readers to a range of recent debates on 1848, with special focus on the revolutions' European dimension and on the commemorations of 1848 during the past 150 years. Since the first edition went to press a number of new works have appeared which approach 1848 in a similar perspective. In the introduction I refer to a seminal collection of essays on 1848 edited in German by the historians Dowe, Haupt and Langewiesche. This work has now appeared in an English translation, *Europe in 1848. Revolution and Reform* (Oxford/New York: Berghahn, 2001.) Robert Evans and Hartmut Pogge von Strandmann edited a useful anthology of short monographic chapters on different 'national cases' of 1848, also containing an essay on '1848 is collective European memory', *The Revolutions in Europe, 1848–9. From Reform to Reaction* (Oxford University Press, 2000). Both works include chapters on Britain. Charlotte Tacke edited a collection on commemorations of 1848 in different parts of Europe, *1848. Memory and Oblivion in Europe* (Brussels: Peter Lang, 2000). An important collection of conference papers looks at 1848 in Central Europe, *Kromerizsky snem 1848–1849 a tradice parlamentarismu ve stredni Evrope* (Kromeriz, 1998). One of the contributors to the present anthology,

Sabine Freitag, has edited a book on refugees who after the revolutions of 1848 fled to England, *Exiles from European Revolutions. Refugees in Mid-Victorian England* (Oxford/New York: Berghahn, 2003). Another contributor to this volume, Simonetta Soldani, together with Heinz-Gerhard Haupt, has edited a special issue of *Passato e Presente* on *1848. Scene da una rivoluzione europea* (No. 46, January–April 1999) with numerous bibliographic references. Concerning the German revolution I would like to point to Brian Vick, *Defining Germany: The 1848 Frankfurt Parliamentarians and National Identity* (Harvard University Press, 2002).

Although some historians still look at 1848 within a framework of national history, this selection of recent publications suggests that during the past five or six years the revolutions' European dimension has become a major focus of research. Likewise, historians ask questions about the revolutions' commemorations, about representations and perceptions of 1848, about subjectivity in relation to the structure of events. Other possible approaches to 1848 – comparing revolutions of different periods or analysing the place of 1848 in revolutionary theory – have not been explored further. (An exception is probably the collection edited by Peter Wende, *Große Revolutionen der Geschichte* (Munich: Beck, 2000) or I. Götz von Olenhusen's anthology referred to in Chapter 10.) The conjuncture of certain trends in historiography seems to confirm once more Benedetto Croce's dictum that 'all history is contemporary'; that our questions about the past are shaped by preoccupations of the present. The historian might regret such 'fashions' within the discipline, but at a time when the humanities and social sciences are under permanent pressure to justify their existence the contemporary importance of historical investigation provides the historian with a perfect *raison d'être*. For different reasons, in many parts of Europe 1848 is still important to the present, even if — or probably because – the focus of historical research has changed over time.

The editor of this volume regrets that one of his authors, Professor Jan Havranek, died before the publication of this second edition. It is certainly a complement to Professor Havránek that one of my students, of Czech origin, complained after reading his chapter that 'the story we learned at school went completely different'.

London and Brussels, May 2003

Acknowledgements

The idea of this book developed out of discussions with friends and colleagues about the changing meanings of 1848 on the occasion of the 150 years celebrations of the revolution. In February 1998, the Centre for European Research at University College London and the German Historical Institute, London invited historians from different parts of Europe to reassess the European dimension in the ideas of 1848 and to analyse the commemorations of the revolution in various periods of European history. The organization of this conference was possible thanks to generous financial contributions from the German History Society, the Royal Historical Society and the History Department of UCL.

I am indebted to all those who contributed with their knowledge, ideas and papers to the conference and to this book.

For the organization of the conference I wish to acknowledge the help and support of Mary Fulbrook and Sue Jones (Centre for European Research and German History Society), Peter Wende and Sabine Freitag (German Historical Institute, London), Kathy Burk (Royal Historical Society), and David French and Rachel Aucott (Department of History at UCL). Many thanks to the Faculty of Arts and Humanities and the History Department at UCL for its financial contribution to the publication of this book.

I owe an enormous debt of gratitude to Sabine Freitag and Rebecca Spang for the ideas and their critical comments on the conceptual outline of the project and on the introduction to this book. I wish to offer special thanks to Nazneen Razwi and Simon Renton for their help and support during the long process of writing and editing, and to Katie Joice for correcting the English of so many non-native speakers. I am grateful to Martin Swales for encouraging me over a long period of planning, to Martin Daunton, Rick Halpern, Bernhard Rieger and Charlotte Tacke for good ideas, to Jaroslava Kubisova, Diana Gibbins, Helen Matthews and Claire Smith for their organizational assistance, to Aruna Vasudevan for not losing her interest in the book, and to Paola, bella compagna, for being so patient with my passion for 1848.

The chapters by Gabriella Hauch, Reinhart Koselleck, Jan Merk and Simonetta Soldani have been translated by Aileen Derieg, Johannes Haubold, Anita Zelasny and Lesley Leicester Barrett.

London and Brussels, December 1998

Notes on the Contributors

John Breuilly is Professor of Modern History at the University of Birmingham. Previous publications include *Nationalism and the State* (2nd edn, Manchester and Chicago, 1993), *Labour and Liberalism in Nineteenth Century Europe: Essays in Comparative History* (Manchester, 1992) and *The Formation of the First German Nation-State* (London, 1996). His current research interests are a comparative cultural history of bourgeois elites in mid-nineteenth-century Hamburg, Lyon and Manchester and a study of the modernization of German lands in the nineteenth century.

Sabine Freitag is a Research Fellow at the University of Cologne and worked previously for the German Historical Institute in London. She is author of *Friedrich Hecker. Biographie eines Republikaners* (Stuttgart: Steiner Verlag, 1998) and the editor of *Die Achtundvierziger. Lebensbilder aus der deutschen Revolution von 1848/49* (Munich: Beck, 1998). She is co-editor of a multi-volume series, *British Envoys to Germany, 1816–1866*, published by Cambridge University Press, and of *Mord und andere Kleinigkeiten. Ungewöhnliche Kriminalfälle aus sechs Jahrhunderten* (Munich: Beck 2001). Currently she is working on a history of criminal law, culture and policy in England, 1877–1930.

Gabriella Hauch is Professor at the Ludwig Boltzmann Institut für Gesellschafts- und Kulturgeschichte in Linz and President of the International Labour History Conference. Previously she taught History, Women and Gender Studies at the Universities of Linz, Innsbruck and Vienna. She is author of *Frau Biedermeier auf den Barrikaden. Frauenleben in der Wiener Revolution 1848* (1990) and *Vom Frauenstandpunkt aus Frauen im Parlament 1919–1933* (1995). Currently she is working on political elites in Austria and on perspectives for a new political history.

Jan Havránek was Professor Emeritus of Modern Czechoslovak History at the Charles University, Prague. His publications included textbooks on modern Czechoslovak history, works on the use of statistical methods in history and studies on the modern history of Central Europe. He was co-author of *A History of Charles University 1802–1990* (Prague, 2001). He died in September 2003.

Axel Körner is Lecturer in Modern European History at University College London. After studies in Bonn, Berlin and Lyon he wrote a PhD at the European University Institute in Florence. His publications include *Das Lied von einer anderen Welt. Kulturelle Praxis im französischen und deutschen Arbeitermilieu. 1840–1890* (Frankfurt am Main, 1997) and (together with C. Gerbel et al.) *Urbane Eliten und kultureller Wandel. Bologna, Leipzig, Linz und Ljubljana* (Vienna, 1996). He is currently working on a cultural history of Bologna between 1860 and 1920.

Reinhart Koselleck is Professor Emeritus for Theory of History at the University of Bielefeld. He is the author of *Kritik und Krise* (English translation: *Critique and Crisis: Enlightenment and the Pathogenesis of Modern Society*, Cambridge, MA: MIT Press, 1988), *Preußen zwischen Reform und Revolution* (Stuttgart, 1967), *Vergangene Zukunft* (English translation: *Futures Past: On the Semantics of Historical Time*, Cambridge, MA: MIT Press, 1985) and co-editor of *Geschichtliche Grundbegriffe. Historisches Lexikon der politisch-sozialen Sprache in Deutschland* (9 vols). Currently he is working on the political iconography of the violent death.

Jan Merk is Director of the Museum of the Margraviate in Müllheim/Baden. He has been a research assistant at the University of Freiburg and was among the organizers of the 1848 exhibition in Lörrach (FRG), Liestal (Switzerland) and Mulhouse (France). He is co-editor of *Lörrach 1848/49, Essays, Biographien, Dokumente, Projekte* (Lörrach, 1998) and of a special issue of *Allmende* on 1848 (1998). He is currently working on political culture in South Baden during the revolution of 1848/49.

Simonetta Soldani is Professor of Contemporary History at the University of Florence and one of the editors of *Passato e Presente*. She is author of essays on nineteenth- and twentieth-century Italian history and co-edited a special issue of *Passato e Presente* on 1848. She edited *L'educazione delle donne. Scule e modelli di vita feminili nell'Italia dell'Ottocento* (1989) and together with Gabriele Turi *Fare gli Italiani. Storia e cultura nell'Italia contemporanea* (1992).

Rebecca Spang is Lecturer in Modern European History at University College London. She is author of *The Invention of the Restaurant: Paris and Modern Gastronomic Culture* (Harvard University Press, 2000). She is currently interested in money.

Martin Swales is Professor of German at University College London. He is author of *Arthur Schnitzler* (Oxford, 1971), *The German Novelle* (Princeton, NJ, 1977), *The German Bildungstroman* (Princeton, NJ, 1978), *Thomas Mann* (London, 1980) and *Epochenbuch Realismus* (Berlin, 1997). He is currently working on a study of tragedy, drama and opera in nineteenth- and twentieth-century Germany.

Part I
Introduction

1

The European Dimension in the Ideas of 1848 and the Nationalization of Its Memories

Axel Körner

Veit Valentin and the political meanings of 1848/49

In 1931 Veit Valentin concluded his famous history of the German revolution of 1848.[1] Still considered a standard work,[2] it completely changed the historical view of the revolution. Unlike other German historians who looked at 1848 only as a function of the process of German unification, Valentin analysed the making of the revolution within the framework of economic change and social conflict, intellectual critique and the crisis of states. Moving away from the – in Germany – traditionally negative image of barricades and social movements, Valentin viewed the revolution as an early example of democratic mobilization and civil society in Germany.

At the time, the book was understood as an apology for parliamentary government, which during the years of the late Weimar Republic was under permanent attack by anti-democratic forces – the communist party on the left, conservatives and the new national-socialist movement on the right. Politically motivated critique of his work as historian was not new to Valentin. He had been barred from teaching for the first time in 1917. His interpretation of the revolution of 1848 contributed to his reputation as a politically committed historian for which two years later, in June 1933, he was removed from his positions as lecturer and archivist in Berlin and Potsdam. The year 1848 still represented a crucial point of historical and political debate. Being forced to leave Nazi Germany, Valentin accepted an invitation to teach German history at University College London[3] where he published the English translation of his *1848. Chapters of German History*.

Apart from his focus on political and social mobilization, Valentin also tried to understand how the ideas of the revolutionary movement of 1848 changed throughout the revolutionary experience. In particular, he was interested in the relationship between the internationalist ideals of the revolutionary movement and its nationalist claims – one of the crucial questions of 1848. In the conclusion to his history of 1848 he describes how nationalism, through the political development of the revolution, overshadowed the initial internationalist idealism: 'The popular movement of 1848 . . . ended with the conviction that nationalism and internationalism are contrary poles.'[4]

The review of Valentin's work as historian draws our attention to two aspects. First, Valentin's biography exemplifies the political meaning of histories and memories of 1848 during the late Kaiserreich, the Weimar Republic and the rise of Nazi Germany. Second, Valentin emphasizes the relationship between the changing concept of nationality as part of the experience of 1848 and the internationalist ideals of the revolutionary movement. Changing political meanings of 1848, illustrated through its commemorations, and the dichotomy between nationalist claims and internationalist ideals were at the centre of a conference organized at University College London in February 1998, sixty-five years after Valentin had been invited to this institute.

This introduction explains how these two aspects – the political meaning of the commemorations and the dichotomy between nationalist claims and internationalist ideals – are related to each other. The view on Valentin's work at the beginning served to draw the attention to these aspects which have been neglected by most historians of 1848. The second point of this introduction illustrates how commemorations of 1848 became *national* commemorations. A third point looks at 1848 from a macro-perspective, relating various national cases of revolution to each other and looking for common features. The fourth point shows that 1848 was seen at the time as a European rather than a national event, and that despite nationalist claims Europe was an important reference-point in revolutionary discourse. The last point looks at the construction of histories and memories of 1848 in a national context which constituted the backbone of its commemorations. The sections of this introduction correspond to the organization of the book which concludes with Reinhart Koselleck's question: how European was the revolution of 1848/49?

Histories, memories and commemorations of the revolution of 1848

Historians analyse 1848 most of the time within a national context. Little attention is paid to the fact that 1848 took place in many different regions and countries of Europe. Even many comparative histories of 1848 only look at the major places of the revolution – Paris, Berlin, Vienna. One reason for this tendency is that the national question constituted a major element of most revolutions of 1848. However, another reason is that commemorations of 1848 concentrated on the place of 1848 within the political history of nation-states.

It is difficult to draw a clear line between the revolutionary activities of the years 1848/49 and the beginning of their commemorations: obsequies for Robert Blum in Germany or celebrations for the victims of the June barricades in Paris were late signs of revolutionary activity, but they also constituted the first commemorations of past events which in turn formed the content of the collective memory of 1848 within specific social or political milieus.[5] When analysing the ideas behind revolutionary events and the commemorations of the revolution we note that through the process of commemoration a European revolution was transformed into many national revolutions.

As Veit Valentin wrote, 1848 marks a watershed: the point when nationalism and internationalism became 'contrary poles'.[6] Various chapters of this book look at the international dimension of the ideas of 1848: the revolutions were seen at the time as a European event, the overthrow of a European order through a European revolution, a European 'springtime of peoples'. However, within the history of its commemorations 1848 developed more and more into a 'national' event. Independent from the question of whether 1848 was seen as a positive or a negative episode within the 'national' history of a country, historical interpretations of the revolution have traditionally favoured a national focus, analysing the revolution as part of the political, social and cultural making of nation-states.[7] In academic historiography as well as in the collective memories of various social groups 1848 has served to legitimize or to delegitimize different political approaches to questions of 'national' significance. Political and social movements often referred to 1848 within the context of national debates; the memory of 1848 developed into a question of national politics.

This process of nationalization has had its impact on the content of historical commemorations. Maurice Halbwachs has explained how present concerns shape the collective memory of the past.[8] Hence, the national approach to 1848 is understandable for a period of European history characterized by the formation of nation-states. National historiography integrated the social, cultural, economic and political development of European societies into a framework of national categories. Within this process also the memories of 1848 became national memories, even if they were divided by political, social and regional cleavages, formed by different experiences of the revolution.[9] In 1898 Italian moderates and republicans had two separate marches for the commemorations;[10] however, the topic of commemoration was still the Italian Risorgimento. The famous Badensian Cradle Song represents a regional tradition of commemoration, but in the song the father was killed during the civil war for the German constitution.[11] In most commemorations we find very few references to the international or European dimension of the revolution. Only the socialist tradition kept to a certain extent an international view of the history of European revolutions, exemplified in the celebrations of 18 March which commemorated simultaneously the victims of 1848 and the victims of the Commune.[12]

If through its commemorations 1848 became an event of national rather than European history, historians interested in the relationship between history and memory should reconsider 1848 from the perspective of this national–international bipolarism, and analyse both the international consciousness expressed in the ideas of 1848 and the process of nationalization within the commemorations. National movements existed well before 1848, but in these early concepts nationalism and internationalism were not yet the 'contrary poles' which Valentin describes. The experiences of 1848 created this polarity and thus explain the nationalization of its commemorations. To analyse this relationship between international ideas and national commemorations – not on a strongly comparative basis but from a European point of view – is the aim of this book.[13]

A macro perspective on 1848

Three chapters of this book discuss common features, connections and comparable aspects of the revolutions in 1848. The aim of this part of the book is to reconnect disparate events, to compare the causes, development and outcome of major sites of revolution, and to point out some general aspects of the 1848 experience which previous works have neglected. The book does not provide a complete or monographic overview on 1848, but bibliographic references point to more detailed works on the topic and introduce the Anglo-American reader to some results of recent research published in French, Italian, Czech and German.[14]

Marx understood the revolutions of 1848 as being closely connected. Theory-led approaches, based on a defined model of explanation, are an invitation for comparison and for a European, transnational perspective on the history of 1848. Seminal works such as those by Jonathan Sperber and Roger Price have explained 1848 by comparing social conflict and periods of crisis before and during the European revolutions.[15] Peter N. Stearns, who claims that 'each revolution must be assessed in its own context', notes that the revolutions 'interacted to a limited extent'.[16] Below John Breuilly claims that the revolutions of 1848 are comparable and connected, but that after the opening stages constitutional and political debate led to the nationalization of a once European framework. Differences as similarities between the European revolutions of 1848 invite comparison from the historian's point of view and contribute to our understanding of change over time in European societies.

Is it possible to speak of 'connected events'? Despite the overwhelmingly national focus of most histories of 1848, some works do draw attention to the aforementioned 'interactions'. Even historians of Italy explain the overthrow of the old order in a European context,[17] and this despite the fact that here commotion was evident since 1846, the beginning of the Pius IX papacy, and thus long before the outbreak of the revolution in the rest of the continent.

Similarly in Poland uprisings started in 1846. However, Norman Davies described the Polish 1848 as the 'Springtime of Other Nations':[18] Poland was not yet in a position to constitute itself as a revolutionary nation. In diplomatic terms the events in France played a central role within the revolutionary landscape of Europe: all over the continent people feared or hoped for French intervention. If with regard to Lamartine's foreign policy this turned out to be much less important than previously expected, the emphasis of revolutionary discourse on French events deserves historical interest for different reasons. First, the experiences of 1789 and 1830 played a symbolic role in the European conception of revolution. In consequence, the Paris February Revolution of 1848 appeared a key event in the further European development. Moreover, most revolutionary movements, especially in the European periphery, maintained close links with exiled communities in Paris, and some of them were more strongly represented in the French capital than at home.[19] Third, an examination of Italian or German revolutionary language illustrates their dependence on French concepts and the frequent translation of French 'keywords' into other European languages.[20] In Romanian the word 'burhghez' appears for the first time: a translation of the French 'bourgeois'.[21] In order to study the language of the French Revolution Robert Blum, member of the Frankfurt parliament, asked his wife for several volumes of Lamartine's *Histoire des Girondins*.[22]

Contemporary revolutionary discourse does not only reveal connections with events in France. Some historians emphasize the role of events in Eastern, South-Eastern and Central Europe for developments during the years 1848/49.[23] With regard to the German revolution of 1848, and more specifically the radical movement in the German South-West, one should not underestimate the impact of the constitutional battles in Switzerland:[24] 'Im Hochland fiel der erste Schuß' recalls one of the famous songs of the revolution by Ferdinand Freiligrath. Jacques Godechot pays considerable attention to the catalysing effect of the Italian revolution,[25] and indeed most of the Italian states had granted liberal constitutions to the restless masses before the revolution in Vienna had even started.[26] It is impossible not to see the destabilizing effect that the Italian revolutions had on the Habsburg Empire, or not to view the events in Vienna as part of the revolution in the rest of the German Federation.

There are further connections to be underlined. Economic developments show interaction between the European capitals during the outbreak of the revolution: the February events in Paris caused all European stock markets to crash,[27] and later in the year rumours of Lamartine's resignation provoked similar economic disruption. Many historians draw attention to practices of revolution held in common, especially the building of barricades and the symbolic use of the colour red,[28] and speak of a 'European model' of revolution:[29] revolutionaries in Vienna and Berlin learned from their fellows in Paris. With the radicalization of events in other parts of Europe, red became the colour of all revolutionary movements, and after 1848, the symbol for workers' movements throughout Europe and beyond. In the words of the revolutionary song writer Jean-Baptiste Clément 1848 was remembered as 'le temps de cerises'.[30] Europe appeared to have become a common space of communication and revolutionary activity. The public sphere was enlarged through the participation of the lower classes, in some cases including the rural population. Revolutionary demands were more or less the same all over the continent: democratization and a parliamentary system; in the most backward regions 1848 meant the end of feudalism. Political debates about how to realize these claims took very similar forms: conflicts between constitutional monarchy and republican rule, between liberals and radicals. In contrast to 1793, not the Guillotine, but the desire for constitutional order governed the revolutionary regimes.[31]

In the accounts of contemporary observers the revolution is almost always described as a failure, even in such differing interpretations as those of Marx[32] and de Tocqueville.[33] The basis for most evaluations of 1848 is the idea that history is a teleological process. Hence, historians try to find out if 1848 represented a step forward or a step backward on some defined path of progress. Evaluations of 1848 during the second half of the twentieth century differ from those of Marx or de Tocqueville. The comparative frameworks of social historians contributed to these new critiques. In pointing out similarities between the revolutions in Germany and France, Wolfgang Mommsen has presented an argument which challenges the theory of a German 'Sonderweg' originating in 1848[34] – also putting in doubt A. J. P. Taylor's famous interpretation of 1848 as the crucial point in history when Germany failed to turn. Merriman concludes his study of the revolution in France with the statement that 'France was not ready for a republic',[35] a view which complements interpretations of German history and thus again challenges the theory of a German 'Sonderweg'. Most of the more recent accounts, and especially the commemorations in 1998, view 1848 in a positive light, interpreting the events of 1848 as a watershed in the process of politicization and development of a bourgeois public sphere: 1848 was an 'apprentissage' (Agulhon) for later political formations,[36] not only in France, but on a European level.[37]

(When historians, social scientists or social and political 'communities of commemoration' evaluate 1848 as a positive or a negative development they are viewing the events from their specific political standpoint.) However, the politics of 1848 were not only about constitutional and national claims. Gabriella Hauch, in her contribution to this book, analyses gender conflicts during the revolution.[38] While the public image of gender was modelled and restrengthened through the revolutionary and especially the parliamentary experience, 1848 also challenged – within a limited space and for a short period of time – traditional gender relations and provoked temporary progress in the emancipation of women. In the aftermath of the revolution women benefited from a transfer of ideas and experience. However, 1848 did not have a profound and long-lasting effect on gender relations. The women's movement, at the end of the nineteenth century, did not recognize significant improvements regarding their political programme. The example demonstrates the difficulty of measuring the success or failure of the revolution with respect to historical 'spaces of experience' and 'horizons of expectation' (Koselleck).[39] While we are well informed about the part which 1848 played within the careers of politicians of the time,[40] and while we have vast documentation at our disposal regarding the role of 1848 within the history of national movements in various regions of Europe, it seems more difficult to assess historical experiences of 1848 on a broader basis, in other words to make evaluations which go beyond the narrow definitions of political and constitutional progress. Contemporaries often did not share historians' and politicians' criteria of success. Martin Swales' contribution to this book reveals, through a broad survey of contemporary European literature, uncertainty and uneasiness about the significance of 1848, a sentiment which was not invented by later generations of historians. People in the aftermath of the revolution were unsure what 1848 meant: did it portend change or stagnation?[41]

If the outcome of the revolution remained uncertain, people never-theless understood the outbreak of the revolution as spelling the end of the old order, 'der Höllensturz der alten Welt'.[42] This is true for Europe as a whole. Even those countries which did not have a revolution themselves were involved in the events. It was the revolutionary tide in Europe which bestowed upon the Netherlands a constitution still in use, and constitutional reform in Sweden, as in Belgium, aimed to prevent the Revolution from overflowing from the rest of the continent.[43] Although Russia was not directly affected, its army – in the role of the revolution's gravedigger – was one of the main actors of the revolution, and 1848 is described traditionally as a key event in Russian history.[44] While in Spain the 1840s are described as a period of political instability, the years of the revolution in Europe saw the dictatorship of Narváez, who was able to prevent major insurrections.[45] Nevertheless, 1849 was the year of the foundation of the Partido Demócrata whose programme reflected the European revolutionary experience. Thus, 1848 affected the whole of the continent: the causes, developments and effects of the various revolutions can be seen to a large extent as connected events. Moreover, as Reinhart Koselleck reminds us in the conclusion of this book, 1848 was the last revolution which could not be attributed to the consequence of a defeat in a war between countries.[46] Never before or since 1848 has Europe witnessed a situation in which at almost the same time, all over the continent, an established political regime was overthrown and temporarily replaced by a new order.

The European dimension within the revolutions of 1848

As the comparative approaches of social historians again reveal, it was not only by chance that the events which caused the old order to fall occurred all over the continent at the same time. Eric Hobsbawm sees the 'first and last European revolution' as the 'culmination and logical product of the era of dual revolution' and the 'expected and predicted' consequence of an economic process which in its social and political significance concerned Europe as a whole.[47] Based on a very different theoretical framework, Lewis Namier sees 1848 as the 'the revolution of the intellectuals'. He admits differences within the political, social, and economic developments of Europe, but claims with reference to Lamartine's *Histoire de la révolution* that there was a common 'ideological, and even literary' denominator: 1848 was 'the product of a moral idea, of reason, logic, sentiment, and of a desire . . . for a better order in government and society'.[48] The economic causes of 1848 have been analysed in the works of social historians cited above, but the pan-European ideas of the revolutions of 1848 still need to be considered in more detail. If Mazzini's 'Young Europe' and various other European associations were not responsible for 1848 from an organizational point of view, intellectuals all over the continent were, nevertheless, engaged in the creation and communication of ideas and debates responsible for the radical change.

In 1998 some commentators on 1848 draw attention to 'a European vision' – viewing the revolution as a first attempt to create a European federation.[49] Within the political context of its 150th anniversary, historical commemorations of 1848 are part of a process of legitimizing the process of European integration. Today not only politicians, but also historians emphasize the concepts of Europe during the revolution. Simonetta Soldani interprets the Italian 1848 as a 'rapprochement to Europe'.[50] Hartmut Kaelble sees 1848 as the key element in a history of Europe which culminates not any longer in the nation-state but in the unification of Europe.[51] Wolfgang Mommsen re-evaluates the 'European vision' of 1848, recognizing within revolutionary ideas an anticipation of Woodrow Wilson's programme and later concepts of European integration. He draws the attention to the fact that Mazzini saw his 'Europe of free peoples' as a federation of nation-states.[52] Nevertheless, as Koselleck explains in the conclusion of this book, the idea of Europe was used as a reference point during liberation from oppressive regimes, but was not the cause of the revolution.

The national question constituted a key element of the revolution. At a glance this might appear to contradict ideals and dreams compressed into the word 'Europe'. If the concept of 'nation' did not yet exclude ethnic and linguistic plurality,[53] there was, however, already a debate in progress about the dangers of nationalism and patriotism for a humanist understanding of the world. 'The nationality of the free nation is humanity,' stated Arnold Ruge, Hegelian journalist, member of the Frankfurt parliament and along with Ledru-Rollin and Mazzini one of the founding members of the 'European democratic committee'.[54] 'Freedom has no nationality', Ruge continued.

Only a 'political people' – a people constituted in political terms as opposed to ethnic definitions – is free to act; only a people which is liberated from despotism and princely rule represents a value in itself. Who belongs to a prince is a slave everywhere. On this basis Ruge spoke in favour of the 'principe humanitaire' and against 'patriotism, nationally motivated hatred, and the primitive instincts of the peoples'.[55] The chapters by Jan Havránek, Jan Merk and Sabine Freitag in this volume demonstrate that there was indeed a debate about the 'national' as opposed to the 'universalist' character of revolutionary change. Contrary to Ruge's 'principe humanitaire' quoted above, authoritarian concepts of change, like the Prussian reforms and Bismarck's German unification, were based precisely on the principle of 'national character'. 'Reform' or 'revolution from above' constituted the contrary pole to the universalism of civil and human rights proclaimed since the enlightenment and the French Revolution.[56]

In 1844, when Ruge wrote his work against patriotism, European intellectuals imagined that one day European peoples would unite in a struggle for liberation against despotic princely rule. Only during the years 1848/49 did the debate about 'national' versus 'universalist' concepts of freedom become a matter of concrete politics. Particularly in the Habsburg monarchy, 1848 represents the birth of conflict between various nationalities. Different concepts of how to deal with the national question were discussed. One concept was the idea of an Austrian nation, respecting ethnic and linguistic plurality, and accepting the Emperor as supranational authority; the administration of the state and the dominant culture would remain German. In this way, for example, the political programme of 'United Slovenia' (Zedinjena Slovenija) claimed the unification of all Slovenians as an autonomous entity under the flag of Habsburg. Another concept was based on the idea of a German nation-state: Austria would lose Hungary, the Italian territories, Galicia and Dalmatia, but at the same time maintain the German primacy over Czechs and Slovenians.[57] It was not only the German element that was perceived as a danger for national minorities: after experiencing the linguistic nationalism within the Hungarian assembly the national minorities within the Hungarian territory were intimidated by the idea of a Hungarian nation and preferred the idea of a multi-ethnic Empire.[58] Jan Havránek's contribution to this volume illustrates the complexity of the national question in the 1848 Habsburg Empire, and analyses the concept of Bohemian patriotism as a movement against both Czech and German nationalism.[59]

The question of national borders and of who would belong to the new German nation-state destroyed much of the initial idealism in the Frankfurt parliament.[60] Power became an essential component of the concept of nation and led to worrying aggression in the debate.[61] As illustrated by the parliament's claims on the Dutch province of Limburg, even international law was considered secondary with regard to questions of 'national' interest. The year 1848 also signified the end of formerly widespread German sympathy for the Polish national movement, which had also desperately hoped for a revolutionary *coup de main* from France. Speakers from all political strands in the Frankfurt parliament sustained the idea of sworn enmity between Poles and Germans, rejecting the little support that there was for an independent Poland as 'cosmopolitan idealism'.[62] As Veit Valentin writes, 'this national feeling swamped everything, it turned against Denmark, against Poland and Russia ... it collected patriotic ideas and masses together as a barrier against violently revolutionary, socialistically minded republicanism.'[63] If, in the context of the 150th anniversary, politically motivated analyses of 1848 tend to stress the 'European vision' of the revolution they also tend to forget the national aggression in the debate.

Despite the conflicts regarding the national question contemporaries understood the revolution as a European event and some of them maintained their internationalist ideals. Marx and Engels, from June 1848 onwards, reported regularly on European revolutionary events in the *Neue Rheinische Zeitung*.[64] John Merriman has described the consistent format of political newspapers during the Second Republic in France, always including a column of international news with brief dispatches from the European capital cities; even provincial papers reported international news which they usually culled from the larger Parisian papers.[65] The papers criticized policy towards exiled revolutionaries ('Kossuth chased from France', *Le Peuple*, Marseille) and attacked the government for 'selling out the nation's honour' by sending troops to Rome (*La Civilisation*, Toulouse).[66] A workers' newspaper from Frankfurt, in a report on recent events across the Rhine, described France as the 'great and noble people of brothers', 'the foundation for the European peoples' freedom'.[67] The same paper demanded Polish independence and opposed the decision to allow German deputies from Poland to the parliament in Frankfurt: 'In the streets of Paris, Vienna and Berlin Poles have fought for the freedom of Europe, they fought for our freedom and gave their blood.'[68] In Vienna, democratic papers followed the line of Marx's *Neue Rheinische Zeitung* and took the June riots in Paris as occasion to underline their solidarity with the French workers, whereas the liberal press welcomed Cavaignac's decisive action, protecting the whole of Europe from similar horrors.[69] The radical poet Alfred Meißner saw in the June events a battle which would soon overrun the whole continent.[70]

'One idea flashes through Europe. The old system shakes and falls into pieces.' In these words a popular assembly in Mannheim, as early as February 1848, described what everyone saw happening.[71] The tone is the same as in Marx's *Communist Manifesto*, published in London at the very same time. We find similar metaphors in French revolutionary songs from 1848, analysed by the author of this introduction in his contribution to this book. De Tocqueville, some months earlier, had warned Guizot that 'we are sleeping on a volcano'; Richard Wagner picked up this metaphor and recognized the revolution to be a European event: 'Europe appears to us as a huge volcano . . . Yes, we notice that the old world falls into pieces and a new one emerges, because the sublime Goddess of revolution rages on the wings of the storms.'[72] Wagner published his essay in 1849, when much of the initial European idealism had already passed. Nevertheless, the revolution remains a European event. The chapters by Sabine Freitag, Jan Havránek, Axel Körner and Jan Merk in this book illustrate the various concepts of nationalism, internationalism and republicanism which have been discussed: 'Nationality separates, liberty unites!', 'Liberty is the sun, nationality nothing but a lantern!' Even as late as in January 1851, the police commissioner of Toulouse reported montagnard activities in a 'red coffee-house' called 'The European'.[73] The view of 1848 as a European event still appears in the memory of the so-called 'Eighteen-forty-eighters', who from their exile in the United States or Switzerland reflected on their experiences and about the possible outcomes of the revolution.[74]

Not only the historical actors of the revolution but also their opponents and outside observers recognized 1848 to be a European event.[75] Although the political language of the Chartists refers to Britain's own radical tradition since the seventeenth century,[76] the political establishment and the government saw the Chartist movement in close relationship to the events in Paris and Berlin. Palmerston's 'Waterloo of peace and order' on 10 April was conceived as an intervention against a threefold menace: against revolutionary Paris, against the uprising in Ireland and against the rebirth of Chartism.[77] Prince Louis Bonaparte, still in exile in Britain, also saw the enormous demonstrations within the context of European revolutionary events.[78] Linked to the British case and mentioned above is the question of where to place the Irish Famine within the framework of a European 1848. Only through memory and commemorations did the Famine become part of the founding-myth of Irish nationalism.[79] However, already before 1848 the liberation of Ireland was seen as part of a European movement: in June 1847, at the funeral of Daniel O'Connell, leader of the Irish Repeal Movement, Father Joachim Ventura spoke of 'the revolution which threatens to encompass the globe'[80] – despite the fact that Mazzini did not recognize 'Young Ireland' as part of his league of European peoples because it 'had no distinctive moral contribution to humanity'.[81] Early Europeanism was not free of chauvinist attitudes, either.

Contemporary discourse reveals a remarkable consciousness of the European dimension of the events, but says little about a 'European vision' as part of the revolutionary programme. Only occasionally do we come across concrete plans for European institutions,[82] as they had been discussed by Saint-Simon, Feuquerai, Littré and Bouvet in France, and by Jeremy Bentham and Charles Mackay in Britain. Ledru-Rollin, Ruge, and Mazzini established in London a 'democratic European committee'. Ruge, in his speech to the Frankfurt parliament on 22 July 1848 and confronted by the increasing aggressiveness of nationalist claims, proposed a European convention for disarmament.[83] Together with Julius Fröbel he proposed a European federation of nation-states, similar to the ideas for supranational institutions promoted by Victor Hugo and Louis Bara. The manifesto of the June uprising in Prague also promoted the idea of a European peoples' congress. However, Europe remained an idea without a concrete programme behind it. Jan Merk shows in his article how transnational collaboration between revolutionaries in France, Switzerland and the German south-west collapsed in the face of anti-republican forces. With the exception of future developments within the European labour movement – whose links to 1848 are not of an organizational nature – none of these 'visions' had a long-lasting influence on political movements in Europe. The concept of Europe in the ideas of 1848 was not strong enough to establish an alternative 'concert Européen'. Despite its idealism, Europe was not one of the revolution's priorities.

Commemorations of 1848 in a national context

How were memories of the revolution constructed and communicated? Gabriella Hauch's works on gender relations during the revolution of 1848 provide examples of the creative impact of communication on the construction of memory: despite the considerable role of revolutionary women and female symbolism during the events of 1848, the memory of the revolution was formed through male images, 'brotherhood', 'fathers of the people' and 'sons of the movement'.[84] As already explained with reference to Halbwachs, the content and meaning of memory depends not only on the facts remembered, but on the context of the commemorations, and on experiences made between the remembered facts and the act of commemoration.

Not only do oral accounts and scholarly research create memory, but also more complex forms of communication. The Arts often work as a communicator of memory.[85] Siegfried Kracauer has analysed the impact of changing political regimes in France on the emergence of Jacques Offenbach's *Operette*.[86] We can establish a similar relationship between historical change and the construction of memories. The action, plot or story in a historical novel or a painting with historical content represent ideas which are contemporary with the act of commemoration, not to the remembered event itself. Similarly, the aesthetics which are employed in the artefact are contemporary with the act of commemoration, not with the story which is told.[87] The chapters by Martin Swales, Rebecca Spang and by the author of this introduction demonstrate the role of popular song, the arts, literature and opera in this process.[88]

To an important extent memories are made of myths. Robert Gildea explained myths as 'collective interpretations of the past which serve a specific goal: they are made to create identity, consistency and legitimation within political movements and communities'. How the invention of history through public acts of commemoration serves a national goal is analysed in Rebecca Spang's chapter on the 'First Performances – Staging Memories of the French February Revolution'. The memory frenzy is a recent phenomenon, exemplified in Mitterrand's Bicentenaire, 'l'Année du patrimoine', Nora's *Les Lieux de mémoire* or the celebrations for 'le baptême de Clovis', and has little to do with the actual 'Mosaïque en France' (Yves Lequin) which forms the memories of various ethnic, regional and social communities and milieus.[89] In the history of its commemorations 1848 helped to create contrasting political communities,[90] but had, with the exception of cases like Denmark or Hungary, rather little effect on the creation of national communities.[91] Concerning the history of 1848, there was little agreement between different political groups on how to interpret and remember the events of 1848.[92] However, all these politically diverse interpretations concentrated on 1848 from a national perspective, in which the European dimension of the revolution disappeared.

In Italy, 1848 was a key element within the history of the Italian Risorgimento. Most icons of German nationalism date from the 1830s, but most symbolic images of the Italian nation refer to the revolutionary years between 1846 and 1849.[93] In Denmark, symbols of national unity similarly refer to the 'spirit of 48'.[94] But if in Denmark 1848 is seen as a reference point for national cohesion through the construction of external enemies, the memory of 1848 in Italy, as Simonetta Soldani demonstrates, was for a long time a divided memory – divided politically and regionally. However, these divisions are all about questions of national politics, and therefore an invitation to neglect the European dimension within the revolutionary ideas and the European context of the events.

In France, the historical protagonists of the revolution of 1848 tried to make it as different from 1789 as possible,[95] although the programme of revolution was built upon the memories of 1789.[96] After 1848, people like Louis Blanc rehabilitated the first revolution from its association with terror,[97] whereas the history of the Second Republic remained a topic of disagreement and secondary importance. After the debacle of the Second Empire, 1848 represented for some people, especially socialists, a reference point for the legitimization of the Third Republic. Nevertheless, as Rebecca Spang shows in this book, 1848 could never compete with the Revolution of

1789.[98] Other people blamed the Second Republic for its instability, it being the reason for holding back the national development of France into a Republic.[99] For Daladier, the example of 1848 illustrated that the Third Estate and the proletariat had to stick together in a Popular Front in order to resist attempted dictatorship.[100] There is no doubt that – despite all political disagreement – 1848 always served as a historical reference point.

In Hungary, 1848 similarly served to legitimize the most diverse political regimes: during the *coup d'état* of 1948 the revolution was regarded as an anticipation of the socialist revolution, while later, in 1956 and again in 1989, it was the model for national uprisings.[101] In the spring of 1990 Hungary had a public debate about which chapter of national history would best represent the new Hungary: the first Hungarian king, Stephen; Kossuth and the revolution of 1848; or March 1989. The 15th of March had the advantage that it represented both Kossuth's revolution of 1848 and the first important mass demonstration of 1989. In the end the Hungarians got three national holidays – the 15th of March, the 20th of August (Saint Stephen's Day) and the 23rd of October, which remembered the 1956 uprising. The year 1848 appears to be an essential piece in the puzzle of national history.

In Germany the events of the year 1989 also contributed to a rethinking of 1848's role in German history. In the debate about the new capital of a unified Germany, Berlin and Bonn had to compete with Frankfurt as the birthplace of German democracy.[102] During the years of the Kaiserreich and the Weimar Republic, commemorations of 1848 remained the domain of social democrats and left-wing liberals. Only occasionally did the national liberals join the celebrations.[103] Jan Merk analyses in this book the changing political meanings of 1848 in German history.[104] After 1945, the revolution seemingly represented the only positive tradition in German history on which to build. The Paulskirche, seat of the parliament in 1848 and destroyed during the war, was one of the first national monuments to be rebuilt. The first president of the Federal Republic, the liberal Theodor Heuss, published a history of 1848 and the constitution of the Paulskirche played an important role in the elaboration of the constitutional law of the Federal Republic of Germany (FRG).[105] However, to whom did the revolution of 1848 belong? Was 1848 the revolution of the working class, or was it the first German experience of a democratic parliamentary system – hence a 'bourgeois revolution'? The local government in Berlin commissioned a history of the revolution by Friedrich Meinecke, a decision which was strongly criticized by the Soviet military administration: a 'bourgeois historian' like Meinecke would be sure to neglect the social context of the revolution.[106] The commemorations developed into a conflict over the parliamentary system between, on the one side, the future state party of the German Democratic Republic (GDR), the Social Unity Party (SED), and the democratic parties, the Social Democratic Party (SPD) and the Christian Democratic Union (CDU), on the other.[107] This conflict did not allow for a debate within a larger, European context. The commemorations served a goal in national politics. Most Germans in the Western Republic continued to be rather ambivalent about the idea of revolution. Although they recognized in the Paulskirche an important element of parliamentary tradition, the revolution itself, the republican movement and the civil war for the German constitution in 1849 all continued to be seen as rather negative episodes in the formation of a German nation-state. This view only changed during the years of the Brandt era which fostered more progressive attitudes in German society. Revolutionary students in 1968 identified with the radical movement of 1848.[108] The Federal Republic's first social-democratic president, Gustav Heinemann, especially contributed to the creation of a new image of Germany's revolutionary tradition. With few exceptions, the political interest in 1848 remained during all these years one of national history.[109] For most of the 150 years of commemoration, Hegelian teleology of the nation state made the history of 1848 a *national* history.

The political primacy of European integration during the 1990s has changed this long-lasting concentration on the national perspective in revolutionary history.[110] The German celebrations for the 150th anniversary of the revolution, including countless exhibitions, conferences and new publications, emphasize a European approach to the events. The president of the Federal Republic, Roman Herzog, during his visit to Belgium in July 1998, pointed out that the constitutional debate in the Frankfurt parliament was inspired by the Belgian model of 1830.[111] The vice-president of the SPD, writing in the party organ *Vorwärts*, entitled her article on 1848 'Revolutionary Vision. 150 years after 1848 a unified Europe becomes reality' and it was printed on a blue background and decorated with golden stars.[112] Laurent Fabius, president of the Assemblée nationale in France, invited historians from all over Europe to celebrate the 150th anniversary of 1848. Memories of 1848 have started to legitimize the process of European integration. At the end of the twentieth century, the nation-state as political reference point is being replaced by a new political entity. In this way, the meaning of historical commemorations changes.

Notes

1 V. Valentin, *Geschichte der Revolution von 1848–49*, 2 vols (Berlin, 1930/31).
2 W. Siemann, *Die deutsche Revolution von 1848/49* (Frankfurt am Main: Suhrkamp, 1985), p. 11, now in English: *The German Revolution of 1848–9* (London: Macmillan, 1998).
3 V. Valentin, *Geschichte der Deutschen* (1947), (Munich: Droemer, 1979), p. 12; English: *The German People* (New York: Knopf 1946). On Veit Valentin, see E. Fehrenbach in: H. U. Wehler, (ed.), *Deutsche Historiker*, vol. I (Göttingen: Vandenhoeck & Ruprecht, 1971), 69–85.
4 Quoted from the English translation: *1848. Chapters of German History* (London: Allen & Unwin, 1940), 458.
5 Manfred Hettling describes how from early on revolutionary activity was replaced with funeral celebrations, obsequies and commemorations for the victims of the revolution: *Totenkult statt Revolution. 1848 und seine Opfer* (Frankfurt am Main: Fischer, 1998). See also C. Tacke, 'Feste der Revolution in Deutschland und Italien', in D. Dowe, H.-G. Haupt and D. Langewiesche (eds), *Europa 1848. Revolution und Reform* (Bonn: J. H. W. Dietz Nachf., 1998), pp. 1045–88. A rich collection of newspapers and pamphlets illustrating the overlapping of revolutionary activities and commemorations is 'Kleine Kollektionen: Robert Blum' at the Internationaal Instituut voor Sociale Geschiedenis' (IISG) in Amsterdam.
6 Valentin, *1848*, p. 458.
7 For an overview concerning the question of 'national' revolution versus 'European' revolution see H. Kaelble, '1848: Viele nationale Revolutionen oder eine europäische Revolution?', in W. Hardtwig (ed.), *Revolution in Deutschland und Europa 1848/49* (Göttingen: Vandenhoeck & Ruprecht, 1998), pp. 260–78, 266 ff.
8 M. Halbwachs, *Les cadres sociaux de la mémoire* (1925) (Paris: Albin Michel, 1994). Idem, *La mémoire collective* (Paris: PUF, 1968).
9 Following Maurice Halbwachs this differentiation is based on experience and communication within specific social groups who form their own collective memories: ibid., p. 12.

10   See the examples by Simonetta Soldani in this volume.

11   'Sleep, my child, don't cry,/The Prussian's going by./He killed your
     father at his door,/He made your wretched mother poor./Keep very still,
     if you'd be wise, / Or he'll find ways to shut your eyes./Sleep, my child,
     don't cry,/The Prussian's going by.' Valentin, *1848*, p. 420. See also
     Jan Merk's interpretation in this volume.

12   B. Bouvier, 'Zur Tradition von 1848 im Sozialismus', in: Dowe et al., *Europa
     1848*, pp. 1169–200.

13   For a comparative approach see J. Sperber, *The European Revolutions,
     1848–1851* (Cambridge: Cambridge University Press, 1994). See also the
     recent article by the same author: 'Eine alte Revolution in neuer Zeit.
     1848/49 in europäischer Perspektive', in C. Jansen and T. Mergel (eds),
     Die Revolutionen von 1848/49. Erfahrung-Verarbeitung-Deutung (Göttingen:
     Vandenhoeck & Ruprecht, 1998), pp. 14–36. P. N. Stearns, *1848:
     The Revolutionary Tide in Europe* (New York/London: Norton, 1974).
     W. L. Langer, *The Revolutions of 1848* (New York, 1971). J. Godechot, *Les
     Révolutions de 1848* (Paris: PUF, 1971). R. Price, *The Revolutions of 1848*
     (London: Macmillan, 1988). Dowe et al., *Europa 1848*. A systematic approach
     to the problem of a comparative history of 1848: Kaelble, '1848'. Rather
     out of date: P. Robertson, *Revolutions of 1848. A Social History* (Princeton,
     NJ: Princeton University Press, 1952).

14   A detailed bibliography, divided by countries, in Stearns, *1848*, pp. 251–62.
     Especially on Germany: D. Langewiesche, 'Die deutsche Revolution von
     1848/49 und die vorrevolutionäre Gesellschaft: Forschungsstand und
     Forschungsperspektiven', *Archiv für Sozialgeschichte*, XXI (1981) and XXXI
     (1991). On France see the detailed bibliography in *Revue d'Histoire du XIXe
     siècle* (1997), n. 14, 129–99.

15   Sperber, *The European Revolutions*. Similar Price, *The Revolutions of 1848*,
     and more detailed idem, *The French Second Republic. A Social History*
     (London: Batsford, 1972).

16   Stearns, *1848*, p. 5.

17   G. Candeloro, *Storia dell'Italia moderna*, vol. III: *La Rivoluzione nazionale*
     (Milano: Feltrinelli, 1960), pp. 9–22, and especially S. J. Woolf, *Il Risorgi-
     mento Italiano*, vol. II: *Dalla Restaurazione all'Unità* (1979) (Torino: Einaudi,
     1981), pp. 530–44; in English: *A History of Italy, 1700–1860: The Social
     Constraints of Political Change* (London: Routledge, 1979).

18   N. Davies, *God's Playground. A History of Poland*, vol. 2, (Oxford: Claren-
     don Press, 1981), p. 340.

19   Ibid., p. 342. For the Romanian movement see L. Maier, 'Die Revolution
     von 1848 in der Moldau und in der Walachei', in Dowe et al., *Europa
     1848*, pp. 253–82. A.-L. Seip, 'Die Revolution von 1848 in Norwegen', in
     ibid., pp. 437–54, 425. J. Belchem, 'Das Waterloo von Frieden und
     Ordnung. Das Vereinigte Königreich und die Revolution von 1848', in
     ibid., pp. 327–50.

20   S. Soldani, 'Annäherung an Europa im Namen der Nation. Die italie-
     nische Revolution 1846–1849', in ibid., pp. 125–66, 130. W. Steinmetz,

'"Sprechen ist eine Tat bei euch." Die Wörter und das Handeln in der Revolution von 1848', in ibid., pp. 1089–139, 1097 ff. A. Körner, *Das Lied von einer anderen Welt. Kulturelle Praxis im französischen und deutschen Arbeitermilieu* (Frankfurt am Main: Campus, 1997), pp. 215–49.

21   Maier, 'Die Revolution von 1848 in der Moldau und in der Walachei', p. 279.
22   Steinmetz, '"Sprechen ist eine Tat bei euch"', p. 1109.
23   G. Schödl, 'Jenseits von Bürgergesellschaft und Staat. Die Völker Ostmitteleuropas 1848/49', in Hardtwig, *Revolution*, pp. 207–39, 210.
24   See the article by Jan Merk in this book; also Siemann, *Die deutsche Revolution*, p. 55.
25   Godechot, *Les Révolutions de 1848*.
26   Woolf, *Il Risorgimento Italiano*, vol. II, p. 546.
27   R. Hachtmann, 'Die europäischen Hauptstädte in der Revolution von 1848', in Dowe et al., *Europa 1848*, pp. 455–92, 461.
28   On the symbolic use of the colour red in revolutionary activity: R. Brécy, 'Le drapeau rouge', *Revue d'histoire moderne et contemporaine*, 2 (1975), 262–8. J. Merriman explains how 50 soldiers were sent to a village near Amboise to remove from the bell tower of the church a weather cock which had been painted red: *The Agony of the Republic. The Repression of the Left in Revolutionary France. 1848–1851* (New Haven, CT and London: Yale University Press, 1978), p. 96.
29   E. J. Hobsbawm, *The Age of Capital 1848–1875* (1975) (London: Abacus, 1997), pp. 25 ff. Woolf, *Il Risorgimento Italiano*, vol. II, p. 532. W. J. Mommsen, *Die ungewollte Revolution. Die revolutionären Bewegungen in Europa 1830–1849* (Frankfurt am Main: Fischer, 1998), pp. 120 ff.
30   R. Brécy, *La chanson de la commune* (Paris: Les Editions Ouvrières, 1991), p. 26.
31   For a comparative overview on these aspects see Sperber, *The European Revolutions*, pp. 148–94. H.-G. Haupt and D. Langewiesche, 'Die Revolution in Europa 1848. Reform der Herrschaftsordnung – Nationalrevolution – Wirkungen', in Dowe et al., *Europa 1848*, pp. 11–42, 13–19.
32   See the articles published in the 'Neue Rheinische Zeitung', *Marx-Engels-Werke* (MEW) (Berlin: Dietz, 1956 ff.), vols 5, 6, 7. K. Marx, 'Die Klassenkämpfe in Frankreich 1848 bis 1850', *MEW*, 7; idem, 'Der achtzehnte Brumaire des Louis Bonaparte', *MEW*, 8. See also F. Engels, 'Die deutsche Reichsverfassungskampagne', *MEW*, 7; idem, 'Revolution und Konterrevolution in Deutschland', *MEW*, 8.
33   See Rebecca Spang's chapter in this volume.
34   Mommsen, *1848*. A very different interpretation with regard to 1848 and the German Sonderweg: R. Kühnl, '1848 und der deutsche Sonderweg. Eine gescheiterte Revolution und ihre Folgen', *Blätter für deutsche und internationale Politik*, 3(1998), pp. 337–47.
35   Merriman, *The Agony of the Republic*.
36   M. Agulhon, *1848 ou l'apprentissage de la République* (Paris: Seuil, 1973). M. L. Stewart-McDougall analyses 1848 from a different perspective, explaining the events by the precipitation of political struggle: *The*

Artisan Republic. Revolution, Reaction, and Resistance in Lyon. 1848–1851
(Mc-Gill-Queen's University Press, 1984).

37   Sperber, *The European Revolutions*, 148–78. Haupt / Langewiesche: 'Die
Revolution in Europa 1848'. Siemann, *Die deutsche Revolution*, 223–8.
Stearns, 1848. W. Kaschuba, '1848/49: Horizonte politischer Kultur',
in: Hardtwig, *Revolution*, 56–78, 68. H. A. Winkler, 'Der überforderte
Liberalismus. Zum Ort der Revolution von 1848/49 in der deutschen
Geschichte', in ibid., 185–206, 198 ff. Kaelble, '1848', 274.

38   See also G. Hauch, *Frau Biedermeier auf den Barrikaden. Frauenleben in der
Wiener Revolution 1848* (Wien: Verlag für Gesellschaftskritik, 1990).
C. Lipp, ed., *Schimpfende Weiber und patriotische Jungfrauen. Frauen im
Vormärz und in der Revolution 1848/49* (Baden-Baden: Moos, 1986).

39   R. Koselleck, '"Erfahrungsraum" und "Erwartungshorizont" – zwei historische Kategorien' (1976), in ibid., *Vergangene Zukunft. Zur Semantik
geschichtlicher Zeiten* (Frankfurt am Main: Suhrkamp, 1989), pp. 349–75.

40   A document of mockery: K. Marx and F. Engels, 'Die großen Männer des
Exils', *MEW*, 8, 233–335. With the necessary distance of historians:
M. Agulhon, *Les Quarante-Huitards* (Paris: Gallimard, 1975). H. Best, *Die
Männer von Bildung und Besitz. Struktur und Handeln parlamentarischer
Führungsgruppen in Deutschland und Frankreich 1848/49* (Düsseldorf,
1990). S. Freitag, ed., *Die Achtundvierziger. Lebensbilder aus der deutschen
Revolution 1848/49* (München: Beck, 1997). C. Jansen, 'Ludwig Simon,
Arnold Ruge und Friedrich Wilhelm IV', in: Jansen / Mergel, *Die Revolu-
tionen von 1848/49*, pp. 225–46. J. Merk, 'Liberale, Republikaner, Frauen
in der Revolution', in *Lörracher Hefte*, 3: 'Lörrach 1848/49. Essays, Biographien, Dokumente, Projekte' (Lörrach: Museum am Burghof, 1998).

41   No single event of the revolution reveals this uncertainty better than the
reactions to the murder of Robert Blum. See the quotation from Ludwig
Bamberger in: Siemann, *Die deutsche Revolution*, p. 227.

42   D. Oehler, *Ein Höllensturz der alten Welt. Pariser Bilder* (Frankfurt am Main
1986).

43   H. Lademacher, 'Niederlande und Belgien. Bemerkungen zu den Ursa-
chen revolutionärer Abstinenz', in: Dowe et al., *Europa 1848*, pp. 351–88,
369. G. B. Nilsson, 'Schweden 1848 und danach – Unterwegs zu einem
'Mittelweg', in ibid., 437–52, 438.

44   Haupt and Langewiesche, 'Die Revolution in Europa 1848', 12 ff
L. Thomas, 'Russische Reaktionen auf die Revolution von 1848 in Europa',
in Hardtwig, *Revolutionen*, pp. 240–59.

45   W. L. Bernecker, *Sozialgeschichte Spaniens im 19. und 20. Jahrhundert*
(Frankfurt am Main: Suhrkamp, 1990), p. 113.

46   See also L. Namier, *1848: The Revolution of the Intellectuals* (1946) (Oxford:
Oxford University Press, 1957), p. 4. Valentin, *1848. Chapters of German
History*, p. 457. Stearns, *1848*, p. 7. Kaelble, '1848', 272. Sperber, 'Eine alte
Revolution in neuer Zeit', p. 31.

47   Hobsbawm, *The Age of Capital*, pp. 14, 40.

48   Namier, *1848*.

49 H. Wieczorek-Zeul, 'Revolutionäre Vision. 150 Jahre nach 1848 wird ein geeintes Europa Wirklichkeit', in *Vorwärts*, 7(1998).
50 Soldani, 'Annäherung an Europa im Namen der Nation'.
51 Kaelble, '1848', p. 273.
52 W. J. Mommsen, 'Die nationale Frage in der Revolution von 1848/49', *Blätter für deutsche und internationale Politik* (1998), pp. 348–58, 348.
53 Haupt and Langewiesche, 'Die Revolution in Europa 1848', p. 40.
54 A. Ruge, 'Aus einem offenen Brief zur Verteidigung des Humanismus an Robert Eduard Prutz', in P. Wende (ed.), *Der Patriotismus* (Frankfurt am Main: Insel, 1990), pp. 85–98, 92.
55 Idem, 'Der Patriotismus' (1844), in ibid., pp. 7–84, 21, 32, 40 ff.
56 Kühnl, '1848 und der deutsche Sonderweg', pp. 342 ff.
57 J. Křalka, 'Revolutionen in der Habsburgermonarchie', in Dowe et al., *Europa 1848*, pp. 197–230, 200 ff.
58 Ibid., pp. 202–9.
59 See also the comparison of Eastern European peoples in Schödl, 'Jenseits von Bürgergesellschaft', pp. 219 ff. Another example for the revolution in a multi-ethnic territory is Tyrol: T. Götz and H. Heiss, 'Die Nation vom Rande aus gesehen. Nationale, konfessionelle, regionale Konfliktlinien in Tirol 1848/49', in Jansen and Mergel, *Die Revolutionen von 1848/49*, pp. 150–71.
60 Siemann, *Die deutsche Revolution*, p. 226.
61 Mommsen, 'Die nationale Frage in der Revolution von 1848/49', p. 349. Kühnl, '1848 und der deutsche Sonderweg', p. 340. Sperber, 'Eine alte Revolution in neuer Zeit', p. 28. Götz and Heiss, 'Die Nation', pp. 162 ff.
62 T. Nipperdey, *Deutsche Geschichte 1800–1866. Bürgerwelt und starker Staat* (Munich: Beck, 1983), p. 627. H. H. Hahn, 'Die polnische Nation in den Revolutionen von 1846–49', in Dowe et al., *Europa 1848*, pp. 231–52, 251. Robert Blum denounced the new Germans' 'youthful' nationalism: Mommsen, 'Die nationale Frage in der Revolution von 1848/49', pp. 353 ff.
63 Valentin, *1848. Chapters of German History*, p. 423.
64 *MEW*, vols 5, 6, 7.
65 Merriman, *The Agony of the Republic*, p. 26.
66 Ibid., p. 32.
67 *Allgemeine Arbeiter Zeitung*, 20 May 1848 and 10 June 1848, reprint (Frankfurt am Main: Sauer & Auvermann, 1968), p. 10.
68 *Allgemeine Arbeiter Zeitung*, 24 May 1848, pp. 21 ff.
69 W. Häusler, *Von der Massenarmut zur Arbeiterbewegung. Demokratie und soziale Frage in der Wiener Revolution von 1848* (Vienna and Munich: Jugend & Volk, 1979), p. 268.
70 Ibid., p. 275.
71 Siemann, *Die deutsche Revolution*, p. 61.

72   R. Wagner, 'Die Revolution' (1849), anonymous in *Dresdner Volksblättern*, in D. Mack (ed.), *Ausgewählte Schriften* (Frankfurt am Main: Insel, 1974), pp. 114–22, 114.

73   Merriman, *The Agony of the Republic*, p. 100.

74   See the examples of the revolutionary priest Anton Fürster in Vienna, and of Ernst Violand, one of the heads of the Viennese revolution: Häusler, *Von der Massenarmut zur Arbeiterbewegung*, pp. 426, 433. Also Freitag, *Die Achtundvierziger*. On the exiled revolutionaries in Switzerland: A. Körner, 'Deutsche Asylanten in der Schweiz. Flüchtlinge während des Vormärz und der 1848er Revolution', *Die neue Gesellschaft / Frankfurter Hefte*, 7(1993), pp. 648–51.

75   See, for example, the account of the revolutionary events in a popular encyclopaedia of the time: *Die Gegenwart. Eine encyclopädische Darstellung der neuesten Zeitgeschichte für alle Stände* (Leipzig, 1848), quoted in W. Pöls (ed.), *Historisches Lesebuch 1815–1871* (Frankfurt am Main: Fischer, 1966), pp. 148 ff.

76   W. Steinmetz, 'Sprechen ist eine Tat', p. 1090. On the language of Chartism: G. Stedman Jones, *Languages of Class. Studies in English Working Class History. 1832–1982* (Cambridge: Cambridge University Press, 1983).

77   Belchem, 'Das Waterloo von Frieden und Ordnung', p. 340. On Britain in 1848 see also M. Finn, *After Chartism: Class and Nation in English Radical Politics* (Cambridge UP, 1993), ch. 2, 'English radical responses to the revolutions of 1848–1849' pp. 60–105. D. Large, 'London in the Year of Revolutions, 1848', in John Stevenson ed., *London in the Age of Reform* (Oxford: Blackwell, 1977), pp. 177–212. G. Claeys, 'Mazzini, Kossuth, and British Radicalism, 1848–1854', in *Journal of British Studies*, 28, 3 July 1989, pp. 225–61.

78   L. Girard, *Napoléon III* (Paris: Fayard, 1986), p. 84.

79   Concerning the recent debate see C. Tóibín, 'On the history of the history of the Irish Famine', *London Review of Books*, XX (30 July 1998), pp. 17–23.

80   Namier, *1848: The Revolution of the Intellectuals*, p. 3.

81   Robertson, *Revolutions of 1848*, p. 408.

82   An overview about the ideas of political unification during the revolutionary period: F. Chabod, *Storia dell'idea d'Europa* (1961) (Rome/Bari: Laterza, 1995), pp. 122–57. P. Renouvin, 'L'idée d'Etat-Unis d'Europe pendant la crise de 1848', in *Actes du Congrès historique du Centenaire de la Révolution de 1848* (Paris, 1948), pp. 31–45.

83   A. Ruge, 'Rede Arnold Ruges in der 45. Sitzung der Deutschen Nationalversammlung in der Frankfurter Paulskirche', in idem, *Der Patriotismus*, pp. 99–113.

84   G. Hauch, 'Frauen-Räume in der Männer-Revolution 1848', in Dowe et al., *Europa 1848*, pp. 841–900, 843. See also her article in this book. Similar Körner, *Das Lied von einer anderen Welt*, pp. 315–25.

85   J. Assmann calls memory stored in artefacts like songs or images 'cultural memory'.

86   S. Kracauer, *Jacques Offenbach und das Paris seiner Zeit* (1937) (Frankfurt am Main: Suhrkamp, 1994), pp. 97, 107 ff.

87 See on this relationship C. Dahlhaus, *Wagners Konzeption des musikalischen Dramas* (1971) (Munich: dtv, 1990), p. 49.
88 See also Hettling, *Totenkult statt Revolution*, pp. 133–87, 188–98; and Kaschuba, '1848/49: Horizonte politischer Kultur', pp. 61 ff.
89 P. Nora (ed.), *Les lieux de mémoire*, 7 vols (Paris: Gallimard, 1984–92). English: *Realms of Memory: Rethinking the French Past* (New York: Columbia University Press, 1996). Y. Lequin (ed.), *La Mosaïque en France* (Paris: Larousse, 1988). For a critical approach: J.-P. Rioux, 'La mémoire collective', in J.-P. Rioux and J.-F. Sirinelli, *Pour une histoire culturelle* (Paris: Seuil, 1997), pp. 325–53.
90 See the articles by Soldani and Spang in this book. For a comparative view on the commemorations of 1848 in the French and German left: Körner, *Das Lied von einer anderen Welt*, pp. 215–49. Bouvier, 'Zur Tradition von 1848 im Sozialismus'. Also Hettling, *Totenkult statt Revolution*, p. 38.
91 Hettling, *Totenkult statt Revolution*, pp. 46, 192.
92 This only changed on the occasion of the 150th anniversary, in 1998. Benedikt Erenz describes a national agreement concerning the revolution, reaching from the extreme left to the right: 'Ja, er lebet noch! Mit Freiheitsgugelhupf und Heckerhut, DKP und Wolfgang Schäuble: Ein pralles Bürgerfest in Offenburg läutet die 150-Jahr-Feiern der 48er-Revolution ein', *Die Zeit*, 19 September 1997. See also U. Speck, 'Nachgeholte Revolution 1848. Später Sieg', in *FAZ*, 20 May 1998.
93 Kaschuba, '1848/49', p. 66. Soldani, 'Annäherung an Europa', p. 129. On the construction of national identity during the Risorgimento see now Alberto M. Banti, *La nazione del Risorgimento. Parentela, santità e onore alle origini dell'Italia unita* (Rome/Bari: Laterza, 2000).
94 S. B. Frandsen, '1848 in Dänemark: Die Durchsetzung der Demokratie und das Zerbrechen des Gesamtstaates', in Dowe et al., *Europa 1848*, pp. 389–420, 418.
95 R. Gildea, *The Past in French History* (New Haven, CT: Yale University Press, 1994), p. 35.
96 Körner, *Das Lied von einer anderen Welt*, pp. 237–43.
97 Gildea, *The Past in French History*, p. 36.
98 Ibid., p. 43. Idem, 'Mythen der Revolution von 1848', in Dowe et al., *Europa 1848*, pp. 1201–33, 1206.
99 P. M. Pilbeam, *Republicanism in Nineteenth-Century France, 1814–1871* (London: Macmillan, 1995), p. 31. Concerning the uncertainty about the evaluation of 1848 see also the article by Martin Swales in this volume.
100 Gildea, *The Past in French History*, p. 52.
101 P. Niedermüller, 'Geschichte, Mythos und Politik. Die Revolution von 1848 und das historische Gedächtnis in Ungarn', in Hardtwig, *Revolution*, pp. 32–55, 41–49.
102 K. V. Beyme, *Hauptstadtsuche* (Frankfurt am Main: Suhrkamp, 1991), p. 114 concentrates on Bonn and Berlin, neglects Frankfurt, but gives a valuable overview of the debate.

103 Hettling, *Totenkult statt Revolution*, pp. 188 ff.
104 See also Siemann, *Die deutsche Revolution*, pp. 7–16. Winkler, 'Der über-forderte Liberalismus', pp. 196 ff., and Kaschuba, '1848 / 49', p. 61. An excellent analysis of the meaning of 1848 in various social and political milieus in Germany: T. Mergel, 'Sozialmoralische Milieus und Revolutionsgeschichtsschreibung. Zum Bild der Revolution von 1848/49 in den Subgesellschaften des deutschen Kaiserreichs', in Jansen and Mergel, *Die Revolutionen von 1848/49*, pp. 247–67.
105 E. H. M. Lange, 'Grundgesetz: Entscheidung für die Freiheit. Das Werk von Bonn im Wandel der deutschen Verfassungsgeschichte', in *Deutsche Verfassungsgeschichte. 1849–1919–1949* (Bonn: Bundeszentrale für politische Bildung, 1989), pp. 105–13, 107.
106 L. Demps, '18.März 1948. Zum Gedenken an 100 Jahre Märzrevolution in Berlin', in Hardtwig, *Revolution*, pp. 11–31, 14.
107 Ibid.
108 R. vom Bruch, 'Die Universitäten in der Revolution 1848/49. Revolution ohne Universität – Universität ohne Revolution?', in ibid., pp. 133–60, 134.
109 Kaschuba, '1848/49', p. 57.
110 The first signs of this change were visible in the late 1960s. One fruit of Willy Brandt's new Ostpolitik was a German–Polish commission of historians that worked on recommendations for history books to be used in German and Polish schools. They presented the uprising in Krakow, in 1846, as the start of the 'European springtime of Peoples'. Hahn, 'Die polnische Nation in der Revolution von 1846–49', p. 231. This is not only an interesting example of a European approach to the history of 1848; it also demonstrates how the perspective of central Europe changed from the 1970s: whereas before the historical link with Poland's eastern neighbour was privileged, Polish historiography now rediscovered its roots in the western part of the continent.
111 P. Hort, 'Streicheleinheiten vom großen Nachbarn', *FAZ*, 15 July 1998.
112 Wieczorek-Zeul, 'Revolutionäre Vision'.

Part II
A European Perspective on 1848

2
1848: Connected or Comparable Revolutions?[1]

John Breuilly

Introductory comments

The easy answer to the question in the title is – yes to both. What happened in one place had connections to what happened elsewhere, e.g. the February Days stimulated popular demonstrations in south-west Germany which in turn influenced the mood of government and opposition in Vienna, Milan and Berlin (to take just the other three sites of serious urban conflict in March). News of Metternich's overthrow contributed to the March insurrection in Berlin. And so on. We can study the mechanics of these connections, e.g. the impact of newly installed telegraph lines which transmitted news and rumours with unprecedented speed, the way railways could take people into some towns to participate in demonstrations, the ways in which print media helped convey a sense of *European* revolution. The difficulties lie not in displaying connections but in establishing why they existed and how significant they were.

As for 'comparable', given that it is essential for comparative history to pay attention to differences as well as similarities, provided only that comparison proceeds within a single framework, deploying one or another concept of revolution to provide such a framework in relation to the various revolutions of 1848 should provide a firm basis for a comparative history of the revolutions. The challenge is actually to do this, not the principle of doing it. Furthermore, if 'comparable' means 'essentially similar' rather than 'capable of being compared', the question becomes more difficult and interesting.[2]

I. Connections

So far as connections are concerned, the important question is *why?* Some historians date the beginning of the 1848 revolution to the January unrest in Palermo. In a pedantic way that is correct; in the calendar year 1848 this was the first important revolutionary event. However, the real beginning was in Paris. Palermo did not create 'connections' in the way that Paris did. No one suggests that the February Days in Paris were inspired by the events of Palermo whereas there are clear connections between the February Days and the wave of demonstrations and popular movements which swept into other countries in the following weeks.

One can trace at least four kinds of connection. The first is confined to France. A centralized political system meant that events in Paris rapidly acquired national significance. There was a tradition established by earlier sequences. These began in 1789 and continued through 1792, 1794, 1799 (in an anti-revolutionary way). The sequence was only interrupted in 1814–15 when first Napoleon and then the Allies carried power from outside into Paris. The 'traditional' sequence resumed in 1830. The connection is an obvious one but requires investigation of the ways in which political elites in Paris and the provinces almost automatically responded to Parisian revolution and why such revolution spread rumours and fed on beliefs at a popular level throughout the country.[3] Less noted are the failed attempts, through inciting revolution in Paris, to spark off such a train of events, as in 1834 and 1839.

There were a complex of connections which catalysed revolution beyond France and I would trace three, all interconnected. First, there was the response of oppositional elites, especially within the south-west German and Italian states. Here the heritage of French occupation and reorganization in the 1792–1815 period had left a legacy of Francophilism and a predisposition to assume that events in France would spill beyond the national boundary, a predisposition which could become a self-fulfilling prophecy. Germans had responded to the July Revolution with rebellion and political change in Brunswick, Hannover and Saxony. Some of the demands raised by demonstrations in towns such as Karlsruhe, Mannheim and Heidelberg almost as soon as news of the February Days were received, pointed directly to French influence – e.g. for village mayors, town councils elected on French principles, trial by jury and the greater use of oral proceedings in the courts.

Second, there was the response of governments. They too had memories and assumptions. The proclamation of a republic in France meant the likelihood of war; a republic would direct revolutionary energies beyond France and repudiate the territorial settlement of 1814–15. Lamartine quickly reassured other powers to the contrary but that itself is testimony to the widespread fear. Generals in Berlin and Vienna calculated how many troops they needed on the French border and how to utilize German Confederal army arrangements and strengthen the western fortresses. They made further assumptions about Polish insurrection, assuming that revolutionary France would support this. Napoleon had done so – the July revolution had been followed by a rising in Congress Poland, and French radicals in 1848 supported Polish restoration.

The third level of action, less conditioned by such memories and assumptions, was that of popular movements. Peasant disturbances in the south-west German states were more a response to the urban demonstrations within their own states than to events in France. These demonstrations indicated weak government which emboldened peasants. Small states in Germany and Italy looked to Prussia and Austria for support and had little idea of resistance when this was not forthcoming in early 1848. As news of government capitulation spread eastwards and southwards this encouraged further opposition and, when filtered through assumptions about 'revolution', demoralized those in power. Generals now calculated how many troops were needed not only on the borders but also in the capital cities to maintain order. Consequently armies began the process of repression in pessimistic spirit, helping explain, for example, acquiescence in Friedrich Wilhelm's decision by the morning of 19 March to capitulate to the insurrection.[4]

In these ways assumptions about connections between revolution in Paris, the rest of France and Europe beyond France, and the perception of limited unrest as harbingers of war and revolution were vital to the rapid and seemingly irreversible collapse of governments, the appointment of oppositional figures to ministries and the escalation of popular action. Opposition was in turn institutionalized and provided a basis for expanding revolutionary action through the removal of legal restraints on freedom of speech, publication, assembly and organization, and the proclamation of elections to numerous constituent assemblies.

However, from about April 1848 connections weakened in so far as they were based on ideological perceptions rather than directly linked interests and institutions. The June Days for example, and their repression, did not seem to have as demoralizing an effect on radical and labour movements elsewhere as the February Days had had an invigorating effect. Indeed, revolutionaries seem increasingly disconnected from one another. Manin in Venice had little to do with Mazzini in Rome; the Hungarian insurgents did not cross the internal Austria/Hungary border to aid the Vienna uprising. Counter-revolutionaries established better connections but directly rather than ideologically. The Russians assisted in suppressing the Hungarian revolution, while Habsburg, French and Neapolitan soldiers restored Papal rule.

Why was there a shift from ideological connections in the opening stages of the revolution but then a rapid decline in such connections, giving way, if there were continued connections, to those of a more direct kind and in ways which shifted the balance of power from revolutionaries to their opponents?

My answer starts with the observation that ideological connections depend upon events apparently following a script known to the actors. Barricades in the capitals, peasant demands for land reform, France as instigator of international crisis: these were 'known' scenarios. People could identify with their 'counterparts' elsewhere: Louis Phillippe's abdication raised the temperature in Vienna; Metternich's flight had the same effect in Berlin, especially when the Prince of Prussia in turn fled, because these were all seen as essentially the same sequence of events. Participants frequently described the early stage of the revolution in terms of a drama based on a master script and capable of repeat performances. Friedrich Wilhelm IV of Prussia wrote to Queen Victoria using the imagery of the revolution as a rising flood which would engulf his small throne and then her much bigger one. Hecker in Paris expressed irritation at the way Lamartine played a part out of his own history of the Girondins during the original French revolution. De Tocqueville recollected events in Paris in terms of a bad play. Marx wrote of history repeating itself, only now as farce instead of tragedy.[5]

The problem was that the script had just two endings in the short term: success of revolution or its early defeat. However, by April it was clear that neither the play nor even Act I had finished in either of these ways. The old authorities had retreated but only in a few places was monarchy overthrown, most notably in France. New men were in charge but men who already felt threatened by continued popular action and radicalization. The April elections to the National Assembly in France gave the first signs that at a popular level forces could be mobilized against as well as for revolution, something that was not in the original script.

People continued necessarily to make assumptions about society and politics in order to feel their way through bewildering and threatening situations. However, now these assumptions worked like tools rather than a script. These tools had to be applied to different problems in different countries. Where direct connections could be made in solving these problems, e.g. where radicals could mobilize electoral support across state boundaries or where military and policing authorities could cooperate, powerful connections could be and were forged. However, these connections usually depended upon adopting methods that operated not at a European level but at state and national level at its widest, and often more narrowly than that. Only if there were prior institutional connections as well as reasonable assumptions about operating within a common political space would linked forms of action develop. Popular mobilization took such different and conflicting forms after the initial revolutionary phase that assumptions about the 'people' and the 'popular will' ceased to be relevant even if the phrases were still trotted out. Radicals now had to work on the specific grievances of this or that region or group and had to connect those grievances to some novel institutional framework such as elections to a state or national parliament.

Conservatives concerned to mobilize opinion against revolution or coordinate policing measures also had to devise rhetorics and organizations that operated within limited political spaces and with given (even if newly formed) institutions. People had less time to look at what was happening in 'someone else's revolution' and, even if they did, could not easily work out what that meant for their own revolution. To use a spatial analogy – 'width' was replaced by 'depth'. The revolutions entered unknown territory and in so doing demanded more concentrated attention and energy. And so connections decreased in significance. Writers like Marx continued to seek to work out the lessons of one revolution for another but increasingly this involved hard intellectual labour and innovation (displayed most vividly in *The Eighteenth Brumaire of Louis-Napoleon*) which did not lend itself to ideological simplifications that could mobilize people.

This decline in connections did not mean that the revolutions in different countries became less and less like one another and acquired unique, perhaps national characteristics. One can observe differences in the patterns of revolution and counter-revolution as one moves from west to east and north to south and these can be linked to political, economic, cultural and confessional differences. However, there were similarities too.

II. Comparisons

To conduct comparison it is necessary to establish a common framework within which each case can be analysed. It helps if this framework is constructed at a level which is neither too general (e.g. abstract theories of revolution) nor too particular (e.g. specific occupations or political values). The first makes connection to 'real' events too arbitrary; the second is too easily distorted by slightly different contexts. I would suggest three medium-level frameworks within which comparisons can be made: economic, cultural and political.

Central to any framework must be some concept of a revolutionary situation. Predictable, stable power relations have fractured; there are instead competing (and constantly emerging and changing) power blocs and no one can be sure which of these will eventually prevail. Assumptions about how economic relationships are to be handled, which cultural norms provide a reliable basis for understanding and action, how authority is to be constituted and exercised: all these are cast into question. Only when the revolution has ended, i.e. when stable and predictable power relations have been restored (whether by revolutionaries or their opponents), can people return to old assumptions or trust in new ones.

Economic relationships

I use the term 'economic' rather than 'social'. Social histories of revolutions are usually framed in terms of occupational sectors and classes and their inter-relationships. Clearly other kinds of 'social' groups exist – constituted by common ties such as religion, political values, region or ethnicity – and are much clearer if one recognizes that occupational/class analysis is only one kind of 'social' analysis.

Such an analysis assumes that groups defined in economic terms share collective characteristics and common forms of action and senses of solidarity. On this basis one can see if particular groups displayed similar patterns of behaviour and belief and entered into similar relations with other groups seen as either allies or opponents.

I can only point briefly to one or two areas in which such comparisons seem well-founded. Best documented is that concerning the artisanal labour movement. Although other kinds of manual workers played important parts in collective action in 1848, it is generally agreed that artisans displayed the highest levels of organization and formulated the most advanced programmes. Furthermore, it has been persuasively argued that the most active artisan groups were located in a range of expanding occupations which were being penetrated by merchant capital but not being destroyed from outside by major technological innovations.[6]

To take this comparative analysis further one can combine a conjunctural with a structural approach. The conjunctural approach would focus on the short-term impact of the 'hungry years' of the mid-1840s upon these craft trades, above all increased unemployment or semi-employment. There is also an important cultural dimension in terms of the ways in which artisans redeployed their assumptions about the dignity of skilled work in an anti-capitalist direction which could draw upon new social theories.[7] By 1848 such workers were ready not merely to act against perceived threats to their work (machines, freedom of competition) and to demand job creation schemes, but also to organize in occupational and supra-occupational ways in support of more positive yet general visions about economic organization (*Organisation du Travail, Organisation der Arbeit*). Growing uncertainty about the trajectory of the revolution pushed a minority of these labour activists towards a more radical position, while a larger number belatedly tried to 'depoliticize' their efforts in order to avoid the terrible dangers associated with political defeat.

The structural approach stresses not merely economic recession and harvest failure in the mid-1840s but also the peculiar features of 'capitalism without industry' which structured direct producer/merchant capital relationships in a special way in a range of artisan trades. Within this perspective artisan action is not seen as a futile attempt either to buck one phase in the economic cycle or to stem the inevitable rise of modern industry but as an appropriate and powerful response to a special type of economic development.

This framework and related research is much better worked out for France and the German lands than for other regions. Some good comparative work also includes England, although the analysis must account for the absence of revolution.[8] We know far less about artisans in the Italian lands or the eastern half of the Habsburg Empire. Maybe artisan movements were not so important in these areas but it may also reflect different concerns on the part of historians, for example, with national and other political conflicts. In any case, we have to establish what, if anything, were the patterns of artisanal organization and action in these areas in order to complete the comparative analysis: differences are as important to such analysis as similarities.

There certainly *were* important differences between France and Germany and between different regions in those two countries. Was this because economic positions and relations differed in important ways (and that will include the significance of artisan workers within the labour force generally) or rather because of cultural and/or political differences? Clearly, for example, the political centrality of Paris, the politicization of all relationships and the scale and intensity of conflict over the National Workshops shaped the labour movement in ways quite unlike elsewhere, even if one might develop a similar type of analysis for the repression of popular movements in Prague, Vienna and Berlin.

It is clear that when we talk of 'economic' positions and relationships we are abstracting from 'real' positions and relationships. People have a plurality of roles and we cannot assume that those which are highlighted by economic categories will be the most important in shaping collective patterns of action in a revolution. Furthermore, even within those economic categories there are different roles available. This is not to suggest that we abandon such analysis. Any set of identities and roles we assume for purposes of analysis abstracts from the 'real'; it is as absurd to privilege 'cultural' over 'economic' categories as it is to attribute significance to 'discourse' rather than 'structure'. Rather we must take different ensembles of positions, interests and discourses and see which combinations most persuasively fit with the patterns of collective action and language that we observe.

Of all social movements those of artisans are the best conceptualized and compared for 1848. In principle there is no reason why one cannot do the same for a category called 'peasant' action. Here I think it will be the differences between France and other countries which will be most striking, rather than the differences between France and the German lands on the one hand and areas to the south and east as is the case for artisans. This is because a key variable concerns the degree to which landed property was held free of any constraints of privilege and to what extent such property was in peasant hands. However, historians have also pointed to important differences in terms of the size and prosperity of peasant holdings, crops cultivated (e.g. viticulture compared to grain), and between zones of plains, hills and mountains. What we do now know is that peasants had a much greater capacity for collective action in pursuit of their interests than was once generally assumed by both conservative and radical observers.[9]

More difficult and less developed are comparisons of groups holding dominant economic positions. There has been, so far as I know, no attempt to compare merchant capitalists or privileged landowners across national boundaries in 1848.[10] One possible reason is that such groups are too small to engage directly as groups in political conflict but rather combine into larger collective formations and in close connection with politico-military forces such as bureaucracies, armies and elite political parties. If that is the case, comparison should shift to the political level, e.g. looking at the way in which new forms of conservatism developed in response to revolution in 1848.[11]

I have left aside the most obvious form of economic comparison, that of class analysis. Surprisingly there has been little sustained effort by Marxist historians to identify common features and goals of a bourgeoisie or a working class across the different countries affected by revolution in 1848.[12] Maybe this is because recognition of great economic differences from both east to west and north to south already suggests that one will not get far with such comparison. In any case, class analysis takes one well beyond the economy. The rather limited nature of revolution in 1848–9 meant, in my view, that extensive patterns of socio-political action and conflict which one might analyse in class terms never had time or opportunity to develop. That is why I think the most useful types of socio-economic comparison will be those that focus on occupational sectors such as those of artisans or peasants.

2 Cultural comparisons

I have little to say about this. The most sustained forms of comparison have primarily used economic or political categories and only introduced 'culture' in the sense of values linked to these categories. Thus one might study artisans in terms of the existence or non-existence of a guild tradition and 'producer' values or radical political movements in relation to traditions of secrecy, conspiracy or populism. Usually the stress is upon differences between various countries and regions though there is no reason why that should be the case.

Three other ways in which cultural comparison could be developed strike me as worth exploring.

First, there is the importance of confessional identities, values and conflicts in 1848. Jonathan Sperber recently sketched out a framework which stressed how established or privileged churches moved more emphatically into strong positions of alliance with restored authority as a consequence of revolutionary failure in 1848–9.[13] Even here the emphasis is upon power relationships and institutions and what remains to be explored is the way in which religion as belief helped shape collective identity and action in the revolutions. In the German case, which I know best, it is clear that the *Deutschkatholiken* (German Catholic movement) and the *Freie Gemeinde* and *Lichtfreunde* (movements of radical, rationalist Protestantism) were important bases for radical action. At the other end of the political spectrum it is clear that many conservatives understood events through a Christian world-view and regarded the restoration of proper Christian beliefs as the basis of any lasting defeat of the revolution.[14]

Second, there is the importance of gender history. Generally speaking 'women's history', so far as 1848 is concerned, has focused on prominent women in the revolution, in particular on the few feminist pioneers but also on movements in which women and feminist values were important, for example in Germany in cases of *Deutsch-Katholizisimus* and the *Freie Gemeinde*.[15] So far as I know, however, a gender history which compares the way in which men and women were assigned (and played?) certain kinds of roles in the revolution in different countries has not been essayed.[16]

Third, one could focus on new capacities for communication developed in 1848–9 (and then rapidly closed down) and how these could alter established senses of individual and collective identity. Revolution broke down stable power relations and conceded new freedoms of speech, assembly, publication and organization. The result was an explosion of printing (both written and caricature), placards, public speaking, clubs, associations and congresses, elections – all forms of action and communication which extended to groups that had never before been able to act or be acted upon in these ways. One could compare the different levels at which this took place, for example along the lines adopted by Siemann in his innovative study of the German revolutions of 1848.[17] Why did one level of communication and action (e.g. that of elections and parliamentary politics) take the form that it did and how did it relate to other levels (e.g. those of interest group organization or the readerships for mass publications)? How did traditional forms of communication and action get redeployed in revolutionary circumstances? Some historians have pointed to the ways in which carnival or song could be used politically.[18]

All I can do is suggest that here is an agenda for future comparative research. At present we only have a few isolated works which make comparisons along these lines, and even those are largely written within national limits.

3 Political comparisons

Revolution is a situation in which there is no single or stable locus of power. This is usually brought about by popular action and involves violent conflict between existing power-holders and those opposed to them. Compared to the 'great' revolutions what is striking about 1848 is that the level of violence was quite limited as was the duration of the revolution. However, within that broad characterization there are important variations. Nowhere else was there a popular rising so massive nor a repression so savage as the June insurrection. Only in Hungary did rebels succeed in institutionalizing revolutionary power over a wide territory in the form of effective local administration and a regular army.[19] Comparisons at the political level could work within the common framework of revolution as involving violence and competing power blocs but should then seek to explain these variations.

I can envisage various ways in which such analysis might be pursued. First, and most obvious, is in terms of broad political currents. Roughly speaking one can distinguish democratic, liberal and conservative positions after the outbreak of revolution. (The democrats wanted to sustain the momentum of change in order to construct a political order in which authority was grounded upon popular consent). (Liberals wanted to use the initial breakdown of authority to construct a political order based on parliamentary consent although insulated from direct popular pressure) (Conservatives wanted to reverse the breakdown of authority and to restore a political order based on acceptance of social hierarchy and traditional authority.) There are problems with these characterizations (e.g. how does one categorize Bonapartism?). There are also finer distinctions to make, e.g. between 'revolutionary' and 'parliamentary' democrats, 'populist' and 'authoritarian' conservatives.

Nevertheless, I think one can conduct a reasonable comparison armed with such distinctions. In a short essay I cannot undertake this here. I would suggest that the most important similarities between revolutions in different countries involved the rise and then destruction of new kinds of democratic movements accompanied by the marginalization of liberal politics and the increasingly effective use of new kinds of populist or policing methods by conservative regimes. This can be linked to the patterns of changes I have already outlined. The lack of a prior crisis meant that oppositional elites (largely liberals) were not ready to assume power on the basis of revolution and generally proved uncertain and ambivalent about how they exercised the fragile power handed to them in early 1848. The weakness of the popular movements that brought down the regimes meant that democrats soon had to realize that they could not immediately establish power on the degree of popular mobilization that existed but must build up much greater popular support. That very lack of popular involvement and the retention of many instruments of power by members of the pre-revolutionary regimes provided conservatives with opportunities to build up support and retake power quickly. The one exception proves the rule. In Hungary it was an established elite of nobles and gentry who took over power and only subsequently found themselves forced to acknowledge that they were engaged in revolution. This was a much firmer basis on which to resist the counter-revolution.[20]

A second level of analysis could be in terms of locales. Some interesting work has been done, for example, on the patterns of revolutionary and counter-revolutionary action in capital cities. In principle similar kinds of comparisons could be mounted for the countryside and the market towns which often acted as their political centres, or for different kinds of larger urban centres.[21] Such comparisons can be conducted both in terms of types of political organization, values and conflict and also in terms of political sociology.

A third level of comparison could be in terms of types of political action and movement. This could be linked to my earlier point about the decline in 'width' and the increase in 'depth' in collective action during the revolution. There are obvious comparisons to make between the patterns of action in the capital cities in the first phase of urban insurrection which is one reason perhaps why the best comparisons of this kind focus precisely on that phase and locale.

However, after that initial phase innovation was required. The proclamation of constituent assemblies and the preparation for elections to those assemblies stimulated such innovation. Elections were in part shaped by traditional forms of influence – the preacher leading his congregation to the polls, landowners and employers seeking to use their economic power to influence voting. Yet the sheer scale and frequency of elections demanded more. Radicals responded most quickly and moved away from forms of 'direct action' (militias, clubs) to those designed to win elections (agitational associations and publications). Their conservative opponents learnt in turn from this. Liberals, formally holding power but feeling threatened by popular mobilization, generally proved the least able to adapt to this new situation. Comparison could focus on the patterns and extent of such innovations and in turn link that to differences between regions and states. Analysis could then extend to pressure group organization which replaced older actions such as petitioning with innovative attempts to influence parliaments and ministries, e.g. artisan congresses and Catholic political associations. Such comparisons could also trace how far such innovations survived beyond the revolution, for example in places which retained some type of constitutionality, and how by contrast others were destroyed or forced underground by repression, or faded away as they came to appear irrelevant to new circumstances.[22]

A fourth set of comparisons would focus on the national dimension of revolution, not merely in terms of national differences but the importance of the national question and nationality conflicts. By its very nature the national perspective inhibits comparison. Yet even if one accepts major differences one can note that there were (three broad zones within which comparisons can be made.) First, largely confined to France, was where the revolution did not call into question the territory of the existing state and where such nationalism as was present was directed beyond national territory. In so far as historians focus upon internal differences, this means that in France national issues are left aside in favour of political and social conflict. The only exception to this is when differences over French policy towards the revolution in other countries both represents competing types of nationalism and leads to internal conflict, for example the May demonstration in Paris in favour of Polish restoration or the radical opposition to French assistance to the Papacy.

Second, there were the German and Italian lands where the national project involved merging a number of states into one. However, there was a major difference in that the principal enemies of German unification appeared as the 'German' states of Austria and Prussia whereas that of Italian unification was the 'foreign' state of Austria.[23] This meant that Italy shared more features than did Germany with the third kind of case where the national project involved separating from the existing state. At the same time, these separatist movements most directly put different nationalisms into conflict with one another and these conflicts have often been assumed to *replace* those based on social divisions elsewhere.

In Germany there is something of a balance between work that focuses on 'social' and 'political' divisions and that on the national question, especially as the fairly 'internalist' analysis of the national question draws attention to related social and political differences. In Italy there is increasingly work on political differences at the level of individual states but the national question still dominates the historiography. This national concern even more completely dominates work on the Habsburg Empire, especially its eastern half. Where a more critical approach has been adopted I think it has both questioned the centrality of the national question to many people in 1848 and also shown that national differences were closely bound up with economic, cultural and political differences. Local radicals were often suspicious of the national movement if it appeared too limited in its democratic values and often preferred to restrict themselves to their own region or state. Popular mobilization often required a social programme, for example that of peasant emancipation, and without that a nationalist movement achieved limited appeal, especially if conservatives were also prepared to make such appeals.

Such issues remain to be explored properly in the third zone of separatist nationalism. This is unfortunate because it tends to mean that nationality is treated as a pre-existing reality whereas in fact I would argue that in many areas this was virtually constructed, and certainly greatly altered, during the revolution. Many people 'learnt' that they were Czechs or Germans in Bohemia and Moravia,[24] or that they were Magyars and Romanians in Transylvania. Different political developments (e.g. the adoption of a different language policy by Magyars) could have led to the assumption of different identities and political positions.

Apart from comparison within each of the three zones, e.g. between the nationalism of 'dominant' and 'subordinate' ethnic groups in the Habsburg Empire (the phrases are less contentious than those of historical/non-historical or large/small), one could also try to see how forms of nationalism varied with political differences (e.g. was there such a thing as conservative nationalism in 1848?) and social constituencies (e.g. did appeals to peasantry take similar forms in different, even conflicting national movements?). British, French and German public opinion supported the Hungarian, Italian and Polish national movements but were generally indifferent or hostile to Slav nationalism. This suggests a common set of assumptions about what kinds of ethnic or cultural identity justified political self-determination and what kinds did not. The prevailing view was that what we would now call dominant cultural groups (and what some at the time termed 'historical nations') were entitled to political autonomy whereas non-dominant cultural groups were at best entitled to a measure of cultural autonomy. Again, I can only outline an agenda for comparison.

Conclusion

This is a speculative essay and I have few definite conclusions. The firmest is that connections based on common assumptions about the nature of revolution were very important at the outset of the revolution but tended to fade away as different revolutions became preoccupied with their own special and unanticipated problems. When this point is reached the historian can only write about the revolutions as a whole either by tracing the new kinds of connections based on direct contacts, whether of cooperation or conflict, or by developing explicitly comparative frameworks along the lines indicated here.[25]

Comparison should always bear in mind that this was a time of revolution. Frameworks of economic comparison can probably best be developed for the study of artisan and peasant movements. Cultural comparisons probably will work best in considering the dimensions of religion (now being studied again after a period of neglect), gender and innovative forms of communication and association and what impact these had on collective identity and action. Political comparison should focus on the major political differences (democratic, liberal, conservative), linking to different social bases and patterns of organization. Negatively the main point of comparisons of the national dimension is to ask what were the conditions of its rapid emergence as a significant source of identity and political programmes; otherwise comparison probably will work best within the three zones of France, Germany/Italy and the Habsburg Empire.

The revolutions arose with little in the way of a pre-revolutionary crisis induced by regime breakdown or war such as one finds before 1640 (conflict with Scotland and between Crown and Parliament), 1789 (financial crisis and the summoning of an Estates-General) or 1917 (crisis induced by setbacks in war). Instead there was a more generalized economic crisis although even that was on the mend after the improved harvests of 1847. It was a climate of opinion based on social fear induced by some of the unrest caused by economic difficulties in 1847 and a sense of revolution as a play waiting to be performed which were important and connecting factors in the initial breakdown of authority. Yet this also meant that it was a superficial breakdown compared to those associated with the 'great' revolutions.[26] That is why so many people have argued that 1848-9 was not a 'real' revolution. However, it was very 'real' in the sense both of appearing so to contemporaries and of involving a breakdown of established authority, if only relatively briefly. Seeking to reconstitute authority was the major preoccupation of political (including national) movements; seeking to advance or defend interests was the major concern of occupational sectors; seeking to impose a set of norms, whether for restoration or permanent change, was the central cultural concern. People had different projects and devised different ways of pursuing those but this common fate of uncertainty as well as shared characteristics (e.g. between artisans or peasants or established churches) also point to important similarities. On this basis a comparative history of the 1848–9 revolutions could in principle be written. I have suggested some of the issues it should explore and the approaches it might adopt. Actually writing such a history is another matter.

Notes

1 This is a speculative essay and it would be inappropriate to provide copious references. I do refer to some essays on relevant topics which have appeared in two German books published to mark the 150th anniversary of the 1848 revolutions. These are: *Europa 1848. Revolution und Reform*, edited by D. Dowe et al. (Bonn, 1998), henceforth *Europa 1848*, and *1848. Revolution in Deutschland* (Frankfurt am Main and Leipzig, 1998), edited by C. Dipper and U. Speck, henceforth *Revolution in Deutschland*. *Europa 1848* is to appear in an English translation.

2 On the methods and advantages of comparative history see my essay 'Making comparisons in history' in *Labour and Liberalism in Nineteenth-Century Europe: Essays in Comparative History* (Manchester, 1992), pp. 1–25.

3 J. Merriman, 'Les "on dit que". Gerüchte und die Zweite Französische Republik', in *Europa 1848*, pp. 1139–66.

4 There were exceptions: Radetzky and his troops had to be forced out of Milan by bitter fighting. Also there appeared to be a repugnance on the part of Louis Philippe and Frederick William IV to retain power by shooting down large numbers of their subjects. The roots of such a governmental morality and why it gave way to less inhibited resort to repression later in 1848 would be worth studying, and again in a comparative way.

5 Rebecca Spang provides some examples of this theme in her essay.

6 See, for example, J. Sperber, *Rhineland Radicals: The Democratic Movement and the Revolution of 1848–1849* (New Jersey, 1991) which does engage in regional comparisons. See also my own essay: 'Artisan economy, ideology and politics: the artisan contribution to the mid-nineteenth-century European labour movement', in *Labour and Liberalism*, pp. 76–114.

7 A pioneering work for France alone which finishes with 1848 is W. H. Sewell Jr, *Work and Revolution in France: The Language of Labor from the Old Regime to 1848* (Cambridge, 1980).

8   Most recently I. Prothero, *Radical Artisans in England and France 1830–1870* (Cambridge, 1997). See now also H.-G. Haupt and F. Lenger, 'Bürger – Kleinbürger – Arbeiter. Klassenbildung/Gesellschaftsreform in Deutschland und Frankreich', in *Europa 1848*, pp. 815–40.

9   I have recently developed some of these ideas a little further, if speculatively, in *Mass Politics and the Revolutions of 1848*, part of *Core Resources for Historians: A Multimedia CD-Rom* (TLTP History Courseware Consortium, University of Glasgow, 1998). See also Ch. Dipper, 'Revolutionäre Bewegungen auf dem Lande: Deutschland, Frankreich, Italien', in *Europa 1848*, pp. 555–86 and W. Höpken, 'Die Agrarfrage in der Revolution in Südosteuropa', in ibid., pp. 587–626.

10 For Germany see two recently published essays in *Revolution in Deutschland*: H. Reif, 'Der Adel', pp. 213–34 and F. Lenger, 'Das Bürgertum', pp. 235–47. For France there remains the magisterial work of A. J. Tudesq, *Les Grands Notables en France 1830–1849*, 2 vols (Paris, 1964).

11 Some such work is appearing for Germany though only at state level. See W. Schwenkter, *Konservative Vereine und Revolution in Preußen 1848/49* (Düsseldorf, 1988).

12 There were the contemporary histories written by Marx and Engels although these focused on France and Germany respectively. Few have attempted to follow in their path and the official marxism of the German Democratic Republic failed to produce anything worthwhile on 1848, being obsessed with establishing both how correct and significant Marx had been in 1848. Some sophisticated marxist analyses have been written for particular cases, such as P. Ginsborg, *Daniele Manin and the Venetian Revolution of 1848–49* (Cambridge, 1979), although ultimately in my view they fail to convince as I long ago argued in 'The failure of revolution in 1848', in *European Studies Review*, 11(1) (1981), pp. 103–16.

13 J. Sperber, 'Kirchen, Gläubige und Religionspolitik in der Revolution von 1848', in *Europa 1848*, pp. 933–60.

14 At a recent exhibition on 1848 held in Frankfurt I was struck by one exhibit, the annotated bible of General Wrangel, the man who dissolved the Prussian National Assembly in November 1848 and restored conservative rule in Berlin.

15 See for example, S. Paletschek, *Frauen und Dissens. Frauen im Deutsch-Katholizismus und in den freien Gemeinden 1841–1852* (Göttingen, 1990).

16 For a couple of relevant essays see S. Kienitz, 'Frauen', in *Revolution in Deutschland*, pp. 272–85; and G. Hauch, 'Frauen-Räume in der Männer-Revolution', in *Europa 1848*, pp. 841–900.

17 W. Siemann, *The German Revolutions of 1848–1849* (London, 1998).

18 See Axel Körner's contribution to this book. There are some relevant essays in *Europa 1848*, notably Ch. Tacke, 'Feste der Revolution in Deutschland und Italien', pp. 1045–88; Willibald Steinmetz, '"Sprechen ist einen Tat bei euch." Die Wörter und das Handeln in der Revolution von 1848', pp. 1089–138.

19 One or two areas in Italy and Germany, notably Rome, Venice and Baden, did organize some significant military resistance to counter-revolution but nothing of the scale and significance of that in Hungary.

20 This is a central argument in I. Deak, *The Lawful Revolution: Louis Kossuth and the Hungarians, 1848–1849* (New York, 1979).

21 See essays in the section 'Stadt und Land' in *Europa 1848*, especially those by R. Hachtmann, 'Die europäischen Hauptstädte in der Revolution von 1848', pp. 455–92; J. Breuilly and I. Prothero, 'Die Revolution als städtitsches Ereignis. Hamburg und Lyon in der Revolution von 1848', pp. 493–534; and K.-J. Hummel, 'Zonen der politischen Stille', pp. 535–54.

22 The two recent collections I have cited before have some relevant essays. In *Revolution in Deutschland* there is a section entitled 'Räume der Revolution' which includes essays on the streets (M. Galius), the pub and café (K. Wegert), the town hall (Th. Mergel) and parliament (U. Speck). In *Europa 1848* there is an essay on militias (R. Pröve), on popular assemblies (W. Siemann) and again on street politics (M. Galius).

23 Like so much else in this essay this is a sweeping statement. German radical nationalists saw Russia as a major obstacle and Italians were well aware that the Bourbon regime of the Two Sicilies opposed unity and, after a brief sympathetic phase, so did the Pope.

24 See the contribution by Jan Havránek in this book.

25 One well-trodden path which traces direct connections is what might be called the diplomatic history of the revolutions. However, that conventional diplomatic history tends to consider 'revolution' as something external to the 'powers' which decide to deal with revolution (or rather with situations produced by revolution, such as the Danish–German conflict in Schleswig-Holstein) in one way or another. There may be something to be said for this approach when considering Britain and Russia as they were external to the revolutions; there is little to be said for it in relation to France, Prussia and Austria, let alone the zones of small states engulfed by revolution in 1848. It is also rare for diplomatic history to adopt an analytical let alone a comparative approach but rather to take the form of narrative which assumes unitary subjects ('states') acting on certain principles ('interests'), a dubious assumption at the best of times and revolutions are not such times.

26 Also in 1789 and 1917 the connection with revolution outside France and Russia respectively was made primarily by the revolutionary regime, through war from 1792 and through Russian attempts to internationalize revolution through the formation of communist parties in other countries. Revolution did not 'spread' as it did in early 1848.

3
Events and Non-Events...Cultural Reflections of and on 1848

Martin Swales

Bertolt Brecht was fond of noting the fact that Shakespeare nowhere in his creative oeuvre mentions – let alone discusses – the most dramatic political event-sequence of his age: the rivalry with Spain culminating in the defeat of the Armada. On the face of it, it was a gift to a dramatist, for it was a constellation that involved everything and everybody: intense public interest, with matters of national integrity and pride very much at stake; there was a striking interplay of battles of words and of physical, military engagements, and a widely shared perception of the world-historical role of the combatants involved. Yet Shakespeare offered no direct statement. To say this, however, is not to say that his art had no engagement with the central experiences of his age. Quite the reverse. But the intense reflectivity – about, for example, political and historical change, about the conflict between sacramental notions of kingship and secular power politics, about the shifting relationships between monarchy, aristocracy and the emergent mercantile classes, about theatre as politics and politics as theatre – was deployed indirectly, by borrowing plots, characters and events from earlier chronicles. This does not mean that great art cannot seek direct confrontation with the immediate present; it merely is to say that it does not *have* to seek that directness.

Moreover, there is an issue of artistic genre which is worth raising at this juncture. The visual arts, because of their manifest ability to capture striking images of events, can frequently find an appropriate mode in which to make a direct statement. In one of the most famous revolutionary images known to us, Delacroix in 1830 depicts

Liberty Guiding the People. Later, Daumier, Meissonier and Millet will provide key glimpses of 1848 through visual statement. And the same will be done in Germany by Menzel's *March Casualties lying in State* and Rethel's *Another Dance of Death*. Let me not be misunderstood. I am not for a moment suggesting that such visual depictions, simply because they are visual and by that token iconic, constitute reportage, dispassionate, documentary evidence. Clearly, issues of mode, convention, of texture and light, and of aesthetic structure are all-important. How allegorical (on the one hand) are such representations? Or (conversely) how realistic are they? Is the mode grand, monumentalizing – or are we manifestly held in the vernacular of humble lives and circumstances? What is the relationship between individuals and groups? How unitary (on the one hand) or (on the other) how disparate are the groups? If there are clearly visualized protagonists in the image, are they expressive of (perhaps victims of ?) the corporate situation? Or are they in some way superior to it? Are they gendered? Is there any erotic charge to be felt – if so, a stylized or an earthy eroticism? My point here is the obvious one: the visual and plastic arts lend themselves readily to the *grand tableau* depiction of major historical events. But even here, the images are not simply, disinterestedly iconic. They are of their very nature mediated. And what they convey is not simple facticity; rather, they mediate the complex mediations of history in the making.[1] And what is true of visual images on canvas also holds good for those mental images that we all carry round with us as memories. In one sense, such precipitates of what we have lived through are underpinned by the claim to (documentary) authenticity, by the sheer authority of the eyewitness observer. Equally, as we all know from our relationship to personal recollections, such memories are ceaselessly reinscribed, renegotiated as our present viewpoint changes. This is not for a moment to invalidate memories as historical evidence. But it is to remind us that memories are not some unmediated image on a photographic plate; they are, rather complexly mediated – and herein resides their historiographical truth.

Almost by its very nature, literature tends to be more indirect, more reflective than the visual arts. As aesthetic theory has long recognized, literature's very medium is linear, sequential. Of course, it can also offer large-scale description, and magnificently so (one thinks of the Battle of the Borodino in Tolstoy's *War and Peace*). But even such panoramic moments have their reflective dimension. The very linearity and discursivity of the linguistic and narrative medium allows it to enshrine and to explore modes of causality. Because (in a way that is not to anything like the same extent true of the visual or plastic arts) it can have access to both the outer and the inner realms, it can articulate the complex flow of reflectivity, the values, temperaments, assumptions, symbols – in a word, the mentality – of a particular age. Even passages of description in narrative, then, are inseparable from registers of discursive commentary.

Before I come to consideration of my texts, I should like to add a further comment on the issue of reflectivity. It seems to me that such reflectivity has a high degree of pertinence where 1848 specifically is at issue. I am not a historian; but I should like to venture the generalization that we are still not quite sure what to make of 1848, whether as a phenomenon within national or European history. Many of the texts that will concern me in this paper seem uncertain what to make of the revolution. There are exceptions, of course. But the majority of my evidence suggests a measure of interpretative unclarity and evaluative unease. One could, of course, attribute this to the fact that high-culture literature is rarely doctrinaire or forthright in its import; rather, it tends to perceive and to articulate complexity at every turn. This one may regret, of course. I shall, however, be concerned to suggest that, where 1848 is concerned, the uncertainty may be a cognitively valuable condition; that, where certain forms of historiography may allow themselves the luxury of unambiguous judgements, the literary mediation may – not in spite of but because of its interpretative multivalence – have much to say about the historical phenomena at issue. The literary picture of the European unrest in 1848 is made up of an untidy corpus of events and non-events, and may on that account be revelatory. In asserting the interpretative intractability of 1848, I am not seeking to imply that other revolutions – for example 1789 – are interpretatively over and done with. Clearly the French Revolution is still passionately contested. But I have the sense that there is a measure of agreement that it does constitute a significant watershed – and that certain primary causalities were operative. Clearly, any attempt to offer an evaluation of its significance would produce a lively debate as to which yardsticks might be more appropriate than others. But the yardsticks would be there, whereas 1848 is a strangely untidy phenomenon, and, by this token, it constantly invites our reflection and discussion. For this reason some of the reflectivity of the literature that concerns me may be genuinely – by which I mean historically – appropriate.

The texts that are referred to in this paper are for the most part literary (although on one or two occasions I shall mention music). Before coming to the works themselves, let me summarize some of the issues they raise:

- What is the prior context that brings about the collapse of the government? How do groups constitute themselves and mobilize?
- What are the essential events of the revolution? In two cases (Paris and Berlin) there is an element of misjudgement as the military overreacts and fires on a demonstration, thus inflaming the situation. In such circumstances even the clearly discernible core of events is problematic and may need reflection and commentary. Are we to talk of the role of contingency (whatever that is)? Should we conclude that better troops, more experienced, more disciplined soldiers would have coped more coolly and thereby not created martyr legends? Conversely, was the situation so explosive that the tension was bound to unload? If so, what were the underlying pressures that converted an unmomentous gathering into a momentous one? Part of the problem with 1848 is that it can be seen as an event and a non-event (in a way that is not true of 1789).
- What kinds of aspiration unite the various revolutionary groupings? Socialist? Utopian? Gradualist? What kind of solidarity is in evidence (for example, between middle classes and workers? between intellectuals and the broader public)? How far do the various national uprisings take note of and learn from each other? How far are they comparable?
- What of the emblematics at work? How do the various participants symbolize their hopes and deeds? (One thinks, for example, of the red-black-gold flag of German unity.)
- What kind of representative forum is under discussion? Councils? Parliaments? Assemblies? Diets?
- What is the role of particular institutions, and what is the mindset that holds these institutions together?
- What is the role of key experiential conceptualizations (such as public/private, licit/illicit, sacred/secular)?

- What forms of debate are in evidence? What is the prevailing discourse (of good sense, sweet reason)? And what of other, marginalized discourses?
- What evaluative criteria are appropriate for judging the success or failure, the progress or the retreat of the revolution? Are ethical judgements – or pragmatic ones – paramount?

I apologize for this bombardment of questions. All I have been seeking to do is to tease out some of the implications generated by the texts that concern me; my sense is that these implications are not merely, and not narrowly, literary – but are, rather, genuinely historiographical in their import. To claim an overlap of literary and historiographical insights in this way is not, I believe, to conflate the two disciplines. Clearly, a historical account of 1848 is falsifiable in a way that a novel is not. But equally many of the hermeneutic processes that inform our negotiation with a novel text are manifestly transferable to the historiographical sphere. At the simplest level, we should not forget that both novels and histories work centrally in terms of a narrative sequence that is sustained not by simple linear contiguity but by notions of causality. The aggregations of 'and then ... and then ... and then' say very little; (hi)stories start to come into focus when 'because ... on account of ... consequently' inform the rhetoric of the telling. However, precisely in our postmodern cultural climate it is important to insist that there were documentable events 'out there', events that have left material traces. To say, in the spirit of Derrida's dictum, 'il n'y a pas de hors-texte',[2] is absurd. But conversely, it is important for us to recognize how abundantly 'textual' that reality out there was. To reiterate a point which I have already touched on: for the historian as for the novelist, many crucial events are moments of human understanding, interpretation, cognition. The difference between an event and a non-event lies not in the empirically measurable, outward scale of the happening, but in its significance – significance as of then and as of now. And significance is a category less of materiality than of interpretation. The input of 'texting' is crucial, for, by being 'texted', matter comes to matter.

Most commentators would, I suspect, agree that the events in Paris are the key inception of the sequence of European unrest. It is, therefore, not inappropriate to begin with France. The years post-1830 see a relatively liberal consensus under Louis-Philippe's kingship. Yet that liberalism goes hand in hand with cupidity and materialism. Stendhal's denunciation of immediate post-Napoleonic France in *Le Rouge et le Noir* is extended to the July monarchy in *Lucien Leuwen*. In both cases experiential inauthenticity is the order of the day as the emptiness of politics casts its pall everywhere. Stendhal's irony ranges magisterially from private to public realms.[3]   Balzac's luridly melo-dramatic imagination expresses both fascination with and outrage at bourgeois culture on the make; money becomes not only a key agent of social life but also a governing metaphor within the *Comédie humaine*. Cognitively, psychologically and financially Balzac's uni-verse moves in a field of force suspended between boom and bust.[4] The 1840s witness an economic crisis as industrial expansion falters. The harvest is poor in 1846. In February 1848, when troops ill-advisedly open fire on a demonstration, the attendant outrage leads to the monarchy being toppled. But many of the socialist, utopian ideas that circulate subsequently are brutally crushed when a workers' rising is put down in June 1848. Louis-Napoleon, nephew of the Great Emperor, becomes President of the Second Republic, but this state of affairs is short-lived because the Assembly is disbanded and Louis-Napoleon becomes the Emperor Napoleon III. The rapid flux of constitutional events raises the question whether the clock has been put forward or back – or has it been just spinning crazily? What has been the nature of the revolution, and what has it achieved? Flaubert's answer is searingly sceptical. Having found unforgettable expression for the stultification of the pre-revolutionary days in *Madame Bovary*, he embarks, in the final version of *L'Education senti-mentale*, on a wonderfully ironic epic of not-quite-connected lives. Frédéric Moreau lives in a world of deferred experience; his emo-tional and cognitive complexity seems well-nigh indistinguishable from his sheer tentativeness. The revolution amounts to very little, it almost passes Frédéric by completely; but then this is true of all experience. There is an all-pervasive climate of drifting, of inauthen-ticity and half-heartedness as bourgeois culture atrophies at every turn.[5] Yet by contrast, other writers do perceive a significant sea-change. Baudelaire registers both the disturbing, fragmenting, displa-cing experiences of the modern urban world and the eerie sense that many of its cognitive modes and forms have not changed to keep pace. That mismatch, captured in the recreation of the Gothic arch by means of steel girders and rivets, is one of the cardinal tensions of European modernity, as Walter Benjamin unerringly recognized.[6]

By contrast with France, Austria, for all that Metternich is finally toppled and a whole regime of censorship is ended, remains more muted. Johann Nestroy, the great satirist of the Viennese stage, is deeply sceptical of what will come out of the 1848 unrest, of what happens when, to paraphrase the title of one of his plays, freedom comes to Chickentown. As always in Nestroy, language wears a dual aspect; it bespeaks both entrapment and creativity. The old discourse of reactionary values rumbles on; many of the new values seem about as hackneyed as the old. And the brilliantly vitriolic scepticism of the commentator figure seems in part to derive its brilliance from the fact that the only begetter of those insights is an onlooker, a commentator.[7] Insight, creativity goes hand in hand with marginality and disempowerment. Both Stifter and Grillparzer have no doubt that, under Metternich's Restoration, the times were out of joint and were inimical to the finer spiritual energies of humankind. Stifter initially supports the revolution, and even allows his name to go forward to the Frankfurt parliament; but then he gets cold feet. All his work post-1848 seeks to espouse the sacramental authority and rightness of gradual, imperceptible processes lying outside human volition and control, and he disparages sudden, transformatory events as being, by ontological definition, non-events. It is, however, part of the stylistic and human distinction of his work that the ideology of conservatism never fully muffles the countervailing energies and intimations. The stately prose of litanesque gradualness is suddenly fractured by brutal discontinuities.[8] Stifter writes very movingly of the human need to make a difference to the bland indifference of the material world. Grillparzer, too, advocates peace and quiet at every turn, but he also acknowledges the erotic, moral and political betrayals entailed by an ethos of 'not rocking the boat'. His historical dramas look back to the early history of the House of Habsburg. In certain figures he discovers individuals who are sceptical and reticent in spirit, but whose innate modesty of action, speech and purpose yet goes hand in hand with the ability to take decisive political action when the occasion demands. The upshot is a strange concoction of utopia and paralysis.[9] Yet not even Grillparzer's advocacy could stem the centrifugal forces at work in the Austro-Hungarian lands. The year 1848 witnesses not only the end of Metternichian oppression, it also sees the constituent nationalities of the Empire asserting themselves ever more vigorously. Franz Joseph comes to the throne in 1848; between then and his death in 1916 he presides in an ethos of masterly, self-mythologizing inactivity over the separatist dismemberment of the old Habsburg dinosaur as the forces of nationalism carry all before them. Yet to say this is to capture only one part of a complex truth. It is important to remember that sometimes that old dinosaur had had a value for people of liberal persuasion and aspiration. In 1848 Bohemia demands equal rights for both languages (Czech and German). The bilingualism (and not monolingualism) is noteworthy, for it indicates that German was not seen as merely the medium of brutal, bureaucratic oppression. In Bohemia the legacy of Maria Theresa was one of strenuously furthered literacy – and with that literacy went a respect for both languages and cultures. We would do well to remember that the revolutionary aspirations across 1848 Europe were accompanied by a complex perception of the forms of community that could best underwrite liberty. Sometimes that form was held to be the unified nation-state, but by no means always. For large numbers of liberals, constitutional guarantees, intelligible administrative structures, decent legislation meant more than the ethnicity of spurious rootedness.

The issue of nationalism complicates matters in Germany. Like Italy, the German-speaking lands are late in achieving united nation statehood. Hence, the forces of liberalism and nationalism are ceaselessly in contestation, sometimes diverging, sometimes overlapping. In Germany, the liberals tend to espouse the cause of 'small German' unity (that is, of a state founded on Prussia, to the exclusion of Austria). The 1830s and 1840s see a number of works from the 'Young German' generation – by Laube, Mundt, Kühne, Gutzkow and Immermann – that lament the constriction and sterility of life in the petty territories that make up the German Confederation.[10] A work such as Kühne's *Quarantäne im Irrenhause* unforgettably modulates *Werther*, Goethe's great novel of protest at the constriction of the inner life, into a terrifying study of the constriction of any sort of life in the penal system of a petty prince. There is, then, no shortage of voices to proclaim the need for change, and some key talents offer a perception of how it is that socio-cultural change comes about. The dramatist Friedrich Hebbel, writing in the Hegelian mode, is one such; constantly he explores the ways in which and the extent to which individual psychology, seemingly private experience, bears the imprint of and fans the flames of the shift of values in the public sphere. In an extraordinary novel set in the immediate aftermath of 1848 entitled *Die Ritter vom Geist*, Karl Gutzkow considers how a post-revolutionary culture may capitalize on the creative energies of the regnerative upsurge. His answer is touching in its helplessness; the novel portays endless associations, societies, groupings, all of which issue manifestos and formulate programmes but have not the slightest idea what to do. (Some sixty years later, incidentally, the years immediately preceding 1914 will furnish Robert Musil with a similar, and similarly exhaustive, Vanity Fair of a well-meaning but anchorless socio-political culture in his masterly *Der Mann ohne Eigenschaften*.) In 1848 Germany, conservative voices (Freytag's *Soll und Haben*, with its hymn in praise of solid German mercantile effort,[11] and Auerbach's love affair with village life in the *Schwarzwälder Dorfgeschichten*) coexist with much more forthright, progressive ones – one thinks of the Low German writer Fritz Reuter, himself imprisoned for seven years, who not surprisingly wrote novels which make no secret of their sympathy for those who seek freedom from oppression. And there are those who modulate from enthusiasm for the revolution to disenchantment and scepticism. One such is Richard Wagner, who in Dresden is forthright in his hopes for national self-transformation, but who swiftly espouses a much more conservative stance. In the late 1840s, at the height of his revolutionary enthusiasm, Wagner starts work on the great project that is *Der Ring des Nibelungen*. He begins at the end – with *Siegfrieds Tod*, which envisages both the initial triumph of the old order and the intimation that, somewhat in the manner of Hebbel, tragedy, the martyr death, will move the world order a notch forward. For the next 27 years Wagner worked on his great epic. The collision of liberationary energies with the abundant recognition of the force – and the forces – of reaction makes the work fascinating in its ambivalence. When the mature Wagner comes to compose the appointed end of the tetralogy which he had sketched years before, he was inclined to make the notion of redemption at the close metaphysical rather than historico-political.[12] Although, as the Chéreau/Boulez centenary *Ring* showed us, the politics can be vigorously reimported into the metaphysics.

Looking back now on 1848 in the German-speaking lands, one wonders if some of the long-established readings still hold true.

A. J. P. Taylor spoke famously of the 'turning point where Germany failed to turn'[13] – and others have written of Germany's failure to join the modern world, of the tragic collapse of liberalism. Hence all the generalizations about the 'special course of German history', the 'belated nation' and so on. But I wonder if we can be so certain in our evaluation of plus and minus, success and failure, progression and regression. To talk of this phase of German history only in terms of failure, of what did not happen – and, above all, in terms of a fatal switching of the points towards unambiguous political disaster – is, I feel, to succumb to the seductions of unexamined normative thinking. The year 1848 was clumsy, untidy, and perhaps this has to do with the fact there were simply too many issues at stake at any one time. And this pluralism militated against the single-minded focus needed for a revolutionary momentum to be generated and sustained. Crucially, there was the ceaseless interplay of and tension between democratic aspirations on the one hand and the desire for national unity on the other. Different territories had their different agendas. Even in liberal circles there was a widespread fear of violent revolution (the negative example of the French Revolution was ferociously potent). There was, additionally, no one capital city to provide the point of symbolic focus; hence, princely rule was never in any thoroughgoing sense challenged. But significant reforms were conceded (greater freedom of the press, an incomparably greater climate of discussion and debate thanks to the Frankfurt parliament were achieved). Admittedly, the Frankfurt parliament was a talk shop, filled with more than its fair share of middle-class intellectuals who no doubt meant well but who had little ability to achieve immediate results. Yet a measure of liberalization came about. And, if one thinks in terms of reform rather than revolution, then Germany's 1848 can perhaps be more justly assessed – as a complex nexus of events and programmes which was too complex to be susceptible of either simple solutions then or of doctrinaire analysis now. The shifting illumination provided by pre- and post-March German literature has, then, a measure of historiographical validity.

Switzerland, by contrast with most other European countries, can celebrate 1848 as a clear milestone, one that marks the emergence of the modern constitutional state. In the early 1830s many cantons were persuaded to introduce a new, liberally minded constitution, the 'Regenerationsverfassung' which, among other measures, envisaged the transformation of the existing, loose aggregation of cantons into a coherently articulated federal state, a 'Bundesstaat' which would be able to take a more vigorous hand in central planning in respect of the economy, trade, traffic and communications systems. Moreover, the progressive cantons were vigorous in their insistence on the secular character of the modern state, and condemned the institutional power of the Jesuits. The conservative inner cantons of Luzern, Uri, Schwyz, Unterwalden, Zug, Freiburg and Wallis resisted these pressures. Luzern appointed Jesuits to key positions in a seminary. The progressive cantons were incensed at this provocation – and at what they saw as the formation of an illegal reactionary alliance, the 'Sonderbund'. Various small skirmishing parties, the so-called 'Freischarenzüge', set off in late 1844 and early 1845 to bring the reactionary cantons to heel. On two occasions, Gottfried Keller, Switzerland's greatest writer of the nineteenth century, was involved in 'Freischaren'. They seem, certainly by his account, to have been half-hearted affairs: on one occasion they never even got as far as Luzern; on another they reached the city gates, but then turned back. Yet finally serious pressure was brought to bear from the Confederation. Troops, under the prudent command of General Henri Dufour, were sent in; the conservative cantons gave way. In 1848 the 'Staatenbund' was transformed into the modern constitution of a 'Bundesstaat'.

In one sense, the events themselves that took place on Swiss soil were modest in scale. Yet their symbolic value was and is considerable. The battle was joined on two fronts: for the soul of the original Switzerland (Schwyz, Uri and Unterwalden were the founding cantons of Switzerland, brought together by the Rütli-Schwur); and for the modern constitutional form of that soul (the more centrist, interventionist federal state in succession to the loose association of cantons). Two of Switzerland's major German-language writers of the time address the central conflicts. Gotthelf in *Zeitgeist und Berner Geist* produces a fiercely polemical novel which uses the contrast between two farming families to embody the contrast betwen old and new ways. There is no contest; Gotthelf's sympathies are unambiguously distributed – the course of the novel is a foregone conclusion. Hunghans and his family, who depart from the traditional faith and espouse newfangled ideas, are not only morally inadequate, they go to rack and ruin, whereas Ankenbenz and his wife remain cautious, God-fearing and, believe it or not, successful. The novel is strident in its didacticism. A much finer example of Gotthelf's craft from this time is *Die Käserei in der Vehfreude*, which seriously, richly and complexly reflects upon processes of institutional and economic change as a small farming community seeks to modernize its business practices by setting up a cheese-making cooperative. Keller similarly reflects on the complex interplay of origins and originality in *Das Fähnlein der sieben Aufrechten* from the *Zürcher Novellen*. In *Die Leute von Seldwyla* he creates a fictitious Swiss village which serves as a model for the social and economic experience of his nation. Time and time again Keller is fascinated by the workings of emblem, myth and symbolization in the lives of individuals and communities. He also registers the imaginative and speculative energies of capitalism, and scrupulously weighs up the interplay of creative and destructive consequences. That same differentiation characterizes his responses to practical politics. He comments, for example, on the 'Freischaren', pointing out that their very half-heartedness served to encourage the reactionary cantons to overstep the mark in the foundation of the 'Sonderbund' – which in turn led to their downfall. In a letter of 1848 he comments on the sheer grandeur of the happenings in Paris, Berlin and Vienna – a grandeur which put the Swiss disturbances to shame. On the other hand, he reflects that the absence of the grand manner produced a subtlety and differentiation in the process of political reform in Switzerland which would be unthinkable on the larger stage – and produced genuine constitutional reform.[14]

In Italy the disturbances of 1848 are inevitably bound up with aspirations for liberation from Austrian rule in the name of national unity and self-determination. In literature there is a clear and significant movement from Romantic and post-Romantic inwardness (Leopardi) towards the historical novel. The crucial transition is effected by Manzoni's *I Promessi Sposi*, in which the rich tapestry of history is quickened by the longing of the two young lovers. In the writings of the subsequent literary generation that passion becomes the aspiration for civil freedom and political autonomy. The key artistic witness to 1848 and its aftermath is, however, to be found less in literature than in music. It is surely no accident that three of Verdi's early operas, *Nabucco*, *I Lombardi* and *Macbeth*, all have great choruses that sing overwhelmingly of the need to end oppression. They become almost battle hymns of the Risorgimento. (Here we are for once concerned with texts whose import and force is unambiguous;

the charge behind those choruses is as clear-cut as it is electrifying.) Moreover, all Verdi's greatest work sings unforgettably of the longing for release from emotional, institutional, cultural, political entrapment – *Rigoletto, La Traviata, Don Carlo, Aida, Otello.*

I have reached the end of my breathless survey. With the exception of Switzerland, where 1848 clearly enshrines a decisive turning point, there is a sense in which, for much of revolutionary Europe, 1848 was and is unclear in its symbolic significance. Clearly, in one sense, the disturbances do relate to and articulate complex underlying currents in the European nineteenth century, to do with urbanization, democracy, modernization and so forth. Even England, relieved not to be part of the unquiet continent, is aware, from Chartism to the passage of the Reform Bill, that the energies for change will not be entirely gainsaid; on the one hand, the influx of refugees from the continent[15] only serves to confirm Whiggish notions of the inexorable, but non-tumultuous, good sense of British historical progress. As regards the major centres of revolutionary activity – Paris, Berlin, Vienna – there is a complex sense of both change and stagnation. Earlier upheavals – the Industrial Revolution in England, the French Revolution – had, as it were, set the seal on modernity. And 1848 can be viewed as part of a chain of aftertremors, with all the attendant movements of reaction and retrenchment. Above all, there is the recurring issue, constantly expressed by the literature and music that we have considered, of the role of the middle classes, of the ethical and political sensibilities of the bourgeois mentality. Is it progressive or regressive, an engine for revolutionary change, or in love with the stifling pall of propriety, closely allied to an ethos of private property and materialism? Is the revolution, then, one that did not quite happen, the one that got away? Or did it get away with a good deal, more than was, perhaps, apparent at the time? The point I am after is that the issues were – and are – complex. If the cultural responses are imbued with uncertainty, this is not, I think, to be understood as an obfuscation of what, on the (historical) ground, was clear-cut. The uncertain, shifting mediations of cultural reflection are part of the historical data. Historical events are themselves heavily mediated entities; they are then remediated by historiography, and by literature, music and the visual arts. Which is not to say that there are no facts, only discourses. But it is to say that sometimes the facts, of which mentality, mood, public opinion, symbolization may be a part, do not obey our rage to discern clarity, purpose, a comfortingly secure taxonomy of rights and wrongs. To such areas of complexly felt experience and uncertainty of signification cultural artefacts often bear thoughtful, scrupulous and, by that token, revelatory witness.

Notes

1 See T. J. Clark, *The Absolute Bourgeois: Artists and Politics in France 1848–1851* (London, 1973); P. Nora, *Realms of Memory: Rethinking the French Past* (New York, 1996); P. Paret, *Art as History: Episodes in the Culture and Politics of 19th-Century Germany* (Princeton, NJ, 1988).
2 J. Derrida, *De la Grammatologie* (Paris, 1967), p. 227.
3 See F. Rude, *Stendhal et la pensée sociale de son temps* (Paris, 1967); A. Jefferson, *Reading Realism in Stendhal* (Cambridge, 1988).
4 See C. Prendergast, *Balzac: Fiction and Melodrama* (London, 1978); C. Prendergast, *The Order of Mimesis* (Cambridge, 1986).
5 See V. Brombert, *The Novels of Flaubert: A Study of Themes and Techniques* (Princeton, NJ, 1968); J. Culler, *Flaubert: The Uses of Uncertainty* (London, 1974).
6 W. Benjamin, *Charles Baudelaire: ein Lyriker im Zeitalter des Hochkapitalismus* (Frankfurt am Main, 1969).
7 See J. Nestroy, *Freiheit in Krähwinkel*, ed. J. R. P. Mackenzie, in Nestroy, *Sämtliche Werke*, 26(1), Vienna, 1995; F. H. Mautner, *Nestroy* (Heidelberg, 1974); W. E. Yates, *Theatre in Vienna: A Critical History* (Cambridge, 1996).
8 See M. and E. Swales, *Adalbert Stifter: A Critical Study* (Cambridge, 1984).
9 See H. Politzer, *Franz Grillparzer oder das abgründige Biedermeier* (Vienna, 1990).
10 See J. L. Sammons, *Six Essays on the Young German Novel* (Chapel Hill, NC, 1972).
11 See R. A. Berman, *The Rise of the Modern German Novel: Crisis and Charisma* (Cambridge, MA and London, 1986).
12 See D. Borchmeyer, *Richard Wagner: Theory and Theatre* (Oxford, 1995).
13 A. J. P. Taylor, *The Course of German History* (London, 1978), p. 69.
14 See J. Rothenberg, *Gottfried Keller: Symbolgehalt und Realitätserfassung seines Erzählens* (Heidelberg, 1976); H. Wysling (ed.), *Gottfried Keller 1819–1890* (Zurich and Munich, 1990).
15 See R. Ashton, *Little Germany: German Refugees in Victorian Britain* (Oxford, 1989).

4

Did Women Have a Revolution? Gender Battles in the European Revolution of 1848/49

Gabriella Hauch[*,1]

The revolution of 1848 was not only a man's business. Women tried to appropriate its revolutionary language, as well as its activities and the resultant new freedoms and rights for themselves. This paper will discuss the different 'battles' that women of different classes and countries fought and then evaluate whether the revolution of 1848/49 was revolutionary for women.[2] The contemporaneity of so-called traditional and modern elements, of violent forms of social protest and the orderly founding of associations marks out the socio-economic, the cultural and the political arena of this era and illustrates the colourful diversity of women's lives and activities throughout the revolutionary year. In order to do justice to these heterogeneous elements, and understand the hopes, aims and interests of the women of 1848, it is necessary to carefully use gender along with other categories, such as class, religion, ethnicity, nationality and age.

The following excursion through the 1848/49 European revolutionary landscape centres around the concept of space, meaning not only geographic locations but also the network of social relationships. This network is drawn from both within and without the institutions of a society and constitutes that society as well.[3] How does the exclusion of women function with regard to the political institutions of the modern age, which are conceived of by men as men's spaces? What conclusions did women draw from this, and what institutionalized women's spaces did they create for themselves? And how were gender relations arranged in the in-between spaces, distinct from institutionalized politics?

* Translated from the German by Aileen Derieg.

'Women, who were strenuously fighting against their exclusion from the meeting...'

With these words an article described the protests of the women of Konstanz, who had forced the commune officials to organize a public discussion on 15 April 1848, on whether the inhabitants of Konstanz agreed or disagreed with the 'Heckerzug', which meant the militant expansion of the revolution. But from the discussion itself, women were excluded.[4] The point was: 'When they say the people, women do not count.' With this sentence in April 1849, Louise Otto voiced her indignation at the exclusion of women in the *Frauen-Zeitung* (*Women's Journal*) that she had founded in Saxony.[5] At that time, citizenship and terms such as freedom and equality as well as the areas of 'the public sphere and politics' were all defined in male terms, regardless of the differentiation of social status. Bourgeois legal works such as the French Civil Code of 1804 as well as the Allgemeine Bürgerliche Gesetzbuch of 1811 in the Habsburg Monarchy regulated private life according to family laws. These legally defined not only the ideal family, but also the dual character of gender. This specificity of gender characterizes the political systems of the modern era from the very beginning up to the present: the bourgeois society as a male project.[6]

The bourgeois demands for the right of political association, the right to vote, the establishment of parliaments, the people's right to bear arms – as the institutionalization of armed masculinity prepared for defence – comprised the dynamics of the first phase of the revolutions. The successful March revolutions of 1848 brought about political clubs and parliaments. With the exception of France, women were not included in these institutionalized male political spaces imbedded in the new constitutions.

Not even their demand to be permitted to listen to political debate was universally accepted, as the example of the City Officials (*Stadtverordnetenversammlung*) in Berlin shows.[7] A two-third majority rejected this proposal. It may have been a point of dispute between conservatives and democrats, but this was usually the only time at which women were mentioned in these institutions. However, there were also women, even if only just a handful, who did not merely accept their exclusion from politics.

For instance, there was a group of Viennese women, who have remained anonymous, who formulated their demands in a four-page pamphlet:

> Beware of believing that we are not filled with the most lively interest in the emancipation of humanity ... We claim the equality of political rights. Why should women not be elected to the Reichstag?[8]

Unfortunately, it was not possible to find a published response to this pamphlet. It was written in that turbulent period, following which the workers were granted the vote in the Habsburg monarchy on 10 June.[9] 'It would be false to call suffrage universal, if at least half of all the subjects are excluded,' the pamphlet continues. It refers to the suffrage they demand as an 'undeniable, inalienable, innate and unassailable right of the female sex'. This is in contrast to the 'difference idea' or the position of most of the women of 1848, who hoped to attain 'their' rights and recognition through defining themselves as the complementary sex.[10] This hope was usually disappointed. Indicatively, it could be argued that the more suffrage was based on the individual rather than on social status, the more men were included in suffrage as individuals, and the more women were excluded.

Thus the Frankfurt merchant's wife Clothilde Koch-Gontard found it 'quite discomforting to be a mere woman, always an onlooker'.[11] She, like Malwine von Meysenbug, had already secretly gained access to the Paulskirche in April 1848,[12] where they hid in the pulpit to listen to the discussion of the preliminary parliament. This was before the councils of the National Assembly and, for example, the Viennese parliament were opened to women in the summer of 1848. These women's role as passive participants was also acceded to them by several associations, which were politically mostly democratic. The reaction of the public – usually a creation of male chroniclers – to these politically interested women was ambivalent. The issue divided not only democrats and liberals, but even democracts themselves.

Aside from hymns of praise along the lines of 'it is a promising sign of the times when even women grasp the stuff of politics'[13] other reactions have left significant traces in the political fabric that are still present today. Women, who were present at political assemblies, were said to neglect their families, the care of their children and wifely duties.   The politically interested woman was ultimately seen as a threat to the state.

This discourse was also steeped in the power of erotic attraction, which apparently spontaneously emerged between the representatives and the women onlookers. More gallant types welcomed the 'circle of democratic women' among the 'eagerly listening audience' of the Democratic Club in Berlin.[14] Ruder reactions characterized the women watching from the galleries as 'immoral and licentious, parading in pomp and display, coquetting and ogling'.[15] The presence of women seems to disturb the supposedly gender-neutral integrity of the male space of institutionalized politics – which results, according to men's fantasies, in chaos and anarchy. Even today, women representatives have been and are still sexually harassed and denounced by their male colleagues who command the power of definition – and the later the evening, the more vulgar the remarks. This is evident in the stenographic protocols of the Austrian National Parliament.[16]

In 1848, the contradictions between the supposed gender neutrality of the revolutionary ideals of freedom and equality and male conceptions of politics provoked women to direct and specific criticism – even if there were not many of these women and they only demanded 'equal rights' in certain points. The vast majority lived and acted in concurrence with the gender-specific dichotomization of institutionalized politics. Aside from spectacular, individual lives, such as that of George Sand or Louise Aston, who attempted to break out of the bourgeois corset, one alternative was to create women's spaces alongside the men's spaces.[17]

'I shake hands with you to create our pact as Sisters' (Schwesternbund)

With this enthusiastic statement, a so-called 'German woman' sent her congratulations to the founding of the 'Women's Club in Vienna'.[18] At the same time women of Berlin described their intentions of founding their own women's association with 'With our own united strength'. They continued: 'We shall make use of the right of free assembly, which now exists for us as well . . .'[19] Women's associations were not invented *per se* by the women of 1848 seeking an alternative to their exclusion from men's spaces. With the exception of France, the women's associations that emerged in the early nineteenth century were system-stabilizing, loyal to the monarchy, patriotic and oriented towards charity works.[20] This was the case, for instance, in Prussia, as Karen Hagemann most recently showed,[21] at the various 'Charity Associations of Noble Women and Girls' which were founded after 1811 in the Habsburg lands under the patronage of the imperial family and open exclusively to women from the higer ranks of nobility. These types of activities meant extending the radius of the woman's domain, which centred around the family, servants, journeymen and apprentices or the household, to a greater responsibility for others. Irene Stoehr has referred to this as 'organized motherliness'. With a different concept of politics, feminist research has highlighted the political dimension and the public-political character of this involvement. Here, the smooth transition between public and private moved into the foreground – for pre-March and 1848; this is especially evident in the studies on Württemberg under the direction of Carola Lipp.[22] These types of associations were also founded in the years 1848/49: associations for embroidering flags for the newly established national guards, associations dedicated to works of charity in an awakened 'national' interest, etc.

At this point, however, in keeping with the motto 'our own', the attention should be turned to those associations that defined themselves explicitly as associations for the emancipation of women. These were associations for women who saw themselves as political individuals and who created a democratic structure for their associations, in other words for women from every class and confession on the basis of a common programme with the aim of fighting against their social discrimination or to improve their own situation in professional, political or legal spheres. And, of course, to fight for more choices, regardless of family connections.

With this definition it is difficult to grasp the diversity of all the 'Democratic Women's Associations' that were formed in the lands of the German Federation, usually during or after the failure of the revolutions. This does not mean that their political character should be questioned, but in most cases the reason for forming the association came from others – and not from the women themselves. For instance, there was the 'Humania', founded on 16 May 1849 in Mainz by Kathinka Zitz.[23] Like a number of other associations, these 1848 women established networks to provide a safe existence for prisoners, fugitives and their families, and to organize escape routes and emigration. Even though these women were themselves 'emancipated and with a democratic attitude', they entered the public eye – with the exception of the women in the free, German-Catholic communities[24] – primarily involved in these relief services. Or is this the result of the androcentric perspective in historical science?[25]

One example is Auguste Scheibe, board member of the Democratic Women's Aid Association in Dresden. I was able to find out more about her through the letters of Ferdinand Kürnberger, who was 28 years old at that time. Following the suppression of the Viennese revolution at the end of October 1848 the socialist democrat fled to Dresden. After the suppression of the revolution in Dresden in May 1849 he was sentenced to prison from where he was able to escape with the help of Auguste Scheibe – and Kürnberger was bowled over.[26] Habituated as he was to his power of definition, he characterized 'Fräulein Scheibe' as being 'at the peak of contemporary education, able to do justice to the political and social questions of our day' and uniting 'the female magnitude of intellect and power of character which commands respect and surprise'. Not only that, but she was also young and very beautiful. He fell in love. In his letter he directly connected his confession of enchantment and his description of the like-minded democratic woman: 'And if I had previously held a narrow-minded, pre-March prejudice against the emancipation of women, it had to vanish at this moment.'

It is particularly interesting that he mentions a 'narrow-minded prejudice' against the emancipation of women here, which now seems outmoded to him. As his letter continues, he maintains that he had also had opportunities to 'admire the dignity of the female sex in its highest form' due to the women who were active in the 'Viennese Democratic Women's Association'. If this is so, then he must have belonged to a small minority. Men with this attitude – as Sylvia Paletschek has shown – were more likely to be found in German-Catholic communities.

One of the more overtly political Women's Clubs was founded in Vienna on 28 August 1848, in the Salon of the Volksgarten.[27] Men were not admitted. In response, the discussion was stormed by men, including a number of national guards, in other words propertied and educated citizens. They smashed windows, took over the room, jumped on the tables, ridiculed the women and threatened to slap them. The women retreated, but not without first agreeing to meet in the late afternoon of the same day. The reaction of these men to women claiming the right of association shows one aspect of the gender-specific resistance struggle against the (women's) emancipation movement that was to be inscribed in bourgeois modernity.

Members of the 'Club des femmes' in Paris experienced similar scenes as a tumult arose on 6 June 1848 during a discussion on divorce laws, and the police came in to clear the hall. The authorities considered this a sufficient reason to dissolve the club. The fact that men also caused loud disturbances during an assembly of maid-servants in April 1848 in Leipzig indicates that aggressively antagon-istic action was not unusual an occurrence.

Unlike its sister association in Berlin, which was to be founded on 14 September 1848,[28] the Viennese Democratic Women's Association defined a threefold objective for itself. The programme comprised three points[29] – the political, the social and the human:

> *political*, to attain enlightenment through reading and educative lectures regarding the welfare of our fatherland, to disseminate the democratic principle in all female circles, to fan the flame of the love of freedom even in the breasts of children at the begin-ning of child-bearing, and also to strengthen German element;
>
> *social*, to strive for the equality of women by founding public primary schools and institutions of higher education, to reform female education and to improve the lot of poorer girls through affectionate elevation;
>
> *human*, to express the profoundly felt gratitude of the women of Vienna for the blessings of freedom by conscientiously caring for all the victims of the revolution.

This programme united the issues of equality, the political education of women, maternal charity toward the female members of the lower social classes and solidarity with the goals of the revolutionary movement. The discussion of the programme did not take place without controversy. At one of the first meetings, Frau Bouvard, a sexton's daughter, called the members of the association 'politically sleepy-heads'. The argument was occasioned by a petition to the Council of Ministers for the repeal of biannual rents that were due – which was rejected by a majority of the members as an undemocratic intervention in private property. In September, a pamphlet appeared in Vienna indicating another fact that might cause divisions among the women. It calls upon the 'German' women of Vienna to become involved in the Democratic Women's Association and hinder Frau Wertheimer, a Jewish woman, from becoming president of the association. In the pre-March period Jewish women of the rich, ennobled city financial bourgeoisie had acquired an important role in the political-cum-public sphere with their salons. However, in the 1848 struggles their religion, unlike that of Jewish men, did not play any role when they demanded the emancipation of their people, their nation.

Although confessions were not explicitly mentioned in the statutes of the association, equal treatment among all members was formally stated in Paragraph 10: 'No differences shall be made among the members because of status. One says simply Frau and Fräulein. Married women have no precedence over unmarried women.' The members were required to be 'of good reputation and liberal-minded character' (Paragraph 7), otherwise they could be barred by a majority vote. In addition, they planned to establish an organization network throughout the empire (Paragraph 31 and 32).

During the two brief months of their existence, they collaborated on the organization of the burial of those fallen in August on 3 September 1848. This was intended to be a public gesture of reconciliation transcending class. Some of their activities were particularly spectacular. On 17 October, several hundred women marched to the Reichstag, and a delegation presented a petition with 1000 signatures calling for the enlistment of the Landsturm, the armed formation of the rural population. This action 'naturally made a nearly ridiculous impression'.

Indeed most of the representatives had hoped that the women would volunteer for nursing duties if fighting broke out. In contrast, the democratic men's associations in Vienna reacted positively to the existence of the women's association – they accepted the women's association as a partner.[30] And so the Women's Association was even a member of the 'Central Committee' of the democratic-liberal associations of Vienna, founded on 30 September. In the discussions at the Odeon, which usually took place before thousands of people, the women of the association held the position of co-organizers and discussion participants – something entirely unprecedented in Europe. Nevertheless, Karoline Perin and the 'Viennese Democratic Women's Association' also encountered distrust on the part of the 1848 activists: 'She has been of no use to us, but has rather caused us damage with the founding of the women's club', was the denouncement following the suppression.[31]

In addition to the political women's associations in France,[32] a 'Democratic Women's Association', which did not admit men as members, was also founded in Berlin on 14 September. The association 'Germania' separated from it on 12 October.[33] On 20 September, the 'Spolek Slovanek' (Association of Slavic Women) was founded in Prague, and the *Slovanská Dennike* (*Slavic Morning Star*) followed in early October 1848.[34]

Let us turn now to a different social milieu, to the first workers' associations, such as the 'Association of Book Printers and Typesetter Journeymen' in Vienna: not only were women not welcome there, but their demands even included the 'removal of female workers'. In other words, even though their condition of employment provided the basis for organization, this did not automatically imply a negation of the gender boundaries. On the contrary, women who had been trained on the job were paid less – and this meant increased competition with men. And the emerging workers' movement, however far removed in actuality, was nevertheless oriented to the bourgeois family, which meant that a woman's place was in the home. Contrary to this, however, the Workers' Association in Berlin did include seperate departments for women, as Rüdiger Hachtmann has shown in his work on Berlin in 1848.[35]

This means that the creation of these institutionalized women's spaces corresponds to the dichotomous character of gender – even though the protagonists were demanding gender equality for themselves. This ambivalence, which has its roots in the very beginnings of the women's movement, is the foundation for 'woman, the exception': from the 'women's question' of the second half of the nineteenth century to the agencies for the equal treatment of women, i.e. at the universities, today.

'...we cannot just fold our hands today and do nothing...Indeed, one can do no more than die'

With these words, Margarethe Adams explained her motivation for participating in the Frankfurt revolt on 18 September 1848, when she was arrested.[36] She was one of about 585 women, who were interrogated and charged with 'carrying stones as weapons and for build-ing barricades'.

Women took part in all the militant struggles of 1848/49.[37] These involved primarily socially and nationally motivated revolts and rebellions or social forms of protest such as caterwauling, which were sustained by the lower classes and decisively influenced the dynamics of the course of the revolution: from the beginning with the March and April revolutions and the achievement of the bourgeois free-doms to the bloody barricade battles that accompanied the suppres-sion of the revolutions in the cities. However, women were also present – in very different roles – at the campaigns of the various (revolutionary) armies and other armed formations.[38] These forms of action mark 'in-between spaces', in which gender categories were more fluid.

If we use the patterns of activity for categorization, it appears at first glance that we have a level of equality before us: women and men both took up weapons, whether these were their tools of work or rifles, and they fought, for example at the battle of the Prater in Vienna on 23 August 1848.[39] Bayonets were raised against men and women ditchdiggers demonstrating against wage reductions.

However, if we examine the discursive level, there is little trace left of equal treatment. The main argument for the brutal handling of the men and women demonstrators and the explanation of why so many women sustained 'stabs to the neck' and head injuries, accord-ing to accounts, was the unseemly behaviour of the women ditchdig-gers. 'Especially the females behaved like furies; the guards were insulted in the roughest, most appalling, most vulgar way,' was the participants' justification.[40] Male protective behaviour could not come into effect in the face of the behaviour of these women – far removed from bourgeois proper comportment. At the time of the August massacre in Vienna, the prospects for the revolution looked dim throughout Europe. The Polish rebellion movement had been put down in April, Prague followed at Pentecost under Windischgrätz, Paris in June and in August, one week before the massacre took place, the Habsburg troops under Radetzky conquered Milan and with it Lombard-Venice. Everywhere conservative and monarchist associations were reasserting themselves.

The change in the political climate meant the end of the celebra-tion of revolution. Barricade fighting signified different types of women bearing or using arms: the cruel woman, the brazen woman and the especially brave and courageously sacrificing woman.

The 'sources' frequently revealed a mixture of the perception and fantasies of the chroniclers, resulting in a bombastically emotional discourse on the woman as revolution or, vice versa, the revolution as woman. Here the longed-for fantasy lover may be found alongside the asexual allegory or the dreaded man-eater. 'Clamorous females' were taken as the consistent sign of increasing uninhibitedness and the end of the respectable and serious people's movement. 'Sources' of this type on women in 1848 deserve our attention primarily because of what they reveal of the phantasmagorias of their authors. The future project seemed to fail, because the presence of women introduced sexuality and sexual diseases were transmitted through sexual intercourse. This, in turn, destroyed male potency – in a double sense.

Simultaneously – corresponding to the mother and whore image of womanhood – women were not only seen as destructive and alien, but also as integrative figures and as proof of the justice of the revolutionary goals.[41] And since some of them gave up their feminine role of being in need of protection, they were that much more regarded as an embodiment of strength for being formerly or properly weak. Particularly in the hopeless final battles in the capitals of the revolution, these women were idealized as being not only the most persevering, but also the bravest. The history of the reception of Delacroix' picture *Freedom Guiding the People on the Barricade* (1831) is an example of this – which may be traced in 1848 to the outer edges of revolutionary Europe all the way to Bucharest.

The Romanian heroine was named Ana Ipátescu.[42] The provisional government was about to be forced by the military to resign, but in the midst of the crowd before the presidential palace, Ana climbed up onto a cab, waving two pistols and shouting, according to the chroniclers: 'Courage children! Death to the traitors!' This so inspired the crowd with courage that they stormed forwards and the military retreated – and Ana was carried into the palace on their shoulders as a heroine. Ana Ipátescu, who was a real person, the wife of a liberal 48er, and this incident, which did actually occur, provide a wonderful study for the way in which heroines or woman as an allegory for revolution were constructed. The men of 1848 hoped in this way to attract more attention from this remote corner of Europe. Two years later, her myth had mutated from the mother to 'Marianne'. The Romanian painter and 1848er C. D. Rosenthal encouraged friends, a husband and wife journalist pair, to write a series of articles for the Sunday papers in London about 1848 in Romania: 'Describe the world of Ipátescu, storming the palace with her hair flowing, half-clothed, with a pistol in her hand; fill your soul with it and it will always be a subject of inspiration for our heroines of tomorrow!'

Allegorical representations of women – subsequently there was the French Marianne, also with bared breast symbolizing the nourishment of the revolution – are symbols for the formation of nations.[43] Further east, she was transformed from the French Marianne into Germania, in the south into Italia, and to Slavia or Bohemia in Prague.[44] An Austria was not among them in Vienna – such is the fragility of the formation of the Austrian state.

In the 'name of the nation', actual women also took up arms. For instance, there was a so-called virgin in the Dresden revolt in May 1849, who fought at a barricade with the 'courage of a lioness' and shot a number of soldiers before she was killed herself.[45]

Thus a martyr was created, even in Louise Otto's *Frauen-Zeitung*, although Louise Otto generally rejected the idea of women imitating men, which would turn them into 'hermaphrodite creatures'. At the same time, however, the question was posed, 'Are men then to be privileged murderers? Are men then indifferent to killing?'[46] Only propertied and educated men were accepted in the 'guards' that were organized after the March and April revolutions. Social segregation was not lifted until the closing battles, but even then women as a social group still remained excluded. The exception was Hungary, the so-called 'people's holy crusade' in the spring and summer of 1849 against the Russian troops that the Habsburgs had called on for assistance. Now, Louise Otto's *Frauen-Zeitung* proclaimed that for women there was no longer time for 'pulling rags, nursing the wounded, sewing clothes and cooking for the army'. For a long time Louise Otto had rejected 'chosen and vain amazonianism'; now women had to become soldiers.[47]

Then there were increased attempts on the part of women to enlist in armed formations, but these attempts were rarely successful and were usually met with laughter by those responsible for enlistment.[48] In addition, there was the possibility of self-armament which meant that women took part in storming arsenals, for instance in Vienna,

Paris and Berlin. And there were women fighting in men's clothing.[49] It should be particularly noted, however, that with the exception of a sexually, emotionally motivated switch of clothing, the woman disguised as a man remains, on the other hand, a figure of ridicule and carnival. Particularly in times of war and revolution, however, even such derogatory expressions as 'virago' and 'mannish woman' are not nearly as bad as 'effeminate man'.[50]

Following this excursion I make my closing remarks. The suppression of the 1848 and 1849 movements meant death, persecution, imprisonment, banishment or emigration not only for the heroes of the movement, but also for the women connected with them, for single women activists and for fighting women who were not prominent figures. It cannot be said with certainty, or rather only a general trend can be detected, that women were punished more severely on an institutional level. Pauline Wunderlich, for instance, was sentenced to life imprisonment for her participation in the barricade battles in Dresden May 1849. A universal statement cannot be drawn from this, even though we may agree with the *Frauen-Zeitung*: 'Could it be that her punishment is to be considered a warning example?' At this level there are also certain examples of the so-called 'privilege of gender'. When Jeanée Deroine and her companions were tried at the end of 1849 under the prohibition of associations, the women were given much lighter sentences, although they were accused of forming a secret political association, attempted overthrow by violent means and conspiracy against the government.[51]

In addition to this, the punishment and humiliation of women is particularily targeted at their physical gender. This was especially true for lower-class women in the course of the victory of the counter-revolutionary troops. Rape and sexual assault are not only a means of destroying self-confidence, but are the most extreme way for men to commit violence against women. Sexual abuse of the female body was seen as a form of humiliation of the enemy warrior. As the liberation movements were suppressed, these circumstances were additionally aggravated by the sadistic reversal of repressed desires for freedom: aggression directed against those who had dared to oppose authoritarian structures and the instances of power. This also happened in 1848/49 in Vienna, Milan and Frankfurt.[52]

At the focus of this article were the women, who had attempted to make the 1848 movement their movement as well. Nevertheless, the potential for conservatism, to which women also contributed, should not be forgotten.

Summary

What significance did the 1848/49 revolution have for women and/ or gender relations?

1 Due to bourgeois freedoms and especially freedom of the press, articulating the needs and demands of women became possible and public, leading to a discussion of an increase of opportunities relating to gender justice and gender difference.

2 There was a transfer of the ideas of women's emancipation. A spatial transfer took place due to emigration to the USA (see the examples of Amalie Struve, Mathilda F. Anneke), Italy (Emma Herwegh). There was also a temporal transfer across generations – in the German women's movement or the women's movement in the Habsburg monarchy, I have noticed increasingly that the mothers, grandmothers or even fathers of the pioneers of the women's movements were '1848ers', who provided their daughters with more education and opportunities.[53]

3 In 1848/49 it became clear how the roles of (bourgeois) men and women were modelled; at the same time, women already living in this corset rebelled and broke out of it, although it was not actually applicable to the great majority.

4 During the revolution months of bourgeois freedom, again with their opportunities for articulation and extended spheres of action, the harbingers of what was to have an enormous impact on the twentieth century were perceived in broad sections of Europe for the first time, thanks to bourgeois freedoms and the dynamics of revolution: a crisis of gender relations. The opponents of women's emancipation were the first to understand, or at least sense the message of women's rebellion: the end of their sole sovereignty.

5 Another issue also became evident – although I have not addressed it here – specifically the frustrations experienced by women over their exclusion and the inclusion of their men and of more and more men in the new forms of institutionalized politics. In light of feuilletons and letter exchanges, the evident discursive, globalizing euphoria about the revolution and relationships must be

questioned, just like the exclusively positive reception of the bourgeois role of women on the part of women themselves.

Notes

1 Thank you to Aileen Derieg, who translated this article in her special, sensible way.
2 G. Hauch, 'Nichtwürdig – emanzipiert – geliebt. Geschlechtsspezifische Aktionen und Diskurs in den Revolutionen 1848/49', in Frauen & Geschichte. Baden-Württemberg et al. (eds), *Frauen und Revolution. Strategien weiblicher Emanzipation 1789 bis 1848* (Göttingen: Silberburg, 1998), pp. 33–57. The opposite position is taken by S. Asche, 'Eine ächt weibliche Emanzipation', *Ariadne. Almanach des Archivs der Deutschen Frauenbewegung*, 33 (1998).
3 G. Hauch, 'Frauen-Räume in der Männer-Revolution 1848', in D. Dowe, H.-G. Haupt and D. Langewiesche (eds), *Europa 1848. Revolution und Reform* (Bonn: Dietz, 1998), pp. 841–900.
4 Seeblätter, Konstanz 18. April 1848, Nr. 93, p. 401, G. Hummel-Haasis (ed.), *Schwestern zerreißt Eure Ketten. Zeugnisse zur Geschichte der Frauen in der Revolution 1848/49* (Munich: dtv, 1982), p. 25 and p. 12.
5 *Frauen-Zeitung*, no. 1, 1849, U. Gerhard, E. Hannover-Drück and R. Schmitter (eds), '"Dem Reich der Freiheit werb' ich Bürgerinnen"', *Die Frauen-Zeitung von Louise Otto*, reprint (Frankfurt am Main: Syndikat, 1979).
6 G. Hauch, 'Rights at last? The first generation of female members of parliament in Austria', in G. Bishop, A. Pelinka and E. Thurner (eds), *Contemporary Austrian Studies*, vol. 6: *Women in Austria* (New Brunswick, NJ and London: Transaction, 1998), pp. 56–82.
7 R. Hachtmann, '"... nicht die Volksherrschaft auch noch durch die Weiberherrschaft trüben" – der männliche Blick auf die Frauen in der Revolution von 1848 in Berlin', *Werkstatt Geschichte*, 1998, pp. 5–30.
8 Gleichstellung aller Rechte der Männer mit den Frauen: oder: Die Frauen als Wählerinnen, Deputierte und Volksvertreter, Wien 1848, Flugschriftensammlung 1848 der österreichischen Nationalbibliothek.
9 G. Hauch, *Frau Biedermeier auf den Barrikaden. Frauenleben in der Wiener Revolution 1848* (Vienna: Gesellschaftskritik, 1990), pp. 139–43. For the Viennese Revolution, W. Häusler, *Von der Massenarmut zur Arbeiterbewegung. Demokratie und Soziale Frage in der Wiener Revolution 1848* (Vienna/ Munich: Jugend und Volk, 1979).
10 K. Offen, 'Liberty, equality and justice for women: the theory and practice of feminism in nineteenth-century Europe' in R. Bridenthal (ed.), *Becoming Visible. Women in European History* (Boston: Houghton Mifflin, 1987), p. 335.
11 C. Koch-Gontard, *Briefe und Erinnerungen*, ed. W. Klötzer (Frankfurt am Main: Fischer, 1969), pp. 62 ff., p. 309.

12 M. von Meysenbug, *Memoiren einer Idealistin* (1876), ed. R. Wiggershaus (Frankfurt am Main: Insel, 1985), p. 124.

13 *Der Freimüthige*, Vienna 1848, no. 131, p. 457.

14 P. Boerner, *Erinnerungen eines Revolutionärs*, vol. II (Leipzig, 1920), p. 23.

15 For Frankfurt, 'Blicke ins Parlament', *Die Sonne*, Stuttgart, 1848, no. 19, pp. 73 f. See also E. Sterr, '"Hat nicht Gott... euch eure Sellung zum Manne angewiesen?" Das Frauenbild in der württembergischen Presse', C. Lipp (ed.), *Schimpfende Weiber und patriotische Jungfrauen. Frauen im Vormärz und in der Revolution 1848/49* (Moos/Baden-Baden: Pfaffenweiler, 1986), pp. 184 ff.

16 Hauch, 'Rights at last?', pp. 81 f.

17 For more details on the dichotomization of political men's and women's spheres and their consequences for the 'New' feminist Women's Liberation Movement, see G. Hauch, 'Aus- und Einschluß. Die Wirkungsmacht der Kategorie Geschlecht', in G. Hauch and M. Mesner (eds), *Vom 'Reich der Freiheit'. Liberalismus, Republik, Demokratie 1848–1998* (Vienna: Passagen, 1999).

18 *Der Freimüthige*, Vienna 1848, no. 11, p. 532.

19 'Der Klub der Frauen an seine Mitschwestern, Berlin 1848', in G. Hummel-Haasis, *Schwestern zerreißt Eure Ketten! Zeugnisse zur Geschichte der Frauen in der Revolution 1848/49* (Munich: dtv, 1982), p. 63.

20 For the Habsburg Monarchy, see G. Hauch, 'Politische Wohltätigkeit – wohltätige Politik. Frauenvereine in der Habsburger Monarchie vor 1867', *Zeitgeschichte*, no. 7/8 (1992), 200–15. For Prussia, see K. Hagemann, 'Nation, Krieg und Geschlechterordnung. Zum kulturellen und politischen Diskurs in der Zeit der antinapoleonischen Erhebung Preußens 1796–1815', *Geschichte und Gesellschaft*, 22 (1996), 577 ff.

21 Hagemann, 'Nation', p. 578.

22 Lipp, *Schimpfende Weiber*.

23 S. Zucker, 'German women and the revolution of 1848. Kathinka Zitz-Halein and the Humania Association', *Central European History* (1980) 237–54.

24 S. Paletschek, *Frauen und Dissens. Frauen im Deutschkatholizismus und in den Freien Gemeinden 1841–1852* (Göttingen: Vandehoek, 1990).

25 Hauch, *Nichtswürdig*, p. x.

26 F. Kürnberger, *Briefe eines politischen Flüchtlings* (Leipzig, 1920), pp. 72–7.

27 Hauch, *Biedermeier*, pp. 144–65.

28 Hachtmann, 'Weiber', p. 13.

29 'Statuten des Wiener Demokratischen Frauenvereins', in Hauch, *Biedermeier*, pp. 235–9.

30 See for more details on the gender relations of the democratic milieus in 1848 G. Hauch, 'Wir hätten ja so gerne die ganze Welt beglückt. Geschlechterverhältnisse im demokratischen Milieu zwischen Komplementarität und Konkurrenz', *Österreichische Zeitschrift für Geschichtswissenschaften*, 4 (1998); B. Bublius-Godau, 'Geliebte, Gatten und Gefährten. Selbstverständnis und politisches Handeln von Ehepaaren in der deutschen Revolution 1848/49', *Geschichte in Wissenschaft und Unterricht*, 49 (1998), 282–96.

31 F. D. Fenner von Fenneberg, *Geschichte der Wiener Oktobertage, geschildert und mit allen Aktenstücken belegt* (Leipzig, 1849), pp. 104 f.
32 H. Grubitzsch and L. Lagpacan, *'Freiheit für die Frauen – Freiheit für das Volk!' Sozialistische Frauen in Frankreich 1830–1848* (Frankfurt am Main: Syndikat, 1980).
33 R. Hachtmann, *Berlin 1848. Eine Politik- und Gesellschaftsgeschichte der Revolution* (Bonn: Dietz, 1998), pp. 514–18; S. Paletschek, 'Wer war Lucie Lenz?', *Werkstatt Geschichte* (1998). Hauch, 'Frauen-Räume', pp. 855 f.
34 M. Moravcová, 'Die tschechischen Frauen im revolutionären Prag 1848/ 49', in R. Jaworski and R. Luft (eds), *1848/49 – Revolutionen in Ostmitteleuropa* (Munich: Oldentourg, 1996) pp. 92 ff; Hauch, 'Frauen-Räume', pp. 800–62.
35 Hachtmann, 'Berlin'.
36 S. Zucker, 'Frauen in der Revolution von 1848. Das Frankfurter Beispiel', *Archiv für Frankfurts Geschichte und Kunst*, 61 (1981), 226.
37 C. Lipp, 'Frauen auf der Straße. Strukturen weiblicher Öffentlichkeit im Unterschichtsmilieu', in Lipp, *Schimpfende Weiber*, pp. 16–25; idem, 'Katzenmusiken, Krawalle und "Weiberrevolution"' and 'Frauen im politischen Protest der Revolutionsjahre', in ibid., pp.122–31. Hauch, *Biedermeier*, pp.167–230.
38 G. Hauch, 'Bewaffnete Weiber. Kämpfende Frauen im Krieg der Revolution 1848/49', K. Hagemann and R. Pröve (eds), *Landsknechte, Soldatenfrauen und Nationalkriege. Militär, Krieg und Geschlechteroldnung im historischen Wandel.* (Frankfurt am Main Campus, 1998), 223–46.
39 Hauch, 'Frauen-Räume', pp. 883 f.
40 In K. Mellach (ed.), *1848. Protokolle einer Revolution* (Vienna: Jugend und Volk, 1968) p. 24.
41 C. Lipp, 'Bräute, Mütter, Gefährtinnen. Frauen und politische Öffentlichkeit in der Revolution 1848', in H. Grubitzsch, H. Cyrus and E. Haarbusch (eds), *Grenzgängerinnen. Revolutionäre Frauen im 18. und 19. Jahrhundert. Weibliche Wirklichkeit und Männliche Phantasien* (Düsseldorf: Schwann, 1985), pp. 71–92. Hauch, *Biedermeier*, pp. 85–119.
42 Hauch, 'Frauen-Räume', pp. 887 f. I am grateful to Lothar Maier, Osnabrück for the information and the translation.
43 M.-L. v. Plessen (ed.), *Marianne und Germania 1789–1889. Frankreich und Deutschland. Zwei Welten – eine Revue. Ausstellungskatalog* (Berlin: Deutsches Historisches Museum, 1997).
44 Moravcová, 'Prag', p. 86.
45 *Frauen-Zeitung*, 1 and 12 (1849), reprint, pp. 39, 42 f, and 109 f.
46 See for more details to women in arms Hauch, 'Bewaffnete Weiber'.
47 L. Otto, 'Der Volkskreuzzug in Ungarn', *Frauen-Zeitung*, 14 (1849), p. 113.
48 *Wiener Gassenzeitung*, 128 (1848), 513.
49 For instance, for the examples of Maria Lebstück (1830–92) and Pauline Pfiffner (1825–53), who were both fighting in Vienna and in Hungary, see W. von Beck, *Memoiren einer Dame während des letzten Unabhängigkeitskrieges in Ungarn*, vol. I (London, 1850), pp. 183–7.

50   S. Becker, 'Transsexuelle – die letzten (echten) Frauen und Männer?', in Sexualberatungsstelle Salzburg (ed.), *Trieb, Hemmung, Begehren. Psychoanalyse und Sexualität* (Göttingen: Vandenhoek, 1998), pp. 100–24.
51   Grubitzsch and Lagpacan, *Freiheit*, p. 113; See also M. Riot Scacey, D. Gay, J. Deroin and E. Niboyet, *La démocratie à l'épreuve des femmes: Trois figures critiques du pouvoir 1830–1848* (Paris: Edition Albin Michele, 1994). J. W. Scott, *Only Paradoxes to Offer. French Feminists and the Rights of Man* (London: Harvard, 1996), pp. 58–88.
52   Hauch, 'Frauen-Räume', p. 897.
53   For instance, for one of the most popular early feminists in *fin de siècle* Vienna, Rosa Mayreder, see H. Bubenicek, 'Wider die Tyrannei der Norm. Impressionen zu Rosa Mayreder', in idem (ed.), *Rosa Mayreder oder Wider die Tyrannei der Norm* (Wien-Köln-Graz: Böhlau, 1998), p. 10.

Part III

Internationalism and Nationalism in the European Revolution

5
Ideas and Memories of 1848 in France: Nationalism, République Universelle and Internationalism in the Goguette between 1848 and 1890*

Axel Körner

Robert Blum in French songs of 1848

In September 1850, the French customs officers in Kehl near Strasbourg confiscated a small booklet, printed in Frankfurt but written in French, with the title *Aux Mânes de Robert Blum*. As its title suggested, the pamphlet was an ode to Robert Blum, the popular German hero of the 1848 revolution, member of the democratic left in the Frankfurt parliament, and later executed during a parliamentary mission to Vienna in November 1848. The French customs officers considered this material important enough to forward the booklet to the public prosecutor in Colmar, who went so far as to ask the minister of foreign affairs in Paris for official assistance in the investigation. During the following six years, police officials in Frankfurt, Stuttgart and Colmar tried to solve the mystery of this anonymous publication, regarded as a conspiracy against the state and evidence for continuing

* This paper is based on documents of the French National Archives and song collections in the National Library in Paris and the Bibliothèque Historique de la Ville de Paris. For a more detailed history of cultural practice in the French Goguette I refer to my book *Das Lied von einer anderen Welt. Kulturelle Praxis im französischen und deutschen Arbeitermilieu. 1840–1890* (Frankfurt and New York: Campus, 1997).

revolutionary activity on both sides of the Rhine. It took the 'Cour d'Appel' in Colmar six years to close the file, eight years after the outbreak of revolution in the streets of Paris.[1]

Officials in France and Germany alike considered the Alsace and Baden to be among the most important centres of the revolution of 1848.[2] In Colmar, Charles Schmidt, an insurgent of the June barricades in Paris, published a bilingual newspaper called *La République du Peuple / Volksrepublik* which in the view of the authorities supported 'communist ideas', 'urging one group of citizens against another'.[3] Since June 1848 the suppression of revolutionary pamphlets, newspapers and booklets had become very common in this frontier region.[4] The booklet to the memory of Robert Blum is not the only evidence for the commemoration of the so-called 'German martyr' within a French context. Pictures, songs and documents of 1848 east of the Rhine circulated in France and honoured the victims of the German barricades. The name of Robert Blum – in France better known than other popular heroes of the German revolution like Hecker or Struve – stands as a symbol for what happened during the years 1848/49 outside France. In the French context, it shows the awareness of the international dimension of the revolution. Pierre Dupont, the celebrated chansonnier of the French Goguette, remembered Robert Blum in one of his most famous songs, 'Le Chant des Etudiants' / 'Students' Song':

> Marchons, sans clairons ni cymbales
> Aux conquêtes de l'avenir
> Et montrons, s'il le faut, nos poitrines aux balles
> Comme a fait Robert Blum, le glorieux martyr![5]

The song was first published in 1848, and later, during the Empire and the Third Republic, reprinted in countless collections of Dupont's works. Another Goguettier from Paris, Charles Vincent, remembered Robert Blum in his widely circulated *Album Révolutionnaire*, dedicating an adapted version of the old revolutionary song 'Les Trois Couleurs' to the assassins of his popular German hero:

> Quoi, c'est au nom de la Grâce Divine,
> Que vous voulez inspirer la terreur!
> Robert frappe, tombe, et sur sa poitrine
> Le sangue jaillit au front de l'empereur.

> Vas près du Christ, pure et noble victime,
> Nous attendrons: le Peuple sait souffrir!
> Tous ces Néros rouleront dans l'abîme:
> Ils ont la force, à nous est l'Avenir.[6]

By the choice of the melody Vincent honours Robert Blum with the colours of the French nation, the 'Tricolore'. In this song the martyr is the object of a holy transfiguration: Robert has given his blood for the people's redemption. He sits next to Christ and awaits the Last Judgement when the 'Neros' of the world will be damned.

In contrast to these songs about Robert Blum, remembrance songs for the French victims of 1848 remained impersonal and abstract. Only a few songs referred to a specific person or to an actual hero of the barricades. One of the songs which entered the collective memory of 1848 in France is 'Les tombeaux de Juin', written by the youthful commander of the barricades and member of the famous secret society 'Les nouvelles Saisons', Charles Gille:

> Ils sont tombés après cinque jours de lutte!
> Ils sont tombés sans nous dire leurs noms;
> Ils sont tombés
> Mais le bruit de leur chute
> Recouvre encore la voix de vos canons![7]

Charles Gille, aged 22 when he wrote this song and an unskilled jobbing-tailor, was once the star of the revolutionary Goguettes in Paris. He commited suicide a few years after the defeat of the Social Republic. His songs in remembrance of the 3000 victims of the June uprising are full of pain and sorrow, but they do not remember actual French heroes of the barricades. Instead, they mourn nameless fallen soldiers: 'Ils sont tombés sans nous dire leurs noms.' Most of the songs in memory of 1848 are songs for the anonymous popular soldier of the barricades. Songs for revolutionaries in exile and confinement remained anonymous as well. In another famous song of 1848, they are remembered as the 'Soldiers of desperation', but their names are never given.[8]

Though they had no detailed knowledge of his biography, his political ideas or his role in revolutionary or parliamentary activity, the French chansonniers of 1848 chose Robert Blum as the international hero of the 1848 revolution. The focus on the German deputy helped the Goguettiers to underline that in their view 1848 was not a purely French political event but a European revolution. This international dimension draws our attention to another contemporary interpretation of 1848 in the French Goguette: 1848 was perceived, again in the words of the Goguettier Charles Gille, as a 'social war';[9] and Pierre Dupont underlines that this social war is in fact an international battle. In his 'Chant des Ouvriers' ('Workers' Song') he describes the revolution as a peoples' fight against the European governments.[10] The songs do not only list revolutionary uprisings in Germany, Italy or Hungary, they also give a social interpretation of these events; similar to Marx's view in his work 'Wage-Labour and Capital', the songwriters of the Goguettes analyse even the socio-political situation in Britain and Ireland within the context of the 1848 revolution.[11] This social interpretation of the events created much more anxiety among the European governments than the liberal claims of the middle classes.[12]

Nevertheless, the ideals and interpretations of 1848 as presented in the Goguette remain on the whole rather unclear. Many French barricade songs of 1848 do not leave the context of French political events. Some songs within the political milieu of the Goguette are not internationalist at all. If Dupont describes the revolution as a peoples' war against the European governments, many Goguettiers understood this claim in the first instance as a revenge for Waterloo. Mazzini's notion of the 'Springtime of European peoples' does not appear in popular revolutionary songs. Victor Rabineau's musical propaganda for a new economic organization of society, inspired by Proudhon's contemporary writings, demonstrates more than anything else his anti-Jewish sentiments: 'Juifs à bout d'artifice, votre règne est passé.'[13] Not all songs were internationalist in their ideals and there was a strong legacy of 1792 nationalism.

Although popular French songwriters did not see the revolution, from an organizational point of view, as an international movement, they recognized its European dimension. This dimension was based on a negative concept of Europe. For the 'people of Paris', 1848 was a revolution against the Europe of the Holy Alliance, the Europe of Metternich, and against 'European diplomacy'. Their idea of Europe was based on the collective memory of negative experiences, reaching from the Middle Ages to the Napoleonic Wars and beyond. It is

not surprising that republican symbolism in France referred exclusively to the classical world, but not to recent examples of European
history (such as Cromwell's Britain or Holland), which were too
closely associated with anti-French positions.[14]

As this paper will demonstrate, the experience of a traditionally
negative concept of 'Europe' – Metternich's Europe of diplomacy –
and the perception of 1848 as a 'social movement' in a larger European context had a strong impact on the later development of internationalist ideals in the French Labour movement during the Second
Empire and the Third Republic. The contemporary discourse of 1848
reveals both a transnational view of the events and their interpretation as a social revolution. Based on this experience, the collective
memory of the French labour movement linked international and
social conflicts of different periods into one single framework, including Waterloo and Sedan; Metternich, Radetzky and Bismarck; the
June Days and the Commune. Interpreting 1848 in terms of a European social revolution appears as a prelude to Internationalism in
the Labour movement of the Third Republic. It was particularly the
connection made between the social and the international dimension of the ideas and memories of the labour movement which
frightened the political regimes in 1848, in 1871 and during the
Third Republic.

Studying change over time means looking for cultural manifestations of change: this is the model Georg Simmel suggests in his work
about conflict in modern culture. Cultural manifestations serve as
records of the process of time.[15] The cultural practice of the French
(and mostly Parisian) Goguettes offers such insights into revolutionary events, into the ideas which circulated among the people of
1848, into the milieu of French workers and artisans, and into the
collective memory of 1848.

The political and cultural context of revolutionary songs: the Goguette

The 1848 'démocsocs', the political representatives of the Social
Republic, formed a political movement rooted within a specific
social milieu: 'the people of June 1848'.[16] The social milieu, as
defined by Rainer M. Lepsius,[17] goes beyond the active members of a
political movement, organized as a political club, a secret society or

a conspiratorial circle. It includes not only the fellows of a political organization as such, but the larger social context shaped by shared experiences, common ideas and collective memories: families, neighbourhoods or workplaces. The relationship between the political movement and its larger social milieu is based on a specific cultural practice. For example, only in exceptional cases were women members of secret societies, but they heard political songs in the local Goguette, and spoke about what they had heard to relatives, neighbours or other women at their workplace. They brought up their children with certain political ideas and with a collective memory of 1789, 1830 or the riots of the 'Canuts' in Lyon. Flyers with political songs and portraits of Raspail or Louis Blanc circulated in the neighbourhoods. After the defeat of the June barricades the families kept songbooks like Charles Vincent's *Album Révolutionnaire* or the famous *Voix du Peuple*.

An abstract political idea like Saint-Simon's doctrine or even the speeches of Louis Blanc or Raspail hardly allows for the evolution of such a socio-political milieu. A political idea needs a cultural communicator which creates a link between political movement and social context. Through cultural practice political ideas are transformed into social reality. With regard to the people of 1848, the writing, singing and publishing of political songs represents an important example of such a cultural practice. They represent the 'low-life' of political literature in this period.[18] The social function of such cultural practice goes beyond the communication of ideas. For the social milieu also the creation of songs itself, the consciousness of having its own culture, has a symbolic meaning. Cultural practice creates traditions and rituals and facilitates emotional ties between individuals and political movements. With regard to the social functions of music, this relationship is of particular interest: the social experience of musical practice creates emotions which are easily remembered and reproduced at a later time, at home or while rereading the same songs in a collection published by members of the political movement. The remembrance of a musical event allows us to rediscover certain images and metaphors, to recall political ideas and the emotions of a social experience at a political meeting. Music, like dreams, allows for the reawakening of what Proust calls the lost memory.

The French Goguettes had their most active years between the late 1830s and the Revolution of 1848.[19] They exemplify a cultural and social context for the communication of political ideas, here more specifically for the political ideas of a radical-democratic and social republic, as they were expressed in the context of the 1848 revolution. Their songs survived repression during the political regimes of the 'Cavaignacs' and Napoleon III and thus represented the memory of radical republican artisans and workers for the long period between the late July Monarchy and the Commune and later during the Third Republic.

Who were the people of June 1848, the people who grew up with the oppositional songs of the Goguette? De Tocqueville described the 'peuple' as 'the classes who work with their hands'.[20] Nevertheless, especially during the years of the July Monarchy, the language of labour in this milieu underwent an important change: language did not any longer demonstrate an artisan identity, but a more proletarian class consciousness.[21] In one of his songs Eugène Pottier describes Cavaignac's bourgeoisie as 'buveurs de sangue'.[22] Though he does not yet mention a conflict between capital and wage labour, he refers to the contrast between rich and poor, between the 'privileged' and the 'people'.[23] The popular milieu of the 'Quarante-Huitards' reproduces the heterogeneity of the French petty bourgeoisie and the peculiarity of the French working class, including independent artisans and small shopkeepers, but also 'born proletarians' whose experience of labour is marked by social decline and capitalist exploitation.[24] Many of these working people were originally skilled artisans and proud to set themselves apart through their own culture, values and ideas from the so called 'dangerous classes', the lumpenproletariat.[25] Historically, they identified themselves with the sans-culottes of the French Revolution of 1789, but since the 1830s new ideas had influenced their political concepts: 'Utopian socialism had started to enter the workshops', as one of the famous Goguettiers describes this ideological transformation in his memoirs.[26] This sociopolitical milieu of impoverished artisans, small shopkeepers and workers built the background for the 'people of June, 1848'[27] – the people of the barricades, radical democrats and socialist republicans, whose concepts still determined the political ideas of the Paris Commune in 1871.[28] Their idea was the application of the revolutionary principals 'liberté, égalité, fraternité' to the 'Social Republic'.[29]

Within this milieu of social republicanism one finds from the late 1830s the Goguette. These were popular meeting places where the people developed its specific cultural practice, influenced by the examples of bourgeois Sociétés Chantantes, traditions of the artisan confraternités and popular freemasonry. The word 'Goguette' comes from the verb 'goguer', an old word for 'se moquer', to tease, understood in the Goguette as political teasing. The 'chansonnier ouvrier' was at the centre of Goguette activity: a worker of the neighbourhood with some artistic aspirations who most of the time was politically active in the local republican and socialist associations. Within his milieu the Goguettier communicated political ideas through songs, often badly written in his own words and sung to popular tunes of 1789 or based on songs which circulated among the people of Paris. People heard these songs not only as customers in the Goguettes themselves, but they also encountered them in widely circulated leaflets, through the political press and in innumerable, locally printed, booklets. These cheap collections of songs represented more than just a means for the preservation of music; they were a kind of popular literature, largely diffused within this social milieu and preserving after 1852 the memory of 1848. During certain periods of the July Monarchy and the Second Republic several hundred Goguettes animated the popular neighbourhoods of Paris and certain provincial towns. The chansons of the Goguettes communicated within a larger social context the values and ideas of popular social republicanism, the collective memories of revolutions, the experiences and hopes of a political movement.

Nationalism, République Universelle and popular concepts of Europe in the ideas of 1848

In order to understand the complexity of the internationalist concepts expressed in the 1848 Goguette songs we have to analyse the origin of the republican opposition's political ideas. Hobsbawm and others have demonstrated that during the revolution of 1789 nationalism prevailed over the universalist claims of the original ideals.[30] For French republican opposition, nationalism stood for the liberation of peoples from their despotic governments, but this also included a leading role for the French nation as the liberator of other peoples. After 1815, nationalism remained an oppositional concept and still during the July Monarchy, when Louis Philippe adopted the Tricolore and transferred Napoleon's remains to Paris, this concept distinguished itself from the official regime through a republican idea of national sovereignty.[31] For the radical opposition, nation and republic were indivisible; popular republicanism claimed the exclusive right to represent the true concept of nation.

In spite of this nationalist tradition within French revolutionary thought, the post-Napoleonic order after 1815 provoked a new international dimension in the ideas of the political opposition.[32] There was an awareness that Metternich's new order of Europe had similar consequences for most European peoples. Moreover, new intellectual networks of communication led to an international dimension in the political debate.[33] Saint-Simonism, which influenced the political ideas of the Goguette very strongly, proclaimed not only a socialist and republican interpretation of Christianity, but also a fraternal and peaceful unification of all peoples and nations.[34] In contrast to 1792, the future republic would not proclaim a European war. Instead, the emancipation of peoples and the République Universelle would evolve as a logical process of civilization.

What did this mean with regard to the concepts of Europe as they were discussed within the popular milieu of the people of 1848? For the Goguettiers, Europe was first of all a negative concept. In thinking about Europe they referred to the post-Napoleonic settlement, to European diplomacy, the Europe of Metternich and Radetzky – a concept in terrible tension with the ideal of a 'République Universelle', understood as a 'République démocratique et sociale', that did not have to fight against other nations anymore. 'What is our interest in the quarrels of the European cabinets?' asks Pierre Dupont in his above quoted 'Workers' Song': 'Let's drink to the independence of the World.'[35]

Some songs of the Goguette offer more concrete examples of their negative concept of Europe. Popular reaction to the Egyptian crises of 1840 gives a dramatic illustration for this. In 1840, Adolphe Thiers' struggle with Britain over Egypt ended in a fiasco. The public response to the international slight to French interests in Africa was a claim to review France's eastern borders. To compensate for his political failure, Thiers himself planned the economic reattachment of Belgium. However, Metternich's Europe would not allow for any of these plans. Moreover, Louis-Bonaparte's attempted *coup d'état* contributed to European preoccupations with French revisionism. In fear of a replay of the Napoleonic Wars, Britain, Russia, Austria and Prussia reactivated their historic Alliance. The republican opposition in France analysed these events not as crises of its own odious regime. Instead, it reawakened the feelings of 1792, now directed against Metternich's Europe:

> Aux armes! Français belliqueux . . .
> Là-bas, un pacte injurieux
> Du Monde refait l'équilibre.
> Quatre Rois ont fait alliance . . .
> Jetons du feu dans la balance![36]

In 'Le quadruple Alliance – Cri d'indigation' the chansonnier Saint-Simonien calls the French people to arms in order to re-establish a European balance in which France would get its fair share. In his 'Marseillaise de 1840'[37] Festeau also describes Metternich's Europe as one of war and hate, but in this song he proclaims a European peace on the basis of free peoples. He opposes the negative concept of Metternich's Europe with a different, popular concept of European peoples. Festeau gives a more concrete sense of this Europe in his song 'Le congrès des Peuples', written just two years before the revolution of 1848: the future Europe does not need borders, 'together we will pull out all boundary-posts'.[38]

Later songs, produced in 1848, are documents of the revolutionary process during which Metternich's Europe was finally destroyed. The Parisian Goguettes sing Metternich's Chiarivari:

> Oh, Metternich, mon ami,
> Mon cher, ton règne est fini.[39]

The Goguettiers' negative concept of Europe actually describes the political landscape of Europe in the time between the Congress of Vienna and the revolution of 1848 rather well. Metternich's system of Europe developed after 1815 into a kind of 'internationalism of counter-revolution',[40] based on the agreement to oppose any attempted liberal or nationalist change to the status quo.[41] Veit Valentin described Metternich as a 'cosmopolitan European' whose answer to revolutionary movements was 'Pax Christiana, European Republic'. This was not a republic of peoples, but of European princes.[42] Contemporaries in Germany discussed the Holy Alliance in a very similar way. Arnold

Ruge, Marx's early collaborator, wanted to replace the Holy Alliance by a 'Council of Peoples', which would organize the European order on the principle of freedom.[43] Later, in the Frankfurt parliament, Ruge presented the same negative concept of European diplomacy as Dupont or Festeau did earlier in their songs: 'Real conventions are peoples' conventions; the wrong ones are conventions of diplomats.'[44]

In the revolution itself the new internationalism was first expressed through references to revolutionary activity outside France. In a song for the popular celebrations taking place on the Champ-de Mars on 21 May, Pierre Dupont sent his support for the revolutions in Italy and Germany, to Poland, and to the only country which had already enjoyed its freedom for several generations: America.[45] Similarly, Charles Gille, Genoux, Vincent, Leroy and Loynel wrote songs with titles like 'La Sicilienne' or 'Aux Italiens', or songs against Pius IX, traitor of the Italian revolutionary aspirations of 1846.[46] All were published in the revolutionary press and later in some of the most famous collections of barricade songs. As in 1830, Poland was again an important topic of revolutionary song, represented by titles such as 'Poland's last cry', 'France and Poland' or 'Poland – Anthem of Resurrection'.[47] In his song 'Vive la République' the Chansonnier Alais claimed freedom for Ireland, Germany and Italy, and Eugène Baillet, founding member of several republican Goguettes before 1848, remembered the republican movement in Switzerland.[48] What happened in France between February and June 1848 was clearly analysed within a European revolutionary context. This European dimension of the revolution was not only discussed in the Parisian Goguettes. Maurice Agulhon mentions a republican youth club in Nantes which started each meeting with a report on revolutionary events in Europe and during which the club's secretary had to complete a map of Europe with labels like 'Révolution allemande', 'autrichienne', 'hongroise', etc.[49] The references to Sicily and the republican movement in Switzerland point to events which dated back to before the French February Revolution. This suggests that the Goguettiers were even aware of the fact that this time, unlike 1789 and 1830, the revolution did not start in Paris, but abroad. Similarly, Armand Marrast, editor of the republican newspaper *Le National*, mentioned in the first public speech to the masses on 23 February the events in Switzerland and Sicily.[50] Before, it had always been France which was seen as the birthplace of revolution, as Louis Voitelain had expressed in an earlier song with reference to the beneficial ideas of 1789: 'Européens, retournez vers vos maîtres!'[51]

For the Goguettiers and the popular social republican movement this 'European dimension' within the revolution represented a fight between, on the one side, the Europe of Princes, diplomacy and alliances, the Europe of Metternich and Radetzky, and, on the other, the Europe of free peoples in their struggle for independence. However, this battle was fought within a vacuum: the Goguettiers never referred to any concrete plans for how to organize this Europe of free peoples. Despite their ideological origins within Utopian Socialism they did not refer to Saint-Simon's idea of a United States of Europe, an idea which had emerged at the time in consequence of the traumatic Napoleonic War experience.[52] Analysing the revolutionary events in 1848 carefully, we also have to note resentment against foreign workers,[53] and in Alsace also against the Jewish population who had hoped for emancipation within the Republic.[54] Singular cases of xenophobic activity in provincial factories did not permeate the politicized milieu of the Goguettiers, but neither was European federalism representative of the ideas of 1848. Instead, the European dimension of the popular republican ideas of 1848 shows that the revolution was conceived as a major turning point in the history of humanity: in the words of another song-leaflet, the day when 'the human being started to hold its destiny in its own hands'.[55] Passing beyond the narrow horizon of national politics, the birth of popular republics all over Europe invites the songwriters to a social interpretation of the revolution, a revolution based on the social, as opposed to the national, division of humanity. A widely distributed song collection of 1848 reproduced Vinçard's 'Appel aux Travailleurs' of 1835, starting with the words 'Prolétaires de toutes terres'.[56]

How did the Goguettiers deal with the historical and revolutionary legacy of France within the context of the liberation of all peoples? The revolutionary songs still illustrate a dichotomy between an awareness of the revolution's European dimension and the conviction that France should play a leading role in the revolutionary liberation of Europe. The year 1848 recalls for many chansonniers the feelings of 1792. As Charles Vincent exposes in his *Album Révolutionnaire*:

> Nous verrons les peuples unis,
> Se modelant sur notre belle France.[57]

France is still seen as playing a major role in the future development of the European revolution. As soon as victory is confirmed, French Republicans will go ahead and fight with their revolutionary brothers and the national movements across the Rhine:

> Aux Armes, Courons aux Frontières!
> Qu'on mette au bout de nos fusils
> Les oppresseurs de tous pays,
> Les poitrines des Radetzkis!
> Les peuples sont pour nous des frères
> Et les tyrans des ennemis.[58]

Again, the 'Europe of the Radetzkys' recalls a negative, pre-Revolutionary image of Europe, as opposed to the Europe of Peoples. Like Dupont, Jaquet, in his song for the Assemblée Nationale, understands the revolution as an occasion for vengeance against the Holy Alliance.[59] Thus these songs express a remarkable distance from the Republic's official foreign policy.[60] The foreign minister, Lamartine, had quickly declared that the new French Republic should not appear as a 'phénomene perturbateur de l'ordre européen'.[61] In an official document to French diplomatic agents dated 4 March, he wrote: 'The proclamation of the French Republic is not an act of aggression against any sort of government in the world'.[62] In spite of popular claims for vengeance against the Holy Alliance, most songs do not suggest a desire to repeat the Napoleonic experience. On the contrary, 'gloire militaire' appears in Rabineau's account of the Napoleonic Empire as a twofold experience: 'all laurels are watered with tears'.[63] For his references to the historical legacy of his family, Louis-Bonaparte, the future Napoléon le Petit, is regarded as the major enemy of the people's social republic. From before 1848 the oppositional milieu of the Goguette had criticized the myth of Napoleon I.[64] Even the popular chansonnier Jean-Pierre de Béranger, often seen as one of the godfathers of the Goguette movement,[65] was denounced by his younger fellow chansonniers for his contribution to a dangerous mystification of Napoleon. Charles Gille taught the history of 1789 and 1792 in his songs, but distinguished between French 'Grandeur' and the cult around Napoleon:

> Glory to the soldier who brought us up,
> But hate to the tyrant who put us in chains.[66]

The Social Republic viewed the European revolution of 1848 as the peoples' victory over Metternich's European order, but it did not suggest any new European order. The references to Italy or Poland and the glorification of Robert Blum do not answer the national question which was in the centre of revolutionary claims throughout the continent. The songs do not reflect the controversial debates about national minorities in the Frankfurt parliament, they do not refer to the national question within the Habsburg Empire, and they do not follow Saint-Simon's or Bentham's positive concepts of Europe. They also do not comment on Ledru-Rollin's, Ruge's and Mazzini's plans for a European democratic convention. However, their remarkable awareness of the revolution's European dimension shows the revolution as a major turning point in European history and as justification for the Social Republic. As the above-mentioned investigation about the commemorations of Robert Blum demonstrates, it was precisely this European dimension in the ideas of 1848 which continued to worry the European governments even after 1852, a Europe which was still perceived as the Europe of the Metternichs and Radetzkys. The French Goguettiers recognized soon that this Europe was about to develop into an even more aggressive order: in the words of another chansonnier 'the Europe of the Bismarcks and Krupps'.

The memory of 1848 in the French labour movement: from République Universelle to internationalism

Revisionist literature on 1848 in France has shown that the movement of the 'Quarante-Huitards' for a Social Republic did not end with Cavaignac's victory and the repression of the June insurrection.[67] Even after Louis-Bonaparte's *coup d'état*, the memory of 1848 remained for a long time a key element within the thinking of the republican opposition and the workers' movement. During the Commune, the ideas of 1848 still represented an important legacy[68] and within the French labour movement radical democracy and social republicanism prevailed for a long time over Marxist concepts. In emphasizing this continuity of ideas and memories I do not mean to suggest that there was an organizational continuity between the opposition of the late July Monarchy and the labour movement of the Third Republic. The Goguettes in particular did not survive as a cultural institution. What did survive, however, was the memory of

1848 as a reference point for later political movements; and if the ideas of 1848 differ considerably from the ideas of the socialist labour movement during the Third Republic there were nevertheless some popular chansonniers in the labour movement who continued to write political songs in the tradition of the Goguette. Their works represent the memory of 1848 in the modern labour movement, and the continuity between 'République Universelle' and 'internationalism'.

References to Charles Gille in particular, the poet of the 1848 barricades, recall the memory of the revolutionary Goguettes during the Second Empire and the Third Republic. After 1852 Rabineau had to veil the political content of his verses, but he still employed Gille's well known tunes for his own songs.[69] Joseph Landragin opened his new song collection with a quote from Charles Gille,[70] and Charles Colmance, in 1867, entitled one of his songs 'Charles Gille':

> Honneur au poète, au martyr!
> Qui vit la liberté du monde,
> Avec les yeux de l'avenir![71]

Forty years after the revolution and 'finally under republican rule',[72] Eugène Baillet published the collected works of Charles Gille.[73] While Charles Gille was remembered only through his songs, other Goguettiers, like Savinien Lapointe and Paul Avenel, played an active role in the political opposition of the Empire and then in the Commune. Several chansonniers of the Commune took part in the socialist Labour movement of the Third Republic, especially the POF. In their songs, the 1848 ideals of a Social Republic merge with the concepts of the modern labour movement.

In the aftermath of colonial expansion and the experience of the Franco-German war, the idealistic concept of the 'République Universelle' was modified. The chansonniers commented broadly on the development of post-1848 international relations. The later Communard Jean-Baptiste Clément challenged the general bellicose climate in Europe with an anti-war song. He describes the anxiety of the young front-line soldier Jacquot during the night before his first battle: Jacquot considers desertion, but fears being seized and executed. Although this means that he has to participate in useless killing, he decides in desperation to wait until the next morning – to be shot and buried on the battlefield.[74] With similar intentions Jules Jouy used the tune of the 'Carmagnole' for a song about the ravens of Sedan: for them the battlefields offer a jolly banquet.[75] In order to set the diplomats' minds at rest, the government of the Third Republic frequently had to intervene against chauvinist songs in the commercial Cafés-Concerts with titles like 'Cochon de Prussien', L'Assassin de Bismarck', and 'Le Vengeur de Strasbourg'.[76] Nevertheless, even after the French defeat, chansonniers in the tradition of 1848 largely rejected populist nationalism. In many songs, Clément tells the sorrows and grievances of young soldiers and their families, but he claims to be 'internationalist' and 'for the union of all the oppressed against the oppressors'.[77] In his introduction to a new edition of songs from 1885 he explains that the French Revolutions were not national revolutions against other European people, but proletarian revolutions. The heritage of the Commune shall not be another European war:

> Silence aux faiseurs de conquêtes
> Aux bourreaux de la liberté!
> Leurs victoires sont des défaites.
> Pour l'humanité
> Place à la liberté!

Another celebrated chansonnier, Eugène Pottier, who later became famous as author of the 'International', represents a final link between 1848, the Commune and the Labour movement of the Third Republic. Although usually associated with the Socialist International or the communist movement,[78] Pottier represents more than anybody else the ideas of 1848 and of social republicanism. His first political songs date from the late July Monarchy, and his first collection, entitled *Workshop Songs*, was published in 1848.[79] Returning from exile, the Communarde participated in a competition of the 'Lice Chansonnière', an association of political and musical veterans of 1848. As a prize for his contribution to the competition, the association offered to publish a volume of his songs from 1848 and 1871.[80] One of these songs was the 'International', written in a hiding-place during the last hours of the Commune while the capital was invaded by Prussian troops.[81] In the songs dating from the Second Empire and the early years of the Third Republic, ideas and memories of 1848 became associated with the modern labour movement. Within this new political context, Pottier's 'lutte finale' became an internationalist concept.

In a song entitled 'Bismarck's speech' Jules Jouy describes the political situation in Europe at the end of the nineteenth century ironically:

> Je veux la Paix; ...
> C'est pour la maintenir que Monsieur Krupp travaille
> Il ne forge du fer que pour l'humanité.[82]

Notes

1 A.N.: BB 18/1487 (A9093), 6.9.1850–13.7.1856, Cour d'Appel de Colmar, Département d'Haut Rhin, Tribunal de Colmars. Since his death in November 1848 the commemorations for Robert Blum were in the centre of revolutionary activity and commemoration: M. Hettling, *Totenkult statt Revolution. 1848 und seine Opfer* (Frankfurt am Main: Fischer, 1998), pp. 52–75. Traditional obsequies were combined with political speeches and civic celebrations. C. Tacke, 'Feste der Revolution in Deutschland und Italien', in D. Dowe, H.-G. Haupt and D. Langewiesche (eds), *Europa 1848. Revolution und Reform* (Bonn: Dietz, 1998), pp. 1045–88, 1066–70, 1080 et seq.

2 See in particular the papers by Jan Merk and Sabine Freitag in this volume.

3 J. Merriman, *The Agony of the Republic. The Repression of the Left in Revolutionary France. 1848–1851* (New Haven, CT and London: Yale University Press, 1978), pp. 32, 37, 219.

4 Ibid., pp. 25–50.

5 P. Dupont, 'Le Chant des Etudiants' (1848), in *Chants et Chansons. Poésies et Musique*, 4 vols (Paris: Houssiaux, 1851–4), vol. 1. Most of these songs were many times reprinted in various contemporary collections of revolutionary songs.

6 C. Vincent, 'Aux meutriers de Robert Blum', in *Album Révolutionnaire. Chants démocratiques* (Paris, 1849), p. 8.

7 C. Gille, 'Les tombeaux de Juin', Bibliothèque Nationale, Recueil de Chansons 1, Ye 7185 (244).

8 G. Leroy, 'Les soldats du désespoir', in *Voix du Peuple*, vol. 1 (Paris, 1848), pp. 224 f.

9 Gille, 'Les tombeaux de Juin'.

10 P. Dupont, 'Le chant des Ouvriers' (Paris: chez l'auteur, 1848).

11 K. Marx, 'Lohnarbeit und Kapital', in *MEW*, vol. 6 (Marx-Engels-Werke, Institut für Marxismus-Leninismus beim ZK der SED, Berlin, 1956), pp. 397–423, 397.

12 W. Mommsen, *1848. Die ungewollte Revolution* (Frankfurt am Main: Fischer, 1989), p. 114.

13 V. Rabineau, 'Les Démolisseurs', quoted by H. Poulaille, 'Les Chansons de 1848', in *Maintenant*, no. 9/10 (1948), pp. 434–502, 476 et seq.

14　P. Pilbeam, *Republicanism in Nineteenth Century France, 1814–1871* (London: Macmillan, 1995), p. 3. On classical models of Republicanism see also Sabine Freitag's paper in this volume.

15　G. Simmel, *The Conflict in Modern Culture and Other Essays* (New York: Teachers College Press, 1968).

16　C. Tilly and L. Hunt, 'The people of June, 1848', in R. Price (ed.), *Revolution and Reaction. 1848 and the Second French Republic* (London and New York, 1975), pp. 170–209.

17　R. M. Lepsius, 'Parteiensystem und Sozialstruktur: zum Problem der Demokratisierung der deutschen Gesellschaft' (1966), in G. A. Ritter (ed.), *Die deutschen Parteien vor 1918* (Cologne: Kiepenhauer & Witsch, 1973), pp. 56–80.

18　R. Darnton, 'The high enlightenment and the low-life of literature in pre-revolutionary France', *Past and Present*, 51, May 1971, 81–115.

19　On similar forms of popular sociability during the years of the Second Republic: Merriman, *The Agony of the Republic*, 51–82, 97 et seq. M. Agulhon, *La République au village* (Paris: Plon, 1970), pp. 207–211.

20　Quoted in R. Price (ed.), *The French Second Republic (Documents of Revolution)* (London: Thames & Hudson, 1975), p. 97.

21　W. H. Sewell Jr, *Work and Revolution in France. The Language of Labour from the Old Regime to 1848* (Cambridge: CUP, 1980), pp. 194 et seq.

22　E. Pottier, 'Les buveurs de sang', *Chants Révolutionaires*, (Paris: n.p; n.d.), p. 108.

23　Körner, *Das Lied von einer anderen Welt*, pp. 155–90.

24　H.-G. Haupt, *Sozialgeschichte Frankreichs seit 1789* (Frankfurt am Main: Suhrkamp, 1989), pp. 179–81. A detailed overview on the structure of the French working class during this period: R. Price, *The French Second Republic. A Social History* (London: Batsford, 1972), pp. 5–30, 56–87.

25　C. Charle, *Histoire Sociale de la France au XIXe siècle* (Paris: Seuil, 1991), p. 57 et seq. J. Rancière, *La nuit des prolétaires* (Paris: Fayard, 1981).

26　S. Lapointe, *Mémoire sur Béranger* (Paris: Havard, 1857), 9. See also Körner, *Das Lied von einer anderen Welt*, p. 171 et seq.

27　Tilly and Hunt, 'The people of June, 1848'. On the social composition of the montagnards see also Merriman, *The Agony of the Republic*, p. 216 et seq.

28　Haupt, *Sozialgeschichte Frankreichs*, p. 193.

29　See M. Agulhon, *1848 ou l'apprentissage de la république. 1848-1852* (Paris: Seuil, 1973), pp. 29–36. See also Merriman's definition: 'Social' in this context means 'to be responsible for the labouring poor'. Merriman, *The Agony of the Republic*, xxi.

30　E. J. Hobsbawm, *Nations and Nationalism since 1780. Programme, Myth, Reality* (Cambridge: Cambridge University Press, 1991), p. 21.

31　C. Nicolet, *L'idée républicaine en France (1789–1924), Essai d'histoire critique* (Paris: Gallimard, 1982), p. 17.

32　Y. Lequin, 'La trace de l'Ancien Régime', in idem, *La mosaïque en France. Histoire des étrangers et de l'immigration en France* (Paris: Larousse, 1988), pp. 323–34. Despite occasional national conflicts between French and

German artisans this internationalization becomes also visible within the exile communities in Paris: W. Schieder, *Anfänge der deutschen Arbeiterbewegung. Die Auslandsvereine im Jahrzehnt nach der Julirevolution von 1830* (Stuttgart: Klett, 1963).

33 L. Namier, *1848: The Revolution of the Intellectuals* (1944) (London: Oxford University Press, 1957).

34 J. Vinçard, *Mémoires épisodiques d'un vieux chansonnier saint-simonien* (Paris: Dentu, 1878), p. 30.

35 P. Dupont, 'Le chant des Ouvriers'.

36 L. Festeau, 'Le quadruple Alliance. Cri d'indication. Octobre, 1840', *Chansons* (1846), p. 244.

37 Idem, 'La Marseillaise de 1840', *Chansons* (1846), p. 319.

38 Idem, 'Le Congrès des Peuples', ibid., pp. 109–13.

39 Sallesede, 'Grand Chiarivari donné a Metternich', *Chansonnier Républicain. 1793–1848, dédié au Peuple Souverain*, p. 163.

40 R. Kühnl, '1848 und der deutsche Sonderweg', *Blätter für deutsche und internationale Politik*, March 1998, pp. 337–47, 341.

41 T. Nipperdey, *Deutsche Geschichte 1800–1866. Bürgerwelt und starker Staat* (Munich: Beck, 1983), p. 100. See also H. H. Hahn, 'Die Revolution von 1848 als Strukturkrise des europäischen Staatensystems', in P. Krüger (ed.), *Das europäische Staatensystem im Wandel. Strukturelle Bedingungen und bewegende Kräfte seit der frühen Neuzeit* (Munich: Beck, 1996), pp. 131–52.

42 V. Valentin, *1848. Chapters of German History* (London: George Allen & Unwin, 1940), p. 15 et seq.

43 A. Ruge, 'Aus einem offenen Brief zur Verteidigung des Humanismus an Robert Eduard Prutz' (1847), in *Patriotismus*, ed., Peter Wende (Frankfurt am Main: Insel, 1990), pp. 85–98, 91.

44 Ibid., 'Rede Arnold Ruges in der 45. Sitzung der Deutschen Nationalversammlung der Frankfurter Paulskirche' (1948), pp. 99–113, 102.

45 P. Dupont, 'Chant rustique pour la Fête du Champ-de-Mars', in *Chansons*.

46 C. Gille, 'La Sicilienne', *Voix du Peuple*, I, p. 135. C. Genoux, 'A. S. S. Pie IX. Rome moderne', *Voix du Peuple*, II, p. 45ff. Vincent, 'Aux Italiens', *Album Révolutionaire. Chants démocratiques* (Paris, l'auteur, 1849), p. 43.

47 A. Loynel, 'A la Pologne', *Voix du Peuple*, II, p. 181. Leroy and Durand, 'France et Pologne', ibid., p. 209. C. Vincent, 'Le dernier Cri de la Pologne', *Album Révolutionnaire*, p. 30. L. Festeau, 'La Pologne. Hymne de Résurrection', *Chansons*, 1846, p. 310. P. Dupont, 'Le Chant des Paysans'.

48 A. Alais, 'Vive la République', *Voix du Peuple*, I, p. 145. E. Baillet, 'Le Cri des Français', ibid., p. 164.

49 M. Agulhon, *Les Quarante-Huitards* (Paris: Gallimard, 1975), p. 96 et seq.

50 Ibid., p. 41.

51 Quoted E. Thomas, *Voix d'en bas. La poésie ouvrière du XIXe siècle* (Paris: Maspero, 1979).

52 G. Duveau, *1848* (Paris: Gallimard, 1965), p. 233.

53 Merriman, *The Agony of the Republic*, 14, p. 155. Agulhon, *Les Quarante-Huitardes*, p. 110 et seq.

54 Especially Alsace and Southwest Germany, where the above-mentioned booklet in memory of Robert Blum was confiscated by the French customs, were the scenes of some violent riots against the Jewish population. R. Rürup, 'Der Fortschritt und seine Grenzen', in Dowe et al., *1848*, pp. 985–1006, 987 et seq. Merriman, *The Agony of the Republic*, 85, 91. On the limits of Jewish emancipation during the revolution of 1848: W. E. Mosse, 'The Revolution of 1848. Jewish emancipation in Germany and its limits', in W. E. Mosse, A. Paucker and R. Rürup (eds), *Revolution and Evolution. 1848 in German–Jewish History* (Tübingen: Mohr, 1981), pp. 389–402.

55 Journet, 'Hymne aux travailleurs', *Au citoyen Barbès, 1er Mars 1848* (Paris: Duverger, 1848), BHVP 29805 (45).

56 J. Vinçard, 'Appel aux Travailleurs', *Voix du Peuple*, II, p. 33.

57 C. Vincent, 'La Liberté', *Album Révolutionaire*, p. 3.

58 P. Dupont, 'Le Chant des Soldats'.

59 Jaquet, *Assemblée Nationale. Chant républicain* (Paris: Proux, 1848), BHVP 29805 (66).

60 Agulhon, *1848 ou l'apprentissage de la République*, p. 42.

61 Agulhon, *Les Quarante-Huitardes*, p. 103.

62 Alphonse de Lamartine in a circular letter to French diplomatic agents, quoted in Price, *1848 in France*, p. 70. Lamartine's policy of non-aggression went so far as to reject the proposal of Prussia's new foreign secretary von Arnim to support Italian unification and the re-emergence of Poland: Nipperdey, *Deutsche Geschichte 1800–1866*, p. 623.

63 Rabineau 'Gloire militaire', *Voix du Peuple*, I, p. 109.

64 Körner, *Das Lied von einer anderen Welt*, pp. 258–64.

65 P. Brochon, *La chanson française. Béranger et son temps* (Paris: Editions sociales, 1956). Idem, *La chanson française. Le Pamphlet du pauvre: du socialisme utopique à la Révolution de 1848* (Paris: Editions sociales, 1957).

66 C. Gille, 'Napoleon', *Chansons de Charles Gille*, p. 41.

67 Agulhon, *1848*. Idem, *La République au village*. Merriman, *The Agony of the Republic*. Price, *The French Second Republic*.

68 Haupt, *Sozialgeschichte Frankreichs*, p. 193. Haupt and Hausen, *Die Pariser Kommune. Erfolg und Scheitern einer Revolution* (Frankfurt am Main: Campus, 1979).

69 V. Rabineau, 'Rabelais' to the tune of Gille's 'Amusez-vous', *Les Filles du hasard* (Paris, 1860), p. 25.

70 J. Landragin, *Mes chansons* (Paris, 1859).

71 C. Colmance, 'Charles Gille', *Oeuvres Complètes* (Paris: Vieillot, 1862), p. 476.

72 These were the words of Gille's brother in law, Mouret, explaining his own apolitical ideas. During the 1870s he maintained, however, a Goguette in Rue Vieille du Temple in memory of Charles Gille. M.-V. Gauthier, *Chansons, sociabilité et grivoiserie au XIXe Siècle* (Paris: Aubier, 1992), p. 47.

73 E. Baillet, *Chansons de Charles Gille* (Cluny, 1887).

74 J.-B. Clément, 'Chanson d'avant-poste', *Chansons* (Paris: Robert, 1885), p. 154. For a similar anti-militarist manifestation see idem, 'O ma France', *Chansons*, p. 98.

75 Jouy, 'La Carmagnole des Corbeaux', *Chansons de Bataille* (Paris: Flammarion, 1889), p. 32.

76 'Titres des chansons contre les Allemands interdites', A.N.: F 21/1331.

77 Clément, *Chansons*, 98.

78 W. I. Lenin, 'Eugène Pottier', *Pravda*, 3 January 1913, quoted in *Arbeiterklasse und Musik. Theoretische Positionen in der deutschen Arbeiterklasse zur Musikkultur vor 1945, Forum: Musik in der DDR* (Berlin: Akademie der Künste der DDR, 1974), p. 125. F. Gel, *Internationale und Marseillaise. Lieder die Geschichte machten. Zwei Reportagen aus 1½ Jahrhunderten* (Prague, 1954).

79 E. Pottier, *Chansons de l'Atelier* (Paris: Naunan, 1848).

80 Idem, *Quel est le fou? Chansons* (Paris: Oriol, 1884). (See preface by the president of the Lice Chansonnière, Nadaud.)

81 The song was composed in 1888 by Pierre Degeyter: Gel, *Internationale und Marseillaise*, p. 170.

82 Jouy, 'Le discours de Bismarck', *Chansons de Bataille*, p. 35. Understood as a military provocation against France, Germany presented its giant Krupp cannon at the Paris World Exhibition of 1867. From that time 'Krupp' became a symbol for a new quality of German warfare. See the illustration in C. S. Maier, 'German war, German peace', in M. Fulbrook (ed.), *German History since 1800* (London: Arnold, 1997), pp. 539–55, 542.

6

National Union or Cosmopolitan Unity? Republican Discourse and the Instrumental Approach towards the German Question

Sabine Freitag

When Friedrich Hecker, a deputy of the second Baden chamber, tried to establish a German republic on 12 April 1848 in Konstanz near the Swiss border, he talked about its advantages as a governmental system and tried to convince his audience that they could govern themselves better then any monarchy ever could. Hecker hoped that his march to Karlsruhe to the palace of the Grand Duke of Baden would become a real mass movement, a 'living mass petition', which would be joined by the dissatisfied Baden soldiers.[1] But instead, one week later, the Baden revolutionaries were soundly defeated by Württemberg and Bavarian troops of the German Confederation. Thus ended the first attempt to establish a republic which was intended to become the nucleus of a future republican German confederation. The second attempt to proclaim a German republic, this time by Gustav Struve on 21 September 1848 under the slogan 'Prosperity, education, freedom for all' (*Wohlstand, Bildung, Freiheit für alle*), was a failure too.[2] And even when a third upheaval broke out in Baden with mass participation by ordinary people – the so-called *Reichsverfassungkampagne*, which intended to force the reluctant governments of Prussia, Austria and Bavaria to incorporate the new Imperial Constitution worked out by the National Assembly at Frankfurt into the constitutions of their respective countries – the radical leaders did not succeed in securing their newly established provisional government.[3]

In recent historical studies there is a huge variety of explanations and interpretations of what kind of political mass movement developed in Baden, and whether it was a political mass movement at all.[4] Judgements are rather contradictory on this point. Jonathan Sperber for example argues in his book on the *Rhineland Radicals* that the upheavals and popular movements during the years 1848/49 throughout west and south Germany were far more than just rural or social disturbances. They had turned into political ones as well. He emphasizes an enormous politicization in which even the peasantry was involved. The political implications of the revolts, so he argues, could not be denied.[5]

Yet in his book *German Radicals Confront the Common People* Karl Wegert, who has researched exactly the same field, comes to the conclusion that it was anything but a political movement:

> The radicals had greater success among people who were vulnerable in a different way...Some were moved by hopes for economic gain, others by a desire for attention, others still were swept into High Politics through misunderstanding...One also encountered a lot of irrepressible characters, men who were naturally extroverted for whom any meeting or rally, political or otherwise, afforded a welcome working milieu.[6]

And the peasants, Wegert claims, joined the meetings mostly for some entertainment or the exchange of local information.[7]

It is not the intention of this paper to discuss the extent to which the common people were politicized in the south-west German upheavals. In the case of many participants it seems obvious that unrest in Baden was primarily fed by continued social discontent. Social, economic and political concerns were mixed together and a great diversity of hopes and wishes were associated with the word 'republic' or – as Jonathan Sperber put it: 'The creation of a democratic, preferably republican government was their answer to the social question.'[8] In other words: the demand for a democratic, preferably republican government was related to economic and social considerations, not to any kind of 'national feelings'. Many of those who participated in the upheavals belonged to social groups which had been directly affected by the socio-economic changes of the previous decade: agrarian crisis, crisis of the crafts and trades, industrialization, modernization, unemployment, poverty. Craftsmen were threatened by technological change and peasants hoped for freedom from the oppressive control of the landlord or the tax collector. They believed that their rebellion would lead to a better life. But it is questionable whether the 'national question' played a crucial role at this level.[9] Even if social unrest was associated with the word 'republic', it was not connected with any expectation of a united Germany. The sense of nationhood could not claim priority over all the other individual interests or concerns. The peasants' sense of group identity or their primary loyalties, for example, in so far as they ever considered them, were more likely to be focused on their village, their region, their religion or sometimes even their ruling royal family. It was still hard for the 'common people' to see themselves as part of a 'nation'.[10]

We must remember that in the first half of the nineteenth century thinking in 'national terms', wanting a united Germany and calling for the creation of a national state was an exclusively intellectual goal, pursued by the urban population, and furthered in particular by members of the educated middle class and students who had been educated at German universities during and after the wars of liberation in 1814/15.[11] Especially in the northern states, and above all in Prussia, national ideas had been generated by the humiliating experience of Napoleonic occupation and the powerlessness of self-defence. As a kind of intellectual compensation educated men like Johann Gottlieb Fichte and Ernst Moritz Arndt favoured the romantic doctrine of a united German nation, defined by common language, culture and history. National self-esteem should be attained by belonging to a cultural nation (*Kulturnation*). The ethnic-cultural nation they had in mind derived from a vague conception of an autonomous, strong German empire such as they believed to have existed in the Middle Ages. In this approach – Friedrich Karl von Savigny's *Historische Rechtsschule* and the late Hegelian school developed in the same direction – the monarchical system as a governmental form turned out almost naturally to be legitimized and confirmed by historical development. But in south-western Germany where political experience was of a different sort the 'national discourse' was used in a different way and for different purposes.

Before I pursue the link between the discussion on republican government and national union, I would like to present briefly some of the influential ideas and real 'models' which might have played a role in creating the republican concept. There never existed, even in radical theory, one single, clear and distinct concept of a republic. Therefore my approach is a very general one which does not go too deeply into the theoretical details of the different radical or individual concepts of democratic theorists. These were much too sophisticated to be widely adopted.[12] In a second step I shall examine the circumstances under which the notion of a 'national state' came under discussion. Here my question is whether the peculiar circumstances in the south-west of Germany caused a more 'instrumental approach' towards the 'national question', i.e. a discussion about a unified Germany – for the radicals preferably under a republic government – without using or appealing to anything like 'national feelings'.

The south-west of Germany, especially Baden, offered a political environment which could support democratic tendencies in every respect. Public life was unusually free and political debate exceptionally vigorous. The early introduction of a constitutional system in 1818 and lively and politically self-contained local communities – as Paul Nolte has recently shown[13] – had made it possible for people to become increasingly familiar with the concept of growing political participation. And real models were indeed not far away.

For many liberals neighbouring France was never regarded as an enemy, nor was its political system rejected as in many other German states confronted with Napoleonic occupation. If we bear in mind that the 'national idea' developed a broad appeal in Germany as an expression of resistance to Napoleon, in the Grand Duchy of Baden things were quite different. Baden did not only emerge from Napoleon's geopolitics as a territorial winner, but as a member state of the Confederation of the Rhine it benefited from the introduction of the Code Civil, which introduced civic legal equality. Those liberals who were influenced by the tradition of rational enlightenment admired France's constitutional system and the guarantee of human rights. In the 1830s there were discussions about a political merger between France and the smaller German states to protect their constitutional system against autocratic monarchical states such as Russia, or even Prussia, in the event of war.[14]

However, in a practical sense the influence of nearby Switzerland seems much more obvious. The loose confederation of independent cantons could be taken as an example of how a republic could survive without any monarchical leadership or government, even though the

Swiss population was a mixture of different languages, cultures and traditions. German liberals – and I do not distinguish between liberals and radicals until the late 1840s – praised Switzerland as a 'born federative state'.[15] But they criticized the lack of a central government for two reasons: the relative weakness against foreign threats and the lack of a Swiss national citizenship which would enable the population to move freely between the cantons (*freies Zuzugsrecht*). In the 1830s the strong national movement with liberal, democratic and centralizing tendencies, initiated by Swiss lawyers and entrepreneurs who were in favour of industrial modernization, was also strongly supported by Baden liberals. The struggle between the agrarian Catholic, conservative cantons and the more liberal, Protestant ones led – as we know – to the Swiss Civil War (*Schweizer Sonderbundskrieg*) in 1847. The result was a federal constitution (*Bundesverfassung*) which was modelled on the American constitution, but turned out to be more democratic: executive power was distributed between seven *Bundesräte*, elected by parliament for a fixed period of time. No single president was elected as the head of the government. The two-chamber system, the *Nationalrat* and the *Ständerat*, showed an orientation towards the American concept of representative democracy and retained the federalist structure of the country; elements of direct democracy such as the 'Volksreferendum' were introduced much later. The constitution guaranteed 'Protection of freedom and the rights of the Swiss confederate'[16]. Those things which seemed absolutely necessary for the industrial and economic development of the country were centralized – for example: measures, weights, coins, the postal system, customs and duties, and the military organization. From now on the central government was responsible for foreign policy and the judiciary, i.e. the system of courts (*Justiz*). But all other areas, such as schools, taxes, police and ecclesiastical affairs remained the responsibility of the individual cantons. What seems interesting is that here we have a 'national discourse' within a republic which supported a central government for economic, strategic-defensive and legal purposes. Centralization was considered to be absolutely necessary to create a homogeneous economic area and to strengthen the country's defensive capabilities. The ethnic mix among the population did not serve as the basis for this national confederation at all.

Historians are still investigating how great the influence of the United States of America was on the idea of a republic in Germany.[17]

Few people had personal experience of its political institutions and social structures. But on the other hand, America was a perfect model for those who were looking for examples. As the influential history professor Carl von Rotteck put it in the early 1820s, in no other country had 'the main demands of pure theory been met in such an enviable richness'.[18] Many German radicals believed that Rousseau's *Social Contract* had been realized in America. Gustav Struve for example referred directly to the American constitution in the Pre-parliament (*Vorparlament*) when he called for a republic with a presidential system in March 1848.[19] But America, like Switzerland, was a nation which did not rely on the ethnic descent of its population but defined itself by its free political institutions. And both countries had already solved the 'border' question.

To the well-known ideas and existing examples of a republican system a further ingredient was added. Theoretical republicanism was a mixture of familiar liberal convictions and something which might be called classical or ancient republicanism. Recent studies have emphasized the influence of this 'theoretical model' transmitted by school and university education.[20] Men like Friedrich Hecker or Julius Fröbel confessed how much they were influenced by studies of the ancient republics of Athens and Rome.[21] And Hecker, shortly before he went to Konstanz, admitted in the *Landtag* how much his republican enthusiasm had been inspired by his ancient studies.[22] It is quite obvious that this idealized interpretation of ancient models was far removed from the historical reality. None the less, 'classical' republicanism could be brought into line with liberal, and especially democratic, convictions. First of all, it was taken as an example of popular sovereignty. Here civil society and political government were brought together, were thought to be identical. The main purpose of this political community, which had been freely created by its members, was to protect everybody's freedom. Even Rousseau's *Social Contract*, which played a crucial role in democratic theories, could be applied to this model. Government had no function other than to guarantee the self-realization of the people. The most important feature of this idealized ancient republic was the mutual cause of social cohesion and the political character of the community. Therefore this 'model' enlarged the active participation of its citizens in political affairs and their selfless commitment to the common good. Because the republic lacks a strong government in an authoritarian sense, it needs the virtue of its citizens to avoid corruption.

Ancient republicanism even fitted into the liberal middle-class ideology.[23] Aristotle emphasized the importance of a strong, independent and frugal middling group for the internal stability of republican society. And this 'middling society' was intended to be something in between the very rich and the very poor, both easily corruptible for different reasons.

In 1847, when liberals and radicals separated over the question of their further political action, it seemed that among many radicals the idea of a political institution called a republic was already well developed and was neither unspecified nor abstract. Many of them knew quite well what popular sovereignty required in practice, how a republic must be organized and what institutions were needed. Of course the German reality of 36 states and four free towns belonging to the German confederation was a considerable obstacle to unification. But even the more moderate liberals – who, as we all know, hoped for national unity and political liberalization to be accomplished gradually without any violent break on the basis of the further development of existing institutions – even those liberals must have been convinced that after all the best governmental form for achieving their goals was a republic. Even for them 'popular sovereignty', the representation of the people, was the only political principle which guaranteed political participation in the way they desired. For different and obvious reasons they became distanced from these ideas and looked for practical cooperation with the monarchical state governments.

Throughout the 1830s and the 1840s the liberal discussion about political participation and liberalization in the German south-west was held without a national state being considered. There were – as far as I can see – three major events which changed this attitude and put the discussion about a 'national state' on the political agenda.

First, the fear of foreign aggression. This was triggered by the *Rheinkrise* in 1840, when France tried to compensate for its failure in oriental politics by an aggressive claim on the 'natural borders' of the Rhine; and by the discussion about the incorporation of Schleswig into Denmark in the mid-1840s, later hotly debated once again in the Frankfurt National Assembly in 1848. Second, the experience of failing to improve the political situation at the level of the individual state. And third the confrontation with the emerging 'social question' which was – in the liberals' view – directly connected with the question of what direction the country's economic development should take.

The *Rheinkrise* in 1840 did not provoke a homogeneous reaction from the left-wing liberals in Baden. Some criticized the German reaction as *Deutschtümmelei,* an extreme display of 'Germanness', others were firmly convinced that France had aggressive intentions towards German territory. But although this event did not give rise to a uniform German reaction, the emotion it generated was nevertheless astonishing.[24] It may have demonstrated to some deputies how effectively this strong emotional reaction could be used for political purposes. When the question of Schleswig was raised in the Baden chamber in the mid-1840s, the reactions of the deputies were ambivalent. Hecker, for example, asked for 'armed volunteers' to support the German minority in Schleswig and fight for its non-separation from Holstein, which belonged to the German Confederation. But at the same time he stressed how urgently the German Confederation needed to be reformed. He therefore combined 'national' arguments with his constitutional ambitions.[25] Men such as Adam von Itzstein, Christian Kapp, Ludwig Weller, Anton Christ and Friedrich Daniel Bassermann acted in the same way. They always kept their main political ambitions in mind, even when Itzstein, for example, asked during the Schleswig discussion, 'whether Germany should always be the victim of other nations'.[26] The aim of this rhetoric was not some kind of *Machtstaat,* but the attainment of a unified country, able to defend itself and its progressive political structure.

This leads to the second cause. It can be argued that the 'national question' was raised at the moment when liberals and radicals in Baden become aware that they had not achieved their goals by their legislative work in the Baden chamber. Every political demand had been hotly debated but most had been rejected by the Baden government, referring to its obligations towards the German Confederation (*Bundesverpflichtungen*). The deputies became aware that they would never succeed in reforming Baden unless they reformed the Confederation as a whole. Whatever they wanted, whatever they decided, they would never achieve it if the *Bund* stayed as it was. Baden still seemed too dependent on the policies of the Confederation. Thus asking for the German Diet to be reformed again revealed an instrumental approach towards the 'national question'. This change of attitude towards the Confederation was described by Heinrich von Gagern to his brother Friedrich as early as 1843:

> Everywhere in the South [of Germany] they are now coming to the conclusion that representative forms alone, without freedom of the press, under the constraints imposed by the federal constitution, and without any further development of conditions encouraging freedom ... do not constitute freedom. In Baden they have resisted the longest, and have tried to find freedom through their constitution. But they were worn down by the outcome of the last Landtag, where the opposition was totally victorious in that it had the majority, but did not have the slightest practical success and was sent home at the end, as if they had been defeated ... What usually we have seen as the conviction of just a few now turns out to be the conviction of the majority: a positive unity, not a mystical one, is now the unanimous cry of all spokesmen. Particularism no longer has any basis.[27]

This 'positive unity, not a mystical one' Gagern mentioned in his letter describes the very concrete wish for national unification defined not by the romantic assumptions of race or ethnic speculations or former medieval greatness, but by democratic laws and broad political participation, and represented by a national assembly.

My third point, which will emphasize the largely 'instrumental approach' towards the 'national question', is the discussion about the German Customs Union (*Zollverein*). In the 1830s most of the Baden deputies had great doubts about the Customs Union, but in the mid-1840s liberals such as Adam von Itzstein, Adolf Sander and Friedrich Hecker started to favour it as an existing structure which could help to unite Germany. However, they did not look to it for purely economic reasons. None of them were businessmen or merchants, for whom the Customs Union could be a source of personal profit. Once again the motivation seemed to be to strengthen the liberal movement by giving it wider backing. Adam von Itzstein had already tried this throughout the 1830s and 1840s by extending cooperation between deputies of different state parliaments (*Landtage*). Supporting the *Zollverein*, which was still dominated by Prussia, did not mean supporting German unification under Prussian leadership to attain some sort of *Machtstaat*. It reflects much more the naive adoption of the ideas of Adam Smith and Thomas Paine on the part of the liberals: the belief that a closed home market (*geschlossener Binnenmarkt*) and free trade within it, the economic interdependencies, the rapid exchange of information and the improved means of communication that would come with it would help to spread democratization throughout the whole country. What deputies like Itzstein or Hecker had in mind was once again an instrumental approach to unification. It should help to democratize the internal structures of the future Germany by pulling walls down, by letting communication spread enlightenment. They hoped that economic prosperity would stabilize conditions inside the state. But uniting Germany – in whatever way – was always a means to achieve the first and primary goal: freedom, by the internal extension of constitutional rights and the power of the *Landtage*.

Jacob Venedey, not a Baden deputy but an early democrat, was sceptical of the *Zollverein* but nevertheless hoped that extending the railway system would promote economic development. He demonstrates the liberals' belief in the connection between economic interdependencies and growing democratization. In 1835 he wrote:

> ...the railroads will bring down all the internal borders in Germany. Ten years after all the large and capital cities are linked together by the railroad, Germany will be a completely different country, and the prejudices which have so splintered the German people up to now, which have so facilitated the rule of its oppressors, will have ceased to exist.[28]

Even Heinrich von Treitschke, the Prussia-orientated historian who was by no means a democrat or republican, knew exactly what further industrial and trade development and exchange would mean at an international level: 'The nature of modern communication is not national, but cosmopolitan. It inevitably tears down the walls separating people from people.'[29]

Without doubt the liberals, and especially the later radicals, were greatly concerned about the social question, about fighting against the unhealthy and unfair development towards something which we later defined as a 'class-divided society'. They might therefore have hoped that the economy itself, free trade released from state controls, would be able to cure these diseases. But believing that the unity of the nation was the fundamental condition for lasting national prosperity, one which could help to solve social problems, was once again to take an instrumental approach to the national question. And seeking unification for economic reasons showed great similarities with Switzerland.

Of course, liberals and radicals differed greatly on the question of what the future German state should look like politically, but their answers to the question of why there should be a national state or why they needed one at all were very similiar. And their reasons seemed to be influenced by instrumental considerations: foreign policy and defence, economic relief or development and the introduction of political reforms and liberalization in every part of the political public sphere. As long as internal political progress always seemed to be prevented by Confederation politics, they had to concentrate their energies on the *Bund*. But this also meant acting at the national level, in whichever way.

Both liberals and radicals were confronted with the question of how to establish the representation of the people at national level. This meant the creation of a national state; even the radicals needed a real territorial body for their future republic. Kant's *Eternal Peace* had not yet been established. And the borders of this republic had to be defined. Friedrich Daniel Bassermann, who became famous for his demand for a German parliament or representation of the German people at the Frankfurt Diet, was thinking about these criteria when he stated in July 1846 in the Baden *Landtag*:

> Language is one tie holding our nationality together. There are provinces, which, although they do not belong to the German Confederation, are regarded as among the best Germans; I refer to the provinces of eastern Prussia. But there is another tie of nationality which is much stronger than language, and that is freedom. The free constitutions of France and Switzerland have triumphed over the language sympathies of German-speaking men.[30]

A German parliament, as Bassermann put it in 1846, would strengthen the sense of nationhood (*Nationalgefühl*), which he saw as the only condition for strengthening 'national power' (*Nationalkraft*). The sequence he mentioned seems to be significant: first a German parliament, then the development of a 'national feeling', which would eventually strengthen 'national power', considered by him primarily as an economic term. But in Bassermann's view, strengthening the sense of nationhood did not mean strengthening the consciousness of being a German in an ethnic sense, but becoming aware and at the same time proud of being a free citizen with political rights in a state that guarantees these rights and is strong enough to do so properly. National self-esteem should arise from internal political progress, the growth of participatory politics. Hecker later applauded this definition and emphasised the necessity of introducing a common German law in all German states to strengthen the 'feeling of belonging together' (*Zusammengehörigkeitsgefühl*).[31]

The discussions in the National Assembly at Frankfurt in 1848 about the basis for the future Germany, and about who should be included and excluded, demonstrated the extreme difficulty of definition since the German Confederation remained a multinational complex. Clear boundaries were difficult to draw at every corner of the German Confederation, which was 'naturally' taken as the basis: Limburg in the west was Dutch, Schleswig in the north was Danish, Posen in the east was Polish and the Tyrol in the south belonged to Austria. Of course, the discussions about Schleswig, but especially about Posen, were highly emotional. There was a great desire to belong to a strong united Germany which would play an important and independent role within Europe. Money was even collected in the various German states in order to establish a German navy (*Deutsche Flotte*). But I would emphasize, as James Sheehan put it,[32] that a left-wing delegate such as Wilhelm Jordan was not speaking for the majority of the assembly when he argued in favour of German hegemony over people obviously culturally inferior, such as the Poles: 'The superiority of the German peoples over the Slavs – with the possible exception of the Russians – is a fact... and against such, I would say, facts of natural history, decrees issued in the name of cosmopolitan righteousness will have little impact.'[33] Jordan's position was probably not shared by most delegates, even if the majority were influenced by the romantic interpretation of a cultural nation.[34] It might be that the radicals, always sensitive to accusations that they were not 'true' Germans, felt far more pressure to convince the audience that they were quite the opposite. The National Assembly itself, as the first real national political institution, might to some extent have promoted these growing nationalistic feelings. But it was only after the failure of the revolution that the effective sense in which these emotions could be used for political purposes became obvious.

We know that the questions of the future Germany's territory and of who was to belong to it were postponed by the assembly because of their enormous difficulty. In the end the Imperial constitution (*Reichsverfassung*) came to a fair and tolerant compromise, and would have protected minorities in an exemplary manner if it had come into effect. Despite all this 'Verbalradikalismus', as Wolfram Siemann put it, this constitution did not aim for military conquest. Karl August Varnhagen von Ense, a former Prussian envoy to Baden in the 1820s, who became more and more radical and republican towards the end of his life, followed the discussions in the National Assembly at Frankfurt. In my view he represents the radical or republican attitude towards an ethnically defined national state:

> How can we decide what we should claim for Germany? There is no satisfactory solution to be had to this mixture of nationalities. We should be satisfied if we come even close to such a solution. In any case, nationality is not the sole, not even the most important basis on which to form states. Shared laws and freedoms are undoubtedly much more important than ethnic ties, especially when these ties have been broken and obscured.[35]

The failure of the revolution may itself have caused nationalism increasingly to overshadow constitutionalism. Liberal political practices were pushed into the background by concern for national unity and power. Their commitment to national unification meant that the liberals largely gave up the original ingredients of their liberal faith to look for a political government ruled by law.

Here the radical republicans, who emigrated to the United States, were much more consistent. One reason why these German republicans were later integrated so successfully into their adopted fatherland was that the political system in the USA showed great similarities to their own ideas of a democratic 'national republic' which did not rely upon the concept of nationality or the ethnic composition of its people. And therefore they could distinguish between nationality and patriotism. There was no merit in loving the country where one was born. It did not require any active decision, but was more the result of chance. Only patriotism (*Vaterlandsliebe*) was the true love of the fatherland, because it consisted of active commitment with a complete disregard for one's own interest. And patriotism was fed by the opportunity for broad political participation. The land of their own choice was a country which guaranteed by law this political participation for the common good, so evidently central and important to their self-perception. In other words, in their opinion, true popular sovereignty came into effect only where active participation was allowed, and where the people and the government were thought to be identical. When German unification was achieved in 1870/71, the men of 1848 celebrated it joyfully. But they assumed that this was merely the first step towards liberating and changing the domestic political structure. Their hope was that now the more liberal and democratic southwest would play a crucial role in democratizing even Prussia. When it became obvious that Bismarck's Germany was still a monarchical and military state , and that it lacked a bill of rights and a real political representation of the people, they were hugely disappointed. In America the 'Forty-eighters' continued to believe that the republic was the right political concept. Even if one or other revolutionary veteran admitted that the proclamation of a German republic in 1848 might have been too early, now the model had proved to be right in practice. The republic would be the future model even for the old continent. Radicals stood firm on the principle of popular sovereignty including its revolutionary consequences. From their theoretical basis a national state defined primarily by the ethnic composition of its people would have been a contradiction in terms. The republican state should be defined in terms of giving its citizens the opportunity for political participation. A republic should be a nation, but defined primarily by its liberal political institutions. It should be prosperous and it should be powerful, not as an aggressive, conquering nation, but as a nation strong enough to protect its political system against foreign aggression and prosperous enough to avoid domestic social tensions. And that is what Friedrich Hecker had in mind when he wrote to a close friend two months before he died: 'Yes, indeed, in 1873 people told me that I was on the right path ... and if I had succeeded, Germany today would be not only free, but also rich and powerful.'[36]

Notes

1   The whole operation is described by Friedrich Hecker, Theodor Mögling and Franz Sigel in F. Hecker, *Die Erhebung des Volkes in Baden für die deutsche Republik im Frühjahr 1848* (Basel: J. E. Schabelitz, 1848; Karlsruhe (reprint): Edition 100 bei ISP, 1998); on Hecker see S. Freitag, *Friedrich Hecker. Biographie eines Republikaners* (Stuttgart: Franz Steiner Verlag, 1998).
2   G. Struve, *Geschichte der drei Volkserhebungen in Baden* (Bern, 1849); A. Struve, *Erinnerungen aus den badischen Freiheitskämpfen* (Hamburg, 1850). A new biography on Struve is forthcoming by A. Reiss, University of Regensburg.
3   The best general treatment of 1848 in Germany is W. Siemann, *Die deutsche Revolution von 1848/1849* (Frankfurt am Main: Suhrkamp Verlag, 1985; 5th edn1993; English translation London: Macmillan, 1998); a classical approach is V. Valentin, *Geschichte der Deutschen Revolution 1848–1849*, 2 vols (Weinheim/Berlin (reprint): Beltz Quadriga Verlag, 1998); shorter general accounts in D. Blackbourn, *The Long Nineteenth Century*, The Fontana History of Germany 1780–1918 (London: Fontana Press, 1997), pp. 138–73; C. Dipper and U. Speck (eds), *1848 – Revolution in Deutschland* (Frankfurt am Main: Suhrkamp Verlag, 1998); on the aspects of European revolutions: D. Dowe, H.–G. Haupt and D. Langewiesche (eds), *Europa 1848. Revolution und Reform* (Bonn: J. H. W. Dietz Verlag, 1998); D. Langewiesche (ed.), *Demokratiebewegung und Revolution 1847–1849. Internationale Aspekte und europäische Verbindungen* (Karlsruhe: G. Braun Verlag, 1998); W. Hardtwig (ed.), *Revolution in Deutschland und Europa 1848/49* (Göttingen: Vandenhoeck & Ruprecht, 1998); a very good overview of research up to 1991 is D. Langewiesche, 'Die deutsche Revolution von 1848/49 und die vorrevolutionäre Gesellschaft. Forschungsstand und Forschungsperspektiven', part 2, *Archiv für Sozialgeschichte*, 31 (1991), 331–443.
4   For example, P. Nolte, *Gemeindebürgertum und Liberalismus in Baden 1800–1850* (Göttingen: Vandenhoeck & Ruprecht, 1994).
5   J. Sperber, *Rhineland Radicals. The Democratic Movement and the Revolution of 1848–1849* (Princeton, NJ: Princeton University Press, 1993), p. 484.
6   K. H. Wegert, *German Radicals confront the Common People. Revolutionary Politics and Popular Politics 1789–1849* (Mainz: Verlag Philipp von Zabern, 1992), p. 321.
7   Ibid., p. 300.
8   Sperber, *Rhineland Radicals*, p. 490.
9   In recent years it has become useful in German historiography to distinguish between the different levels on which the revolutions took place: see W. Siemann, 'The revolutions of 1848–49 and the persistence of the old regime in Germany (1849–1850)', in M. Fulbrook (ed.), *German History since 1800* (London: Arnold, 1997), pp. 106–23; see also Dipper and Speck, *1848*, chs III/IV.

10 J. Sperber, *The European Revolutions, 1848–1851* (Cambridge: Cambridge University Press, 1994), p. 87.

11 H. Schulze, *Der Weg zum Nationalstaat. Die deutsche Nationalbewegung vom 18. Jahrhundert bis zur Reichsgründung* (Munich: Deutscher Taschenbuch Verlag, 1985); J. Sheehan, 'What is German history? Reflections on the role of the nation in German history and historiography', *Journal of Modern History*, 53 (1981), pp. 1–25.

12 An excellent introduction to the theoretical background of radical thinking is P. Wende, *Radikalismus im Vormärz. Untersuchungen zur politischen Theorie der frühen deutschen Demokraten* (Wiesbaden: Franz Steiner Verlag, 1975).

13 See in general, Nolte, *Gemeindeburgertum*, chs II–IV.

14 M. Mayer, *Freiheit und Macht. Studien zum Nationalismus süddeutscher insbesondere badischer Liberaler* (Frankfurt am Main: Peter Lang Verlag, 1994), pp. 53 ff and pp. 88 ff.

15 C. von Rotteck and K. Th. Welcker (eds), *Staats-Lexikon oder Encyklopädie der Staatswissenschaften*, vol. IV (Altona: Verlag Johann Friedrich Hammerich, 1837), 'Eidgenossenschaft, Schweizerische', pp. 611–28, at p. 617.

16 'Schutz der Freiheit und der Rechte der Eidgenossen'.

17 For an older approach see E. Angermann, 'Der Deutsche Frühkonstitutionalismus und das amerikanische Vorbild', *Historische Zeitschrift*, 219 (1974), 1–32; E. G. Franz, *Das Amerikabild der deutschen Revolution von 1848/49. Zum Problem der Übertragung gewachsener Verfassungsformen*, Beihefte zum Jahrbuch für Amerikastudien, vol. 2 (Heidelberg: Verlag Carl Winter 1958); G. Moltmann, *Atlantische Blockpolitik im 19. Jahrhundert: Die Vereinigten Staaten und der deutsche Liberalismus während der Revolution von 1848/49* (Düsseldorf: Droste Verlag, 1973).

18 'Die Hauptforderungen einer reinen Theorie…sehen wir dort in beneidenswerther Erfüllung.' C. von Rotteck, *Allgemeine Geschichte*, vol. 8 (Freiburg, 1826), p. 628.

19 F. S. Jucho (ed.), *Verhandlungen des deutschen Parlamentes* (Frankfurt am Main, 1848), pp. 6–7.

20 P. Nolte, Bürgerideal, Gemeinde und Republik. ' "Klassischer Republikanismus" im frühen deutschen Liberalismus', *Historische Zeitschrift*, 254 (1992), pp. 609–56.

21 Freitag, *Friedrich Hecker*, pp. 18–21.

22 *Verhandlungen der Ständeversammlung des Großherzogtums Baden von 1842 bis 1848*, Protokolle und Beilagen der zweiten Kammer (Karlsruhe, 1842 ff.), 16 March 1848, p. 220.

23 L. Gall, 'Liberalismus und "Bürgerliche Gesellschaft". Zu Charakter und Entwicklung der liberalen Bewegung in Deutschland', *Historische Zeitschrift*, 220 (1975), 324–56.

24 Schulze, *Der Weg zum Nationalistadt*, pp. 80–2.

25 'Motion Friedrich Heckers betreffend die Erhaltungen der Integrität Deutschlands bezüglich auf die Herzogthümer Schleswig-Holstein und

Lauenburg', *Verhandlungen der Ständeversammlung des Großherzogtums Baden von 1842 bis 1848*, Protokolle und Beilagen der zweiten Kammer, vol. 7 (Karlsruhe, 1846), pp. 433–41; F. Hecker and G. Lommel, *Deutschland und Dänemark. Für das deutsche Volk* (Schaffhausen: Verlag J. J. Ziegler, 1847).

26 'Soll denn Deutschland stets die Beute fremder Nationen sein?', *Verhandlungen*, op. cit. (1845), p. 340.

27 'Im Süden ist man nun überall zu dem Resultat gekommen, daß die repräsentativen Formen, allein, ohne Preßfreiheit, unter dem Zwang der Bundesverfassung, ohne weitere Entwicklung freiheitsfördernder Zustände ... Freiheit nicht begründen ... Die Badner haben sich am längsten gewehrt, haben am längsten durch ihre Verfassung und mit ihr Freiheit gesucht. Aber das Resultat des letzten Landtags, wo die Opposition in Majorität vollkommen siegreich auch nicht den geringsten praktischen Erfolg hatte und am Ende nach hause geschickt wurde, als wäre sie besiegt, hat auch sie mürbe gemacht. ... Was wir sonst nur als die Gesinnung weniger annehmen, zeigt sich nun als die Gesinnung der Mehrheit: Einheit, positive, nicht mystische Einheit, ist das fast ungedämpfte Feldgeschrei aller Wortführer. Der Partikularismus hat gar keine Organe mehr.' Heinrich von Gagern to his brother Friedrich von Gagern, 4 January 1843; quoted in W. Klötzer and P. Wentzcke (eds), *Darstellungen und Quellen zur Geschichte der deutschen Einheitsbewegung im neunzehnten und zwanzigsten Jahrhundert* (Heidelberg: Carl Winter, 1957), pp. 262–3.

28 Quoted in R. M. Berdahl, 'New thoughts on German nationalism', *American Historical Review*, 77 (1972), p. 79.

29 'Nicht national, kosmopolitisch vielmehr ist die Natur des modernen Verkehrs; unausbleiblich reißt er die Scheidewände nieder zwischen Volk und Volk.' Heinrich von Treitschke, Bundesstaat und Einheitsstaat (1864), in H. von Treitschke, *Aufsätze, Reden und Briefe*, vol. 3 (Meersburg, 1929), pp. 9–146, at p. 14.

30 'Die Sprache ist ein Band unserer Nationalität, und darum giebt es Provinzen, die, obschon nicht zum deutschen Bunde gehörend, doch zu den besten Deutschen zählen, ich meine die preußischen Ostseeprovinzen. Außer der Sprache giebt es aber noch ein Band der Nationalität, das noch stärker ist, als das der Sprache, die Freiheit. Die freien Staatsverfassungen Frankreichs und der Schweiz haben über die sprachlichen Sympathien deutschredender Männer gesiegt.' F. D. Bassermann, *Verhandlungen der Ständeversammlung*, 4 July 1846, p. 61.

31 *Verhandlungen der Ständeversammlung*, 12 February 1848, p. 126.

32 J. Sheehan, *German History, 1770–1866* (Oxford: Clarendon Press, 1989), p. 688.

33 'Die Übermacht des deutschen Stammes gegen die meisten slavischen Stämme, vielleicht mit alleiniger Ausnahme des russischen, ist eine Tatsache ..., und gegen solche, ich möchte sagen, *naturhistorischen* Tatsachen läßt sich mit einem Dekrete im Sinne der kosmopolitischen

Gerechtigkeit schlechterdings nichts ausrichten.' W. Jordan, in F. Wigard (ed.), *Stenographischer Bericht über die Verhandlungen der deutschen konstitu-tierenden Nationalversammlung zu Frankfurt*, vol. 2 (Frankfurt am Main, 1848), 42. Sitzung , 19 July 1848, p. 1146.

34 Cf. W. Siemann, *Die Frankfurter Nationalversammlung 1848/49 zwischen demokratischem Liberalismus und konservativer Reform* (Frankfurt, 1976).

35 W. Greiling (ed.), *Karl August Varnhagen von Ense, Kommentare zum Zeitge-schehen. Publizistik, Briefe, Dokumente 1813–1858* (Leipzig, 1984), p. 172; quoted in: D. Langewiesche, 'Germany and the national question in 1848', in J. Breuilly, *The State of Germany. The National Idea in the Making, Unmaking and Remaking of a Modern Nation-State* (London and New York: Longman, 1992), pp. 60–79, at p. 65.

36 'Ja mehr noch, 1873 sagte man mir . . . , daß ich auf dem rechten Wege war und hät ich reüssiert, so wäre heute das Land nicht nur frei, sondern auch reich und mächtig.' Friedrich Hecker to Charles Söhner, 25 January 1881, *Friedrich Hecker Papers*, Western Historical Manuscript Division, St Louis, USA.

7
Bohemian Spring 1848 – Conflict of Loyalties and Its Picture in Historiography

Jan Havránek

Conflict of loyalties

During the first half of the nineteenth century, in the eyes of most western European observers, Bohemia was a German country with a large agrarian population still using its Slavonic language. Some were informed about the wealthy and conservative Bohemian aristocracy, which occupied many influential positions in the Habsburg Monarchy, but who at the same time opposed the centralist bureaucracy and defended those traditional privileges connected with the state rights of the Bohemian kingdom of the lands of the Crown of St Wenceslas (Bohemian *Landespatriotism*).

Only a few people knew that during the 1830s and 1840s many things were changing. The Czech national movement was becoming an important political force in the country. Essential to this development was the fact that 90 per cent of the population was able to read and write: obligatory school attendance was introduced in 1775. Prayerbooks, almanacs connected with calendars and other books could be found in the households of many Czech farmers.

In 1847 the *Matice Česká*, publisher of Czech books, had 4500 subscribers. Czech journals were sent not only to the clergy and some Czech-speaking officials, they also had many subscribers among the Czech professionals – millers and peasants in the villages, and brewers, innkeepers and shopkeepers in the small Czech towns. Czech ethnic nationalism had many followers among the students and young intellectuals who were concentrated around the literary and scholarly journals.

The two opposition movements – Bohemian *Landespatriotism* of the traditional aristocracy and the ethnic nationalism of the Czechs which was particularly concerned with the linguistic question – were embodied in one person, František Palacký, the historiograph of the Bohemian estates and the editor of the leading Czech scholarly journal *Časopis českého muzea*, who was since the first days of the revolution recognized as the political leader of the Czechs.

During the 1840s also German nationalism emerged in Central Europe, as a parallel movement to Czech nationalism. The first of these was the stronger and failed to take into account the perspectives of the latter. This attitude is expressed, for example, in the words of Franz Schuselka, an influential German author born in Bohemia, published in 1845 in Leipzig:

> As to the Slavs in Bohemia, Moravia, and Silesia, it turns out a historical necessity that they remain in the union with Germany. they will most probably be absorbed into the German element.[1]

In Prague as well as in other cities in Europe news about the revolution in Paris inspired the political activity of those citizens who were dissatisfied with the lack of a political forum and who were awaiting important changes in the near future. On 11 March 1848 48 Prague citizens, inspired by a small illegal organization called the Czech Repeal, met in the large hall of the inn *Svatováclavské lázně* and demanded democratic rights for citizens everywhere and two specific demands for Prague: the convocation of the common diet and establishment of the common government for the lands of the Crown of St Wenceslas – Bohemia, Moravia and Austrian Silesia – and first and equal rights with German for the Czech language in public affairs. A citizens' committee was elected for the final redaction of the Prague Citizens' Petition which existed, with some changes in its membership, as the most authoritative citizens' representative body *Národní v ybor* (National Committee), until the defeat of the Prague uprising in June 1848. Originally it comprised both Czech and German members, but six weeks later most of the Germans left the committee because of disputes over the representation of Bohemia in the Frankfurt parliament.

Inspired by events in Vienna, on 15 March students met in the *magna aula* of the university and demanded, along with civic rights and academic freedoms, equal rights for both languages in the university lectures and examinations. The friendship between the two national groups in Prague, where at that time about one-third of the inhabitants were conscious of their adherence to the German nation, was also expressed on 18 March in a meeting of 50 writers of 'both languages' in Hotel Erzherzog Stephan. In their resolution they argued: 'that the zealous campaign in which the Czechs demand equal rights for good should not be considered as a disturbance of unanimity.'[2]

The atmosphere of the few days, in which the word *brotherhood* was heard throughout Prague, is expressed in the lines of Friedrich Sacher:

> Jubilate brothers, make the jubilation ring
> in all the elated Bohemian lands,
> since Czechs and Germans live together peacefully
> in their common homeland.[3]

Only when the demands of the Czechs were expressed by their leading journalist Karel Havlíček Borovský on 19 March in his article 'Naše korouhev' (our banner), published in the newspaper *Pražské noviny*, were the different attitudes of both nationalities to public affairs made clear. Havlíček demanded:

1 Withdrawal and secession of the lands of the St Wencelas' Crown from the German Federation.
2 Their self-government with a common diet and government in Prague.
3 Equal rights for both languages in schools, theatres, offices and also on the plaques on buildings. He recommended that the Czechs use their language on plaques in their shop windows. This initiative was generally accepted and in the streets of Prague the Czech language, underrepresented earlier, started to prevail.
4 The elimination of the old Diet of Bohemian Estates and elections for the new parliament respecting the interests of all classes of the country's population.[4]

Although the disputed language of the plaques contributed to the conflict, the real reason for conflict between Czechs and Germans was connected to the existence of the Frankfurt parliament. At the beginning the focus of interest was the question of the participation of František Palacký in the preparatory activities of the meeting of the Frankfurt parliament. Palacký, who was well known among German historians and generally accepted as the representative of the Czechs, was invited to take part in the activities of the Committee of Fifty. He responded to this invitation with a letter dated 11 April 1848. He refused to participate in the activities of this assembly, and justified his refusal at first with historical arguments, i.e. that the relations between the Czech state and the Empire were based on the treaty between the rulers, not on any agreement between the nations. His other arguments were political: small nations in Central Europe were living in anxiety, their autonomy threatened by the Russian universal monarchy, and they feared that if the German Republic destroyed the Habsburg Empire, this would open the door for Russia to gobble up the territory inhabited by small, predominantly Slavic nations.

The only protection against these dangers would be the creation of a state with the Danube as its backbone, meaning the Habsburg Monarchy: if the Austrian imperial state didn't already exist, it would have to be urgently created not only in the interest of Europe but also in that of humanity.[5] This was a classical formulation of the Austroslavist political programme. Palacký nevertheless expressed the eagerness of the Czechs for the *Zollunion* with Germany.

His letter was accepted with approval by the Czechs. Most of the Germans in Czech lands expressed sympathy with the idea of German unification. The National Committee tried at first to find a compromise solution. On 14 April German colours – black-red-gold – were permitted, but not recommended by the Committee. This last compromise was nevertheless followed by the secession of most of the German members from the authoritative leadership of the revolutionary movement, which was respected by the Czechs throughout Bohemia and partly also by the German peasants.[6] This is illustrated by the fact that all Czech and some German peasants sent their demands to this unofficial authority, thinking it their most likely source of aid. When the National Committee finally decided on 24 April not to take part in the elections for Frankfurt, the division of many organizations into distinct Czech and German organizations followed. The association of Prague citizens, which was founded in March and called *Svornost* (*Eintracht*), was divided at the end of April into two organizations – Czech *Svornost* and German *Concordia* – but the real concord ceased to exist. The same process divided the Students' Legion, where the question of the colours of the uniforms led to the split. Originally the colours of Bohemia were used (red and white), but at the end of April the German students turned up with the German tricolour and the Czechs answered with the Slavic white-blue-red.

At about the same time that Palacký was invited to Frankfurt the 'Letter' from the Emperor's Cabinet was given (on 8 April). It was the second, but for the Prague citizens the first *acceptable* answer to their petitions. It promised autonomy for Bohemia and concessions for the Czech language, and was accepted by the Czechs without enthusiasm but nevertheless with a degree of satisfaction. The Germans protested against it because the Germans from Czech lands were not represented: the Viennese born there founded the 'Association of Germans from Bohemia, Moravia and Silesia', led by the physician Ludwig von Löhner, and resolutely protested against the Letter.

The outcome was clear: the people's main loyalty was to their ethnic nation. Czechs were first and foremost Czechs, Germans were Germans. Bohemian patriotism became for the German inhabitants of the country unimportant, for Czechs were identified with their ethnic nationalism. Austrian patriotism was for both nations a conditional one: Austroslavic Austria would be greeted by the Czechs, for the Germans the loyalty to Vienna could be accepted once Vienna was black-red-gold.

In March the Bohemian-German Moritz Hartmann had expressed his feelings in the words: '*Freiheit ist Sonne, Nationalität nur Laterne*' (Liberty is the sun, nationality nothing but a lantern).

Six weeks later a completely different attitude to the problem was expressed by his friend Alfred Meißner in a poem celebrating the victory of Moritz Hartmann in the election for Frankfurt in Leitmeritz on 4 May:[7]

> One Germany great and mighty,
> one Germany strong and free,
> unanimous and harmonious
> with German-Austrians it must be.

The same idea was expressed by Alfred Meißner in one sentence: the age of nation-states is dawning. German-Austria will become a constituent part of Germany.

Under these conditions the Czech national organization *Slovanská lípa* (The Slavic Linden) was founded on 30 April with Mathias Thun as chairman, and a few weeks later the initiative was given to the Prague Slavic Congress. New affiliations proved victorious.

The historiography of 1848 in the Czech lands

The events of 1848 were in Bohemia, as well as in other Central European countries, the starting point of its modern political life. For the Czechs the beginning of their political activity was closely connected with the successful conclusion of the process of reaching their identity as a modern nation. Despite the fact that the events of this year had been prepared by Czech 'patriots' ('vlastenci' in Czech, the more ironical 'die Wlastenzen' in German) they still appeared as a watershed to the coming Bohemian generations. This feeling was expressed in poetry and novels, and in articles in Czech newspapers, but the time for historians' analytical description of these events came much later.

The historiography of the revolutionary year 1848–9 was from its beginnings influenced by the problem of who were the obvious inheritors of the victories of 1848 when the Czech nation became a political player for the first time. The question was: who drew the correct conclusions from the events of the revolutionary year – was it the radicals, who attempted to attract the support of various enemies of the Habsburgs for the Czech national movement during the 1860s, or the liberals who in 1860 concluded an alliance with the conservative Bohemian aristocracy? (Some parallels could be found in the different attitudes of journalists and politicians towards the events of the 'Prague Spring' of 1968 after the victory of democracy in 1989.) In 1860 František Palacký was again accepted as the political leader of the Czechs, and spent a lot of time justifying his political ideas and actions during the revolution. In the third volume of the collection of his shorter works (*Radhost*),[8] wherein, in 1873, he published his most important political articles, one-third were dated from the years 1848 to 1849. He defended his critical attitude towards the conservative aristocrats at that time which led to a conflict with Leo Thun, and also defended his activities against the radical democrats. Most attention was, of course, focused on the attitude of the Czechs towards Vienna and Frankfurt. For many years he was successful in convincing the Czech public of the validity of his interpretation. Only from 1890, 13 years after his death, was his interpretation criticized. Less significant were his critics from the right such as Joseph Alexander Helfert,[9] even though their works were important testimonies of fact. More attention was given to criticism from the left, in the memoirs of Josef Václav Frič.[10] The most important aspects of Palacký's activities in 1848, his attitude to Frankfurt in his Austroslavism, were supported by nearly all Czech politicians and historians.

During the years 1860–90 most of the authors of books and articles dealing with 1848 had been participants in the events. They reprinted their articles and published speeches from the year of liberty – and also published their memoirs. The Czech attitudes to the Habsburg Monarchy and German unification were still relevant. Concerning many points of the revolutionary programme – the autonomy of Czech lands, general suffrage, social questions – no great progress could be registered.

For many decades the revolution was also not subject to profound historical research because the sources from the state and private archives were accessible only in exceptional cases.

During these thirty years at the centre of interest were the politicians, the forty-eighters, and not particularly František Palacký who died in 1876 and who inspired the political strategy of the Czech National (Old-Czech) Party, nor his son-in-law František L. Rieger[11] who inherited from him the leading political position in the Old-Czech Party. Most attention was paid to the man who, during the years 1848–50, was close to Palacký in terms of strategy but was more radical in his tactics. This was Karel Havlíček,[12] the first first-class Czech journalist. Since 5 April 1848 his newspaper, *Národní noviny*, a daily, had 1500 subscribers. Havlíček was respected particularly for his consequent struggle for the Czech national movement and his liberal ideas. His journal resisted the renewed censorship of 1849 and was published up until 19 January 1850 when it was finally banned. Then, from May 1850 to January 1851, he published in Kutná Hora another journal called *Slovan*, but from 16 December 1851 until 29 April 1855 he was expelled from Bohemia and forcibly resettled in Brixen. When he died in Prague on 29 July 1857 hardly any important Czechs attended his funeral. From 1863, since the Young Czechs had begun to criticize Palacký and Rieger in their journal *Národní listy*, they found in Havlíček the martyr of the Czech national struggle. This attitude was expressed in his biography by Karel Tůma, one of the editors of this journal.[13] The picture of the radical nationalist Havlíček as a national hero and martyr was generally accepted among Czech teachers and journalists, i.e. people who influenced public opinion. His Prague grave was visited by nationalist demonstrators, and the song '*Spi Havlíčku v svém hrobečku, Čech se Němce nebojí* (Sleep Havlíček quietly in your grave, the Czech is not afraid of the German)', was very popular. This one-sided picture of Havlíček as radical nationalist was criticized by Tomáš G. Masaryk in his book *Karel Havlíček and the Ambitions and Aspirations of the Czech Political Awakening* (1896).[14] Masaryk argued that Havlíček fully supported Palacký, that he was in fact a political realist and that therefore Masaryk saw Havlíček as a predecessor. In his book Masaryk expressed his attitude towards the events of 1848:

> Without Revolution the improvement was not possible [. . .] Absolutism was defeated in Austria, even when the Revolution was suppressed, i.e. only the armed revolution was suppressed, not the revolution in the heads of men; and that revolution was the most important event of 1848.

Masaryk showed special interest in the social problems of that revolution.

During the 1890s there was for the first time the opportunity to study the revolution using the archival sources. This was done by young historians, such as Zdeněk V. Tobolka, who were influenced by Masaryk's ideas even if they did not fully agree with his interpretation of Karel Havlíček. Tobolka edited the political works of Karel Havlíček[15] and published books about the beginnings of constitutional life in Bohemia[16] and the Prague Slavic Congress in June 1848.[17] To some degree Masaryk also influenced Jan Heidler, another historian who focused his work on 1848. During his short life (1883–1923) he published four books about the revolutionary years, the most important being the analysis of political pamphlets concerning the attitude of Bohemia to Austria published before the revolution, and the biography of Anton Springer, a German activist and later historian of the revolution in Prague.[18] The role of František Palacký in the revolution of 1848 was the object of the study of Masaryk's adversary, Professor of History Josef Pekař, in his biography of Palacký.[19] During the first decade of the twentieth century the historians as well as sociologists such as Emanuel Chalupný[20] discussed the mistakes of the Czech politicians in 1848 and Havlíček's ideas, now accessible in Tobolka's work, were the subject of many discussions among students and young intellectuals.

Books written for the broader community of readers included that of Josef Jakub Toužimský on the 1848–9 revolution which included many pictures and had an attractive title: 'At the Dawn of a New Era'.[21] Its author described the year of revolution as a good year, a year of change, a year of liberty as it had been seen by contemporaries. Interest in the problems of this period was so sharp that even historians with different specializations spent at least some of their time on 1848 and published at least one book about the personalities of the 1848 revolution, for example Václav Chaloupecký[22] and Karel Stloukal.[23]

Full access to all the materials in the state archives in Prague and Vienna and the systematic research of their sources brought new results during the interwar period. The Prague sources gave František Roubík an opportunity to publish, along with many analytical studies concerned with the abolition of the corvée (*robota*) and the peasants' behaviour, a synthesis of all the events that happened during the Czech year 1848,[24] which even today is a very useful book. Karel Kazbunda used the new sources from the central archives in Vienna to write a monograph about the Czech national movement in the first nine months of 1848.[25] For his whole life – he died in 1973 at the age of 87 – he had worked on the biography of Karel Havlíček which he finished just before his death. The manuscript is among his documents and is available to researchers. Some articles have informed us about the rich source of information that this manuscript is, but the attempts to publish this extensive work have been unsuccessful up to now. Hugo Traub published the biography of F. L. Rieger and the history of the failed students' reattempt at an uprising in May 1849.[26] In order to gain the attention of a larger readership some works focused on the daily life of the society at that time, such as the book on life in Prague in the 1830s and 1840s by Naděžda Melníkova-Papoušková[27] and a narrative about the revolutionary year written by a popular author, Eduard Bass.[28]

From the 1920s this revolution was at the centre of interest of a circle of orthodox Marxist journalists and historians; articles published during the 1920s accepted the opinions of Marx and Engels about the Czech movement in 1848 with some reserve,[29] but later the interpretations of Marx and Engels were published in Czech translation[30] and after 1929 the communist historiography accepted their opinions – and that of Lenin and Stalin – as an obligatory directive for the interpretation of the Czech past.[31]

The war years 1939–45 which closed Czech universities and interrupted the publishing of nearly all Czech scholarly journals prevented the emergence of new studies on the problem and so in 1948 attention was focused mainly on the reprinting of older books such as Roubík's synthesis, or the printing of documents from 1848 such as cartoons, songs and literary reminiscences on that year.[32] Arnošt Klíma published a survey of the events in 1848 in Bohemia[33] from a Marxist perspective without dogmatic simplifications. In Kroměříž (Kremsier) a large exhibition was prepared, where the attention was concentrated on the anniversary of the abolition of the corvée. A survey of the activities of the parliament in Kroměříž [34] was published for that occasion.

Two years later a new evaluation of the national past began. Marxist historians – Zdeněk Nejedlý with some reserve and younger students with more enthusiasm – concentrated their interest on the uprising in Prague in June 1848, and radical democrats such as Josef Václav Frič and Emanuel Arnold were their focus of interest and represented their positive heroes of that year.[35] Palacký, on the other hand, was branded as a representative of the Czech bourgeoisie and criticized for his liberal, non-radical position. Quotations of Marx and Engels were used against him. Condemnation of Palacký was the central thesis of a book on the Czech history of 1848 which was published in 1951 by the Soviet historian Ivan I. Udalcov.[36] Emphasizing the role of the radical democrats, he argued that the Czechs were nevertheless not a 'counterrevolutionary nation' as a whole. A positive picture of the radical democrats was also shown in films based on the memoirs of J. V. Frič.

Studies about the activities of the radical democrats continued and in 1958 the Czech philosopher Karel Kosík published a monograph on their role in Czech society during the nineteenth century.[37] His interest was at that time focused predominantly on the democratic

component of their political ideology. He compared the radical democrats with the nineteenth-century European revolutionary democrats.
His book and later articles were perceived by the Czech public as
critiques of the undemocratic nature of the Communist regime. The
Prague Spring of 1968 was being prepared.

New studies about the history of 1848 during the 1950s and 1960s
were relatively rare. A survey of the period (as part of a textbook) was
published by František Červinka,[38] as were monographs about the
Czech political organization 'Slovanská Lípa' by Jan Novotný[39] and
by M. Trapl and A. Přichystal who wrote about Moravia.[40] The most
important book, based on the private archives of aristocratic families
and concerned with the problems of the whole Habsburg state, was
published by Josef Polišenský.[41] All these books contained independent opinions and opposed the official Marxist interpretation which
was represented in the works of Josef Kočí.

The Prague Spring, in which many historians took part and as a
consequence later had problems with publishing their books and
articles, was anticipated through the critique of many historical and
political subjects. The historian Vladimír Kašík wrote the introduction to a new edition of Marx's, Engels's and Lenin's works on Czech
history, published in 1961–4. He explained the sources of Marx's and
Engels's one-sided opinions and did not hide his discontent with the
authors.

The independent attitude of Czech historians to their own past
which was laying the groundwork for the Prague Spring was the subject of a book about Czech historiography on the period of National
Revival up to the Revolution in 1848, written by Ivan I. Udalcov and
published in Moscow in 1984.[42] The book appeared in print relatively
late and so it had hardly any negative consequences for the author
accused of heresy against the Marxist interpretation of past events.
Nowadays we have to appreciate this excellent survey of the Czech
historical literature of that time and the author's careful step-by-step
description of how it became disaffected with orthodox Marxism in
the early 1960s and eventually turned against it in 1968–9. In 1970
ideological censorship and purges were reintroduced, publications
were banned and many historians were dismissed, silenced or prevented from teaching.

To chart the changing atmosphere among Czech historians the
results of two post-1970 conferences are instructive. Whereas the

papers of the symposium in Kroměříž in May 1969, in which historians from Austria and West Germany participated, were never published, the papers of the meeting of Czech and East German historians in Bechyně in September 1973 *were* published. They showed there were still some attempts at original interpretation on the Czech side, but the Marxist orthodoxy was nevertheless fully reintroduced.[43]

During the 1980s the atmosphere somehow changed and a few new interesting books were published. Arnošt Klíma wrote a book about the relations between Czechs and Germans during the Revolution.[44] Otto Urban published a small book about the parliament in Kroměříž,[45] but the most important event in the historiography of that time was the publication of his great work on Czech political history from 1848 to 1918, first in Czech and later in the broader German version[46] which included an excellent bibliography. In 1989 a new book on the revolution in the whole of the Habsburg Empire was published by Josef Kolejka[47] and one year later a book by Jiří Štaif[48] showed a revival of solid analytical studies of the Revolution. Many important new discoveries were brought to light by Jiří Kořalka in his study about the Palacký invitation to Frankfurt, and especially in his large book about the problems of nineteenth-century nationalism which was published in Vienna.[49] His seminal biography of František Palacký was due to be finished in 1999.

Essential for the 1990s is a renewed close collaboration of historians from all the Central European countries – of Austrian, German, Czech, Slovak, Hungarian and Polish historians. This initiative was expressed in November and December 1990 by a symposium in Bad Wiessee in which historians of all these nations took part. The papers of this meeting were published in 1996 and contain an excellent bibliography of the literature which addresses the problem of 1848, particularly information on books and articles published during the last two decades.[50]

We now look back over the 150 years since the revolution. In 1998 two large and a few smaller conferences took place in the Czech Republic which should bring forth some new studies on the period. Unfortunately the same year saw the commemoration of 650 years of the Charles University, 80 years of the independent Czech state, 50 years since the Communist *coup d'état* of February 1948, 30 years since the Prague Spring of 1968. The anniversaries are important for a particular reason: they forced historians to write and publishers to print books – 1998 was a good year in this respect.

Notes

1   'Für die Slawen in Böhmen, Mähren und Schlesien stellt es sich als eine geschichtliche, politische und geistige Notwendigkeit heraus, in der Verbindung mit Deutschland zu bleiben und höchst wahrscheinlich im deutschen Elemente völlig aufzugehen'; F. Schuselka, *Mittelmeer-Ost- und Nordsee* (Leipzig: 1845), p. 273; cf. A. Klíma, *Češi a Němci v revoluci 1848–1849* (Czechs and Germans in the Revolution of 1848–1849) (Prague: 1988), pp. 16, 136.

2   'daß das Eifern und Fordern tschechischerseits, daß sie dieser Gleichberechtigung in allem nunmehr tatsächlich anteilig würden, nicht als Störung der Einmütigkeit verstanden werden soll'; O. Urban, *Die tschechische Gesellschaft 1848–1918*, vol. 1 (Vienna: 1994), p. 58.

3   Jubelt Brüder, lasst den Jubel schallen,
         hoch erfreut im ganzen Böhmenland,
         Da nun Tschechen, Deutsche friedlich wallen,
         Arm in Arm in beider Vaterland.

   F. Roubík, *Český rok 1848* (The Czech Year 1848) (Prague: 1947), p. 243

4   K. H. Borovský, *Dílo* (Works), vol. 2 (Prague: 1986), pp. 142–6.
5   O. Urban, op. cit., p. 61.
6   F. Roubík, *Petice venkovského lidu k Národnímu výboru z r. 1848* (The petitions of the country people to the National Committee in 1848) (Prague: 1954).

7   Ein Deutschland groß und mächtig,
         Ein Deutschland stark und frei,
         Einmüthig und einträchtig
         Deutschösterreich mit dabei.

                                    A. Klíma, op. cit., p. 104

8   F. Palacký, *Radhost 3, Spisy z oboru politiky* (Works about Politics) (Prague: 1873).
9   J. A. Helfert, *Geschichte der österreichischen Revolution im Zusammenhange mit der mitteleuropäischen Bewegung der Jahre 1848–1849*, Bd. 1 (Freiburg: 1907).
10 J. V. Frič, *Paměti* (Memoirs), 4 vols (Prague: 1885–9); 2nd edn, 3 vols (Prague: 1957–63).
11 H. Traub, *František Ladislav Rieger* (Prague: 1922); R. Sak, *Rieger, příběh Čecha devatenáctého věku* (Rieger, the Story of the Czech of the 19th century) (Semily: 1993).

12 K. H. Borovský, *Politické spisy* (Political Works), ed. Z. V. Tobolka, 5 vols (Prague: 1900–3); K. H. Borovský, *Dílo* (Works), 2 vols; 1st vol. ed. J. Korejčík, 2nd vol. ed. A. Stich (Prague: 1986).

13 K. Tůma, *Život Karla Havlíčka Borovského* (The Life of Karel Havlíček Borovský), (Kutná Hora: 1886).

14 T. G. Masaryk, *Karel Havlíček, snahy a tužby politického probuzení*, 1st edn (Prague: 1896); 2nd edn (1904); 3rd edn (1920); 4th edn (1998), quoted below, see pp. 22, 24.

15 K. H. Borovský, *Politické spisy* (Political Works), ed. Z. V. Tobolka, 5 vols (Prague: 1900–3).

16 Z. V. Tobolka, *Počátky konstitučního života v Čechách* (The Beginnings of the Constitutional Life of Bohemia) (Prague: 1898).

17 Z. V. Tobolka, *Slovanský sjezd v Praze r. 1848* (The Slavonic Congress in Prague 1848) (Prague: 1901); Z. V. Tobolka and V. Žáček, *Slovanský sjezd v Praze 1848* (The Slavonic Congress in Prague 1848) (Prague: 1952).

18 J. Heidler, *Čechy a Rakousko v politických brožurách předbřeznových* (Bohemia and Austria in the Political Pamphlets Published before March 1848), (Prague: 1920); J. Heidler, *Antonín Springer a česká politika v letech 1848–1850* (Anton Springer and Czech Politics During the Years 1840–1850) (Prague: 1914).

19 J. Pekař, *František Palacký* (Prague: 1912).

20 E. Chalupný, *Karel Havlíček*, 1st edn (Prague: 1908); 2nd edn (1929).

21 J. J. Toužimský, *Na úsvitě nové doby* (At the Dawn of New Times) (Prague: 1898).

22 V. Chaloupecký, *František Palacký* (Prague: 1912).

23 K. Stlouka, *František Ladislav Rieger a Průmyslová Jednota v prvních letech absolutismu* (František Ladislav Rieger and the Industrial Union in the First Years of Absolutism) (Prague: 1934).

24 F. Roubík, *Český rok 1848* (The Czech Year 1848), 1st edn (Prague: 1931); 2nd edn (1948).

25 K. Kazbunda, *Ceske hnuti roku 1848* (Czech Movement in the Year 1848) (Prague: Historicky klub, 1929).

26 H. Traub, *Květnové spiknutí v Čechách r. 1849* (The May Conspiracy in Bohemia 1849) (Prague: 1929).

27 N. F. Melnikova-Papoušková, *Praha před sto lety* (Prague before Hundred Years) (Prague: 1935).

28 E. Bass, *Četní o roce osmačtyřicátém* (The Reading about the Year Forty Eight), 1st edn (Prague: 1940); 2nd edn (1948); 3rd edn (1963).

29 J. Šverma, *Rok 1848 v Čecháh* (The Year 1848 in Bohemia) (Prague: 1929), J. Šverma, *Česká otázka ve světle marxismu* (The Czech Question in the Light of Marxism) (Prague: 1933).

30 K. Marx , B. Engels, V. I. Lenin and J. V. Stalin, *O Rakousku a české otázce* (About Austria and the Czech Question), ed. G. Breitenfeld (Prague: 1933).

31 P. Reimann, *Geschichte der KPTsch* (Prague: 1931).

32 K. J. Beneš, *Rok 1848 v projevech současníků* (The Year 1848 in the Speeches of the Contemporaries), 3rd edn (Prague: 1948); J. Tichý, *Rok 1848 v obrazech* (The Year 1848 in Pictures) (Prague: 1948); J. Václavková, *Písně*

roku 1848 (The Songs of the Year 1848) (Prague: 1948); F. Hamp, *Čas oponou trhnul. Revoluční rok 1848 v české poezii a próze* (The Times Changed. The Revolutionary Year 1848 in Czech Poetry and Prose) (Prague: 1948); F. Roubík, *Rok 1848 v obrázcích a karikaturách* (The Year 1848 in Illustrations and Cartoons) (Prague: 1948).

33   A. Klíma, *Rok 1848 v Čechách* (The Year 1848 in Bohemia) (Prague: 1948); a new version: *Revoluce 1848 v českých zemích* (The Revolution of 1848 in Czech Lands) (Prague: 1974).

34   J. Spáčil, *Veškerá moc ve státě vychází z lidu. Kronika o kroměřížském sněmu 1848/1849* (All the Power in the State has its Origin in the People. The Chronicle of the Kroměříž Parliament 1848/1849) (Kroměříž: 1948).

35   E. Arnold, *Sebrané spisy* (Collected Works), (Praha: 1954); J. V. Frič, *Politické články z let 1847–1864* (Political Articles from the Years 1847–1864), (Praha: 1956); V. Žáček and K. Kosík (eds), *J. V. Frič a demokratické proudy v české politice* (J. V. Frič and the Democratic Currents in the Czech Politics), (Praha: 1956).

36   I. I. Udalcov, *The Outline of the National Political Struggle in Bohemia in 1848* (Moscow: 1951). The German translation was published in 1953 in Berlin (East), the Polish in 1953 and the Czech in 1954 in Prague.

37   K. Kosík, *Česká radikální demokracie, příspěvek k dějinám názorových sporů v české společnosti 19. století* (The Czech Radical Democracy. The Contribution to the History of the Conflicts of Opinions in the Czech Society of the 19th Century) (Prague: 1958). The sources were edited: V. Žáček and K. Kosík (eds), *J. V. Frič a demokratické proudy v české politice* (J. V. Frič and the Democratic Currents in the Czech Politics) (Prague: 1956).

38   F. Červinka, *Přehled dějin Československa v epoše kapitalismu* (The Survey of the History of Czechoslovakia in the Epoch of Capitalism), vol. I, 1848–1849 (Prague: 1959).

39   J. Novotný, *Slovanská lípa 1848–1849*, vols I and II (Prague: 1975–6).

40   M. Trapl and A. Přichystal, *České národní obrození na Moravě v době předbřeznové a v revolučních letech 1848–1849* (The Czech National Revival in Moravia before March 1848 and during the Revolutionary Years 1848–1849) (Olomouc: 1970).

41   J. Polišenský, *Revoluce a kontrarevoluce v Rakousku* (The Revolution and Counter-revolution in Austria) (Prague: 1975).

42   I. I. Udalcov, *The Historiography of the Czech National Revival. The Last Czechoslovak and Soviet Researches* (Moscow: 1984).

43   *Revoluce 1848–1849 ve střední Evropě. Sborník referátů z mezinárdoního vědeckého sympozia historiků* (The Revolution of 1848–1849 in Central Europe. The Proceedings of the Scholarly Symposium of Historians) (Prague: 1974).

44   A. Klíma, *Češi a Němci v revoluci 1848–1849* (Czechs and Germans in the Revolution 1848–1849) (Prague: 1988).

45   O. Urban, *Kroměřížský sněm 1848–1849* (The Assembly of Kroměříž), (Prague: 1988); 2nd edn (1998).

46   O. Urban, *Česká společnost 1848–1918* (The Czech Society 1848–1918) (Prague: 1982); *Die tschechische Gesellschaft 1848–1918*, 2 vols (Vienna: 1994).

47 J. Kokejka, *Národy habsburské monarchie v revoluci 1848/49* (The Nations of the Habsburg Monarchy in the Revolution 1848/49) (Prague: 1989).

48 J. Štaif, *Revoluční léta 1848–1849 a české země* (The Revolutionary Years 1848–1849 and the Czech Lands) (Prague: 1990).

49 J. Kořalka, *Pozvání do Frankfurtu* (The Invitation to Frankfurt) (Prague: 1990). J. Kořalka, *Tschechen im Habsburgerreich und in Europa 1815–1914. Sozialgeschichtliche Zusammenhänge der neuzeitlichen Nationenbildung und der Nationalitätenfrage in den böhmischen Ländern* (Vienna and Munich: 1991).

50 R. Jaworski and R. Luft (eds), *1848/49 Revolutionen in Ostmitteleuropa* (Munich: 1996).

Part IV

Commemorations of 1848 in National Context

8
From Divided Memory to Silence: The 1848 Celebrations in Italy*

Simonetta Soldani

Indifferent Italy

A hundred and fifty years after 1848, Italy's public memory of the events of what used to be called 'the year of miracles' is dominated by a mixture of indifference and silence. That 'long revolution' brought Italy to abandon neo-Guelph organicism and the theocratic federalist projects of 1846, to adopt modern European liberalism's ideas and projects, to contribute to the 'great European movement' and to radically redesign the boundaries of the possible and the necessary. However, today the lack of interest in these events is so profound as to constitute a collective suppression. Italy's National Library catalogue lists no new monograph on the subject since 1996, and the only valuable study published in the 1990s is Enrica Ciommo's 1993 book on the 'national question' in the South.[1] If we go further back we find little more than an intelligent but circumscribed research on the spreading of the Roman republic – its ideas, events, actors and institutional and political innovations – in the nearby countryside.[2] Recent historiographical attention to the Risorgimento, and to its configurations as memory and myth,[3] does not touch upon 1848, about which we still do not have a good inclusive survey.

It is as though 1848 can no longer arouse collective attention. The stereotypes nurtured up till very recently by school curricula which created detailed cultural *koinés* are dead, and nothing has come forward to replace them. It is thus not surprising that the voice of the

* Translated from the Italian by Lesley Leicester Barrett.

anniversary celebrations has been so feeble, especially in comparison with simultaneous events in Germany, Hungary, Austria and Romania: even the relative lack of attention in France looks less noticeable. Initiatives have been scarce, and mostly promoted out of some sense of duty rather than a genuine cultural and civic urge.

For the 'Five Days' anniversary, for instance, the Milan municipality tried to create an aura of 'national-popular' festivity, with bow and arrow competitions in costume, recollections of the past in the guise of *tableaux vivants* ('The Austrian Garrison at the Castle', 'The Tricolour Flag on the Dome', 'People Rising in Brera', 'The Victory') and a few 'historical conversations' which focused on relevant topics (for instance, *Roots of the Present: the Five Days in Italy's History*), but failed to arouse any historiographical or civic interest.

More robust scholarly initiatives were planned in Turin, with an exhibition of satirical newspapers in collaboration with Paris, Lausanne and Nuremberg,[4] and an international symposium in two instalments, dedicated to *Piedmont in the Restoration* and *The 'Statuto albertino' and Italian Constitutionalism*.[5] In addition there were concerts, films on the Risorgimento and a further set of well-focused, highly interesting events on the issue of religious freedom: a conquest/concession that came to life in February–March 1848. It was illustrated in exhibitions, documentary publications and a conference on *The Emancipation of the Jews in Italy: Between Integration and Assimilation* (this last, however, provided a long-term overview of the state of the art rather than an investigation into the motives and consequences of the 1848 decision). Finally, the last 'capital' of Northern Italy, Venice, organized – besides a historical exhibition and some minor cultural events commemorating the siege experience – an international conference concerning the city's role as a connecting agent among nationalist groups and liberation movements active in Istria, Dalmatia and the Balkans.[6]

When we leave the 'Padania', however, the picture gets even more rarefied: an exhibition at the Museo del Risorgimento in Bologna on the local insurrection against the Austrians; a conference in Florence on the 1847 reforms (too purely descriptive to illuminate the connections with 1848);[7] and a conference in Naples whose focus, as in Turin, was on the eve of 1848, thus leaving the revolution in the background.[8]

To this summary overview one could probably add a few other minor events, but the result would be the same. The scholars' lack of interest is stressed by the silence of the local historical societies and amateur historians, of the libraries, archives, museums, schools and small municipalities, that is to say of that diffuse network whose activism is always the best symptom of a widespread interest in, and participatory questioning of a specific segment of history. Moreover, the very local roots of most celebrations in a few key cities of 1848 produced an emphasis on local peculiarities rather than on the interaction among different fields, realms and grounds of social and political activities and events that were profoundly shaped in intensity and significance by their common pertinence to a single revolutionary phase.

What is most problematic in this Italian silence is its stark contrast with the recent, lively public interest in such topics as the inherent fragility of the Italian nation-state, the uncertain foundations of the very concepts of nation and *patria* and the chronic difficulties of the Italians' relationship with their national institutions. Thence the numerous polemic revisitations of Italy's short and long history, which also touch upon the Risorgimento's specific topics (even though one would have expected a stronger emphasis in a country where neither Fascism nor the Monarchy's fall managed to introduce a true institutional discontinuity between Savoy's Piedmont and Maastricht's Italy). Arguments were advanced against the state's inability to strengthen national identity, or for a civic identity incomparably stronger than the political one. There were those who questioned 'the Italians' weak patriotism' and those who stressed the damage done by 'the less insolent than awkward attempt to give the Italians a state shaped after the Piedmontese one', i.e. after one of Italy's least Italian regions.[9]

That the current debate on the tensions between nation and nation-state could hardly be less academic is made evident by solid facts, such as the Lega's success in the North; the recurrent news of separatist plans developed in the South by the Mafia and subversive right-wing groups; the proliferating projects for a 'federal revolution' and the strengthening of local and regional autonomy; or the growing claims against the inadequacy of the Italian centralized state, inherited from Savoy Piedmont, to face the tensions of this millennium's convulsive ending in the perspective of European unification. And yet no one seems to be interested in using the 1848 anniversary – the year *par excellence* when Italy thought and acted in a federalist and European perspective – to liberate this debate from the abstract models of political 'science' and root it in history's profound concreteness.

Most of those engaged in the discussion fail to free themselves from either short-term political polemics or fancy projections upon the millenary range of history. They do not focus on the moment of origins – those few revolutionary years between 1846 and 1849 during which the notions of *patria*, nation and state were redefined along the current lines and meanings – three years that stand at the core of the issue. Then the hope rose and fell that the Vatican itself could take the lead of the emerging liberal and national movement. Then the foundations were laid for an Italian nation-state born without and against religion; that contrast – it has been observed – represents a world-wide *unicum*, and resulted in a deep laceration given the profoundly Catholic identity of the Italian people.[10]

The problem is that 1848 identifies an event marked by conflict, indeed by multiple, overlapping and clashing conflicts, that took place on different levels and gave rise to memories and founding myths for opposing identities. One could provocatively adopt for 1848 the same formula advanced by Claudio Pavone for the Resistance: namely, that it was simultaneously war for national independence, civil war and class conflict.[11] But in the present environment dominated by calls for 'pacification' among the Italians and a notion of politics as conflict mediation (possibly *a priori*) rather than as an expression of conflicts, those credentials obviously are neither appealing nor stimulating.

Inscribed in popular memory and lexicon as a synonym for chaos and disorder ('fare un Quarantotto', 'sembrava un Quarantotto') that year in fact witnessed a true explosion of politics, which translated into projects and options so strongly connotated as to create identities and memories that were initially atomized and later divided. If Cattaneo noticed that 1848 had taught everyone that 'Italy is not subservient to foreigners, but to its own people', Ricasoli on the other hand acclaimed the 'good job' done by the Austrians in Livorno with the killings of 8 and 9 May 1849. The only common ground was the awareness that the issue of independence did not in any way sum up the 'Italian problem'.[12]

Silence and a divided memory appear to be, in short, two ways to avoid thinking about 1848, so as not to interrogate the issues that it posed and did not resolve. The very fact that the most visible anniversary celebrations of that epoch-making event accidentally coincided with moments of social or institutional crisis in Italy's history – 1898, 1948, 1998 – provided a perfect justification for embarrassment and laziness. Historians as well as militants were prodded to analyse segments of 1848 and celebrate its multiple partial components, thus avoiding a comprehensive assessment of its significance for the history of Italy and the Italians in the last one hundred and fifty years.

Proud as we are of the rediscovered importance of using plurals both in historical descriptions and interpretations – there were many and diverse revolutions, not only on a European scale, but in Italy as well – we risk losing sight of the peculiar feature of the extraordinary revolutionary tide of 1848 (still unequalled in modern history): its basic unity in time and space.[13] Because the continuous interaction of agrarian rebellions, strikes, campaigns for reform and constitution, urban uprisings, spontaneous calls to arms, inaugurations of parliaments, negotiations for custom and political union, constitutional congresses, and proclamations of republican governments force us to think in the singular mode. The revolution was indeed many diverse things in diverse places and for diverse actors, but it was also 'one'.

One state, two countries

The fiftieth anniversary came when Italy was undergoing a crisis which questioned the prevailing conceptualizations of state and nation, their identities, relationships and prospects. In the long '*fin de siècle* crisis', 1898 stands out as the moment when the divergence grew wider between a 'common people' bent on demonstrations and uprisings (in the countryside and the South at first, then in the Centre–North and the cities) and an 'establishment' long tempted by authoritarian, if not reactionary, solutions.[14] However diverse, these temptations found a common ground in the proposal to 'return' to a literal interpretation of the Kingdom's *Statuto* (the cautious constitution enacted on 4 March 1848 by Carlo Alberto, King of Piedmont-Sardinia, the last of the peninsula's monarchs to do so). Such 'return' would have erased the liberal and parliamentarian habits that had meanwhile modified the *Statuto*'s original features, providing for a government responsive to the king and not to the parliament. This was the real issue for those in power, and that's why the only celebrations sponsored by the central authorities were those focused on the *Statuto*, even though it had never been popular among Italians. Its annual celebration on the first Sunday in June had never lost its purely 'institutional' character.[15]

Even the Minister of Education, although open to liberal suggestions, did not recommend the schools to mention the public demonstrations, uprisings and insurrections that had marked the 1848 revolutionary season and had signalled that 'Italy's redemption' included motives and forces which could not be straitjacketed into the narrow Savoy-parliamentarian framework. Unlike the truly conservative groups, however, he took care to present that season as 'the origin and foundations of our country's free institutions', a 'synthesis of accomplished hopes and imminent victories' guaranteed by the parliament's primacy.[16] The parliament was the true 'initiator of Italy's unity', as a centre-left member of parliament had written long before in order to celebrate the Piedmontese parliament's merits.[17]

Yet in the numerous public celebrations of 1848, few teachers and principals portrayed the *Statuto* following the suggestions of the Minister of Education as a charter stressing the role of parliament and citizens' rights, although there were some who dared to present it as a summa of 'Italy's age-old intellectual and social life'.[18] In the many *pamphlets* relating the speeches made in schools, in accordance with the Minister's wishes, mentions of the *Statuto* were usually aimed at emphasizing the primacy of duty and the need for obedience, submission and sacrifice which everyone was supposed to exercise 'for King and Fatherland' (these two terms were so often juxtaposed as to create a genuine hendiadys). Upon reading these more or less successful rhetorical efforts, one has the impression that they were targeted not at active citizens but at subjects devoid of any autonomy, especially when addressed to the low-middle classes or the technical schools' pupils, i.e. groups that had just reached the dignity of full citizenship, and therefore a tenuous degree of nationalization.[19] This is the very reason why the *Statuto*'s celebrations were particularly numerous in the South and in Sicily, where statutory rights (always a possibility rather than a certainty) had recently been systematically violated,[20] and where the only memory of the Risorgimento was of the popular uprisings aimed at expelling the barons and the Bourbons rather than at 'uniting with Italy'.

However, a 'memory of 1848' pivoted on a parliamentary interpretation of the *Statuto* was too biased to withstand the current political struggle. Italian politics in the 1890s revolved around the harsh contrast between those who based the state's legitimacy upon the nationality principle and those who adhered to a dynastic principle, a perspective that has been dubbed 'the bourgeoisie's *coup d'état'*.[21]

In a context of popular uprisings and tensions met by the government with explicit and implicit suspensions of legal rights, intimidating declarations and bloody repressions, the cleavages of 1848 appeared unmitigated and indeed exacerbated by new casualties and new hatred. In May, the army that was supposed to represent the nation hunted down citizens of Milan who were protesting against the high food prices and shot them even in their own houses and gardens. Many thought this to be the logical consequence of the dynastic options of 1848 and of their most recent interpretations.[22] Those who had portrayed Carlo Alberto as the 'magnanimous King', champion of independence from Austria – and who gave credit for the Milan insurrection to those who hoped that the Piedmontese king would rid them of the triumphant populace – could only end up shooting the defenders of an Italy based on people's protagonism: the latter were not seen as political antagonists but as mortal enemies.

The tragedy of May 1898 brought to its definitive crisis the interpretation of the Risorgimento as a 'discordant concord' between winners and losers, which had been laboriously constructed since unification and had seemed to prevail in the 1880s, when 'trasformismo' among the parties had dominated national politics. The difficult balance that had been reached around the 'factor of unity and independence' could not withstand the irruption of the issue of liberty, which questioned the origins and nature of the state, and the role of citizens and their rights in it.

The most resonant episode of this 'fracture of memory' took place on 20 March in Milan. Eleven days earlier the city had been brought to a halt by the grandiose funeral of the radical deputy Felice Cavallotti, killed by a conservative Catholic journalist in a duel. The moderate Catholic municipal government decided to celebrate the 50th anniversary of Milan's Five Days in a spirit of monarchism and national harmony, in tune with the interpretation of 'a perfectly unitary Risorgimento devoid of internal discord'.[23] Those who rejected this provocative falsification had no choice but to go for an explicit confrontation. It was the only way to restate that the memory of the Five Days was not for sale, that a paradigm of compromise could not be stretched to the point of focusing the memory of the Milan revolution on the Savoy house (in August 1848 the House of Savoy had chosen to return the city to the Austrians rather than to be in debt to the protagonists of such a subversive action as the liberation of the city by its inhabitants).

Thus the city was simultaneously crossed by two different demonstrations, each one with tens of thousands in attendance: an official one in the morning, with bands playing the royal march but no speeches, and one in the afternoon organized by republicans and popular associations, with the Socialists' red flags and bands playing Garibaldi's anthem as well as the workers' anthem. The *annus mirabilis* of Italy's national revolution could arouse emotions and passions only if revisited in the light of a 'local' experience perceived as the essential core even for larger projections of identity. The battleground for this contest about the past was defined less by the state's central authorities and institutions than by locally organized political groups and clienteles, and particularly by their spokesmen in the municipalities, who usually represented closed and narrow-minded alliances that, unlike those operating at the national level, viewed liberalism as an utterly alien culture.

The productions by these local notables made clear that 'in the official myth of the Risorgimento there was no room for considering the peoples' Revolution as an essential tool for the Italian rebirth',[24] just as in current politics there was no room for the self-proclaimed heirs to the contents and forms of that Revolution. Just a month after this fracture – which was as much about future prospects as past memories – materialized in Milan, a similar dynamic emerged in Florence. Here the municipality focused the celebrations on the unveiling of statues of the two moderates Peruzzi and Ricasoli, on the very day of the so-called 'Tuscan revolution' of 1859.[25] The democrats saw this choice as a challenge in view of the lack of any other relevant official event (aside from the usual solemn mass at Santa

Croce on 29 May, to remember the Tuscan volunteers who died in Lombardy in 1848).

Thus, the moderates 'celebrated' 1859 rather than 1848, and in a purely local key to boot, while the democrats tried to give voice to the Risorgimento as national liberation not only from foreign, but from domestic oppressors, as a 'people's war' against Austria, under the impress of Giuseppe Montanelli and the Constituent Assembly. But this was not easy given the state of martial law proclaimed after the uprising in Milan. An analogous sequence of events took place over the summer in Bologna, where a solemn commemoration of the insurrection against the Austrians of 8 August, however, could not possibly be eschewed. Democratic societies and popular parties opted to stay out of the official celebrations when they were notified that they could not speak, even briefly, nor carry their flags and sing. Thus they called the citizens to an alternative ceremony where they could sing Mameli's as well as Garibaldi's anthem, pay homage to Mazzini and show the tricolour flag together with white, black or red flags.[26]

There were probably many other occasions marred by such a dynamic of mutual exclusion and self-exclusion. Traces can be found in events sponsored by the early museums of the Risorgimento,[27] in the arguments that divided the editors of the early periodicals on the Risorgimento,[28] or among the members of the Veterans of 1848–1849 and the National Battles Veterans associations. The veterans were largely converted to a 'pacified' reading of the Risorgimento, but they were too proud of 'the nation's redemption' and the volunteers' role in it to consent to a purely statutory interpretation of the Risorgimento which leaned towards Savoy.

Italy was not Germany, and no one could afford to define 1848 simply as a mistake. That crucial year had made clear that the existing situation was unbearable; it had begun projects and processes that could not possibly be ruled out as utopian; it had brought new protagonists on the public scene. These new protagonists included segments of an unmistakably bourgeois ruling class, even though it was eventually the nobility that took the best advantage out of the 'lessons of 1848', as Carlo Cattaneo admitted with bitterness in 1851. The aristocrats had 'learnt how important it is to be organized' and to restructure the state's institutions much more thoroughly than the *homines novi*.[29] The latter – although well aware of the crucial role they had, and could have again, as 'the nation's core' – were still too weak and divided to assume a fully independent leading role.[30]

In *fin de siècle* Italy it was surely legitimate to define 1848 as a revolution, but only as long as the adjective 'national' was prefixed to it, in a way to distance its character from the ghosts of a 'social revolution'. Many, however, continued to use less embarrassing terms. Similarly, having participated in 1848 could be a point of honour only as far as it affected the anti-Austrian struggle, rather than the campaign for citizens' rights and for a state based upon the duty and right to equality and participation, since these were the distinguishing features of any self-styled heir of the Risorgimento's democracy.

This was, in fact, the leitmotiv of many minor events that took place, in spite of current difficulties, wherever a network of lay and democratic societies was active: banquets, subscriptions, wreaths and public homages at graves, monuments or other places sacred to the revolution's memory. In the absence of specific studies this, at least, is what emerges from a screening of newspapers, pamphlets, flyers, cheap engravings, etc. Those demonstrations that remembered 'another Risorgimento' (and that were not based on critical rethinking, but on appropriating different segments of the past and constructing civic and political genealogies for the present's sake) were experienced by militants and tiny local democratic élites as one of the few tools available to assert the continuing existence of 'another Italy'.[31]

As long as the present was marked by discrimination and repression, the language of memory could not possibly talk of 'national reconciliation', but only celebrate one's own diversity and construct one's own past. The obvious aim was to give historical depth and legitimacy to the current coalitions and demands. Another aim, however, was to further strengthen the men defeated in the Risorgimento and the labour and socialist movement, a precious though burdensome legacy connecting past and present revolutionaries.

Initially, the renewed struggle between those who saw only insurrections and 'people's' governments in 1848 (as witnessed by many essays on Lombard and Venetian cities) and those who credited every conquest to the monarchy brought no advancement either in public memory or in historiography. But the Democrats' decision to challenge any attempt to give 1848 a purely dynastic colouring threatened the moderates' cherished image of a linear and monolithic Risorgimento, thus reopening a discourse on past and future.

As Gaetano Salvemini wrote in the Preface to his splendid essay on the *Partiti politici milanesi* (the only remarkable historical work from that poisoned period), no one could look forward to the future if the conspiracy of silence against 'the most dangerous names, such as Cattaneo and Ferrari' remained unbroken, if Mazzini remained 'a pale icon of unity' and Garibaldi 'just one of Vittorio Emanuele's lieutenants'.[32] The insistence on unanimity and on the Savoys' central role could not – as he wrote – unite and 'pacify'. It would only prevent a collective reckoning with the country's history and with the ghosts of a past that could not be denied. This became evident in the early twentieth century, when new studies began to appear which gave dignity to new research approaches and interpretations. Their 1848 included rebels and insurgents in the South and in the countryside, agrarian struggles and social conflicts, federalists and republicans. It was a history of discontinuities and irrepressible conflicts which could not be erased from collective memory and reflection.[33]

Between the Guelph anvil and the Communist hammer

The 1898 celebrations had been conditioned by the overtly reactionary politics of the moment. Fifty years later, the 1848 centenary was ensnared by the Cold War and the breakdown of anti-fascist unity. The celebrations of 'the peoples' springtime' coincided with an electoral campaign marred by exasperated conflicts. That campaign ended in the defeat of a socialist–communist alliance, the 'People's Front', which had assumed as its symbol the image of Garibaldi, and the triumph of the Christian Democracy: alien to the Risorgimento tradition, the latter appeared as the natural heir of the 'organized Catholics', always the anti-Risorgimento instrument of the Catholic church. A few months later, the attempted murder of the Communist Party secretary Palmiro Togliatti at the door of the parliament brought the country to the verge of civil war, opening up a wound that would take a long time to heal.

There could be no more abrupt political and cultural turning from the years of the Resistance and of the country's difficult reckoning with Fascism. In those years, the call for a Risorgimento to be 'completed' in continuity with the defeated democratic potential of 1848–9 (many partisans talked about 'insurgence as a way to resurgence') had seemed so obvious and was so widely shared as to become one of the principles of the Resistance that many had labelled it a 'second Risorgimento'.[34]

It was not by chance that the republican constitution was (and still is) shaped around the same political project the democrats had fought for a century earlier. Written down by a constituent assembly elected with universal suffrage, the constitution begins with a solemn set of *fundamental principles*, just like the Roman constitution of 1849. Also the anthem selected to replace the royal march goes back to the Roman republic: *Fratelli d'Italia* was composed during the siege by one of Mazzini's followers, and that's why it had long been barred from official celebrations.

But in 1948, with the sharp right-wing turn of Italian and international politics, the 'public discourse on revolution' could no longer reconnect to the democratic and republican experience of 1849. At the opening of the centenary celebrations Italy seemed to downplay even its own republican choice, with the election of a president, Luigi Einaudi who had opted for the monarchy in the 1946 referendum. Rather than a common experience amounting to a controversial but precious shared asset, the legacy of 1848 was once more a patrimony to be divided between the political contestants in accordance with the needs and power relations of the present.

For instance, the issue of federalism – so crucial in 1848 – was symptomatically left aside by the celebrations, and it became even impossible to publish Carlo Cattaneo's complete works. The contemporary political establishment had no interest in his republican and federalist views: in the aftermath of the immediate postwar secessionist tensions (particularly strong in Sicily), every party adopted rather more centralist attitudes than those outlined in the recent constitution.

In relation to the more recent past, the celebrations managed to erase the Fascist appropriation of 'popular' figures and experiences (like Garibaldi, Mazzini or the war volunteers) and to cut down to size the role of Carlo Alberto and the House of Savoy, in spite of the monarchists' and moderates' protests. The latter found a prestigious spokesman in Benedetto Croce, who swore on the 'complementarity' of Mazzini and Carlo Alberto for Italy's fortunes.[35] Moreover, the celebrations paid unprecedented attention to the revolution's Europe-wide scope, which was explored in an uneven collection of essays bound long to remain a crucial piece of scholarship, and in a conference – promoted by the Accademia dei Lincei – that was as balanced as it was cautiously open to innovative issues.[36] However, the widespread reaction against those who were impatient or dissatisfied with an interpretation of 1848 just as 'a struggle for the common ideal of national independence' (or, at best, for a vague notion of 'liberty') proved that fear of change and a 'need for stability' were quite pronounced even among historians.

Culturally as well as politically it was the Christian Democracy (CD) that gave representation to these anxieties. Moderates of every colouring and faith were gathering under the CD's wings, thus passively ferrying onto republican Italy men and institutions of the past, as well as its values, assumptions and mentality. The party's dominant role was not used in order to highlight those ideas, figures and groups of liberal catholicism that a century before had opened crucial divisions in the establishment, and that could now serve as inspiration for reconceptualizing a crucial turning point in the Catholics' course towards a secularized and nationalized idea of politics. On these issues, the most innovative and fruitful suggestions came rather from Antonio Gramsci's reflections on the *Risorgimento*, written in the 1930s and published in 1949.[37]

Instead, Christian Democratic politicians used the Catholics' role in the 1848 rupture either to play down events already planned or to give visibility to moderate and even conservative opinions, while the Church's hierarchy went as far as to propose an overtly reactionary reading of 1848 as a 'deviation' from the proper course set by Pius IX's farsightedness, and as 'a historic failure' due to the restlessness of 'agitators' and of the 'low people' that they excited. There was even a Catholic newspaper that dared to invite 'Let us not celebrate 1848' and the CD's daily, *Il Popolo*, published a single article, this one stressing *Metternich's humanity*, while the journal *Civiltà cattolica* hosted two brief articles which argued that the revolution's most important result was the renewed 'spiritual unity of Europe' under the banner of religion.[38]

Even the great liberal intellectual Benedetto Croce advised Naples's (monarchic) mayor to 'abolish the planned celebrations', as a due reverence for the 'feeling of timidity' provoked by the prospect of 'raising one's eyes' to 'the noble ideals and heroic actions of the past'.[39] The CD-led Rome municipality chose, 'with clerical unscrupulousness', to dedicate the centenary to a single Pope's volunteer who had died in the siege of Vicenza.[40] Most municipalities run by the right-wing or the centre-right opted for silence, with the consent of the central government (which did not budget any funds for the celebrations) and the full support of all those private local actors – banks, corporations, wealthy citizens – who had good reasons to loathe the celebration of such a revolutionary year.

Those who did not belong to this moderate majority could not but indict such management of the celebrations. The Left raised its finger against the 'Catholic clique' and those 'Anti-Risorgimento forces' which (according to one liberal and progressive historian who was then studying the relationship between *Church and State in Italy in the Last Century*) appeared 'closer to Pius IX than to those who had fought against his theocratic desires'.[41] These anxieties were magnified by the absence, among Catholic laymen, of any significant distancing from the Vatican's 'resounding effrontery'.[42] The clerical-fascist Egilberto Martire proclaimed 'God for Italy, Italy for God', thus raising the spectre of a true desire for a 'neo-Guelph reconquest' of the nation.[43] Even some historians were prepared to extol Pellegrino Rossi as the 'martyr' of good Vatican governance and his death as the cause for the 'failure' of the moderate, liberal, neo-Guelph project.[44]

The left-wing forces – whether democratic and bourgeois or communist and proletarian – took an opposite attitude towards the celebrations. They wanted to highlight the solidarity among different social and political groups around progressive goals, the role of the revolutionary movement's most advanced forces, an open and cooperative notion of nationality and the existence of 'another genealogy' in which to root their own national legitimacy. But they also wanted to emphasize the historical dignity of that very subject, the people, that a century ago had surfaced to public life soon to be expelled from it, with devastating consequences for the whole country. As a young and insightful 'reporter' of the centenary observed: 'The masses that – in the course of a few months – had appeared upon the scene and then vanished were exactly those "Italians" whom many later regretted had not been "made" when Italy was "made".'[45]

Newspapers and journals of the 'progressive' groups, parties and movements rushed to publish memoirs, recollections and biographies aimed at rooting names, faces, battles and events in the collective imagination. They did so to shape an identity made of active participation in the conquest of political democracy, national independence, solidarity among the peoples and also social change. *Rinascita*, the Italian Communist Party's cultural monthly, published an engaging special number open to a variety of contributors and issues. The space given to Marx and Engel's *Communist Party Manifesto* was large but not preponderant, while numerous essays dwelt upon the liberal, moderate and neo-Guelph protagonists of 1848. The main emphasis, however, was on the need to pay attention to economic conditions and fluctuations, to social groups and their relations, to the struggles for social and economic issues.

Similarly, the 'red' cities (with socialist-communist local governments) promoted public lectures and exhibitions aimed at a non-specialist audience in order to emphasize the people's agency and the 'hope for change' of 1848. The conferences they organized strove to mediate between different positions and generations, but they usually gave more visibility to speakers who talked about 'social issues', 'socialistic ideas', 'sparks of class struggle' and the likes. In Perugia, for instance, the municipal and provincial governments invited to a conference the 'pure liberals' and the anti-idealistic and anti-elitist historians, but also the younger historians who had waged their battles around the 'social dimension' of 1848.[46] Latent tensions were thus brought to the surface, and they were all the more volatile for their political and cultural connotations, given the predominant role of a stale idealistic historiography that rejected any discourse liable to be connected to Marx's hated 'materialism' and to the primacy of 'economic factors', as had already happened in the conferences which took place in Palermo, Milan and Rome.[47]

The Prime Minister Alcide De Gasperi gave the opening speech at the historical conference on the Milan 'Five Days'. But even though he had clearly been influenced by German social catholicism (when he was a subject of the Habsburg Empire in Trento), he decided to argue that the 'Five Days' proved that – contrary to what Marx wrote – 'the supreme force that dominates events' is not the economy, but the 'spiritual forces'.[48] Other speakers praised class harmony as opposed to class struggle, and tried to exorcise those years' uprisings as germs of the 'barbarism' that was currently in danger of surrendering Italy to the heirs of 'the invaders that 15 centuries ago had submerged the Roman civilization'.[49]

It would certainly be exaggerated to claim 'a Left-wing primacy in the celebration' and an 'inversion' in the cultural and moral assessment of the Risorgimento's protagonists – as did Franco Valsecchi, a prestigious historian of a strongly conservative political and historiographical bent.[50] The new approaches and issues did not grow into a fully fledged 'historical revision' of the moderate-monarchic interpretation, and their innovative contents appear far less ground-breaking to our eyes than to their contemporaries who were outraged by statements such as those of Emilio Sereni, a communist politician and a great historian of agriculture, who pointed out the role of sharecropping in the deep-rooted power of the Tuscan moderate party, or of Delio Cantimori, the famous historian of the Counter-reformation, who insisted on the 'genuine continuity of actions and ideas' between 1848 most radical groups and the Bolshevik revolution.[51]

Yet various elements appeared genuinely innovative, especially in a context such as the Italian one, which had experienced a precocious rejection and disappearance of early twentieth-century historiographical assumptions on the linkage between socio-economic dynamics and liberal-national demands. On virtually every relevant occasion we can find someone arguing – both factually and theoretically – for an analysis aimed at giving historical concreteness to people's conditions of life and work, and at breaking the absurd barrier between a social and a political approach, between social and national claims, between struggles for political liberty and those for social justice.

The volumes of proceedings of the 1848 centenary conferences reveal an interest much more diffused than one would assume from the views and anathemas of history's 'pontiffs'. Even the studies promoted by Benedetto Croce and published by the *Società napolitana di storia patria* include numerous essays whose main theme is the controversial connection between the Southern agrarian struggles of 1847–8 and the assertive emergence of new classes and political ideals.[52] It was an issue that was given immediate relevance by the large ongoing agrarian mobilization 'for land and democracy' (particularly acute in the spring and summer 1948), and that has not been investigated except peripherally in a few studies of the early twentieth century.[53]

The true protagonists of that clash, however, were no longer the municipalities, the schools or the popular societies. The stage was now occupied by the newspapers and magazines, which published excerpts from forthcoming lectures and conferences, magnified the most heated arguments, hosted politicians' and opinion-makers' comments, stimulated debate and vitriolic responses. Given the expanding circulation of the press, the main actors and audiences of this battle around the 'memory of 1848' became those groups who were entrusted with the formation of public opinion and the transmission of a new image of the past.

On the other hand, the popular classes to which everyone referred, and which, fifty years earlier, had been protagonists of the celebrations, had apparently lost any interest and agency in the effort to assert a different intepretation of the 1848 revolution. Even the 1949 ceremony in Rome, which put an end to the outrageous boycott of Giuseppe Mazzini's statue (it had been waiting since 1904 to be unveiled on the Gianicolo[54]), had little popular participation. Even more negligible was the presence of the popular parties' militants. Mazzini (the man who – as Cattaneo had written – 'considered even the disasters to be victories, as long as the fight was maintained') was now merely an icon of the Republican party, a tiny but crucial component of the centrist coalition. This seems to confirm an opinion already voiced while the war was still raging: 'The attitude the Italians assume toward the Risorgimento still implies . . . a choice that precedes any historical evaluation.'[55]

In those months marked by the unstoppable ascent of the domestic and international Cold War it became clear that of all the 1848 icons only Marx and Engel's *Manifesto* (just reprinted in an important edition by Emma and Delio Cantimori[56]) could still arouse heated, contrasting passions. But it did not belong to the same story of nation-building and nation-state formation, although it had numerous and important contacts with it. Today, even the *Manifesto* is nearly ignored by admirers and critics alike. At best, it re-emerges as a fragment of an antiquarian memory tendered only by specialists and devotees: a further proof of the actual flight from the roots of our own recent history that is rapidly swallowing 1848 in the quicksand of indifference and that threatens to estrange us from ourselves.

Notes

1 E. Di Ciommo, *La nazione possibile. Mezzogiorno e questione nazionale nel 1848* (Milano: Angeli, 1993).
2 F. Rizzi, *La coccarda e le campane. Comunità rurali e repubblica romana nel Lazio (1848–1849)* (Milano: Angeli, 1988).

3   See for instance B. Tobia, *Una patria per gli Italiani. Spazi, itinerari, monu-menti nell'Italia unita (1879–1900)*. (Bari and Rome: Laterza, 1991); U. Levra, *Fare gli italiani. Memoria e celebrazione del Risorgimento* (Turin: Istituto per la storia del Risorgimento italiano, 1992); *Il mito del Risorgimento nell'Italia unita*, special issue of *Il Risorgimento*, 1–2, 1995.

4   Le rivoluzioni del 1848 e l'Europa delle immagini, Turin, 1998.

5   Il Piemonte alle soglie del 1848 (7–10 October), Lo Statuto albertino e il costituzionalismo italiano (12–14 October). These initiatives are to be followed by two publications on the same topics: *1898–1998, dallo Statuto albertino alla Costituzione repubblicana* and *Milleottocentoquarantotto. Torino, l'Italia, l'Europa*, edited by Umberto Levra and Rosanna Roccia.

6   La rivoluzione liberale e le nazioni divise, 5–6 June 1998.

7   Le riforme del 1847 negli Stati italiani, 20–21 March 1998.

8   The conference, organized by the *Deputazione napoletana di storia patria*, was titled, Personaggi e problemi: Stato e società alla vigilia del 1848, and took place on 26–28 November.

9   See, for instance, S. Lanaro, *L'Italia nuova. Identità e sviluppo* (Turin: Einaudi, 1988); G. E. Rusconi, *Se cessiamo di essere una nazione. Tra etnodemocrazie regionali e cittadinanza europea* (Bologna: Il Mulino, 1993); E. Galli Della Loggia, *La morte della patria* (Bari and Rome: Laterza, 1995); A. Schiavone, *Italiani senza Italia* (Turin: Einaudi, 1998), from which I quote Carlo Dionisotti's statement on Piedmont (*ivi*, 100). For a scholarship more detached from current public arguments see I. Porciani, 'Stato e nazione: l'immagine debole dell'Italia', in S. Soldani and G. Turi (eds), *Fare gli italiani. Storia e cultura nell'Italia contemporanea* (Bologna: Il Mulino, 1992), vol. I, pp. 385–428; and G. Turi, 'Patria e Nazione nel linguaggio politico italiano', *Passato e presente*, 46, 1998, 37–55.

10 G. Rumi, 'La riconquista guelfa. Speranze e reticenze nel centenario dell'Unità', *Il Risorgimento*, 1–2, 1995, 523.

11 C. Pavone, *Una guerra civile. Saggio sulla moralità della Resistenza* (Turin: Bollati Boringhieri, 1991).

12 C. Cattaneo, *Dell'insurrezione di Milano nel 1848 e della successiva guerra. Memorie* (1849), now in idem, *Il 1848 in Italia. Scritti 1848–1851*, D. Castelnuovo Frigessi ed. (Turin: Einaudi, 1972), p. 273; B. Ricasoli, 'L'assedio di Livorno del 1849. Diario', M. Nobili and S. Camerani (eds), *Nuova Antologia*, 1782, 1949, 113–27. Cattaneo was a democratic politician and social writer; Baron Ricasoli was a moderate.

13 For a recent re-assessment of the question see M. Hanagan, 'Dalla Rivoluzione francese alle rivoluzioni', in P. Bairoch and E. J. Hobsbawm (eds), *Storia d'Europa*, vol. V, *L'età contemporanea* (Turin: Einaudi, 1996), 637–73.

14 On the relevance of this cleavage in the building of the Italian state, and in the shaping of two contrasting myths of the Risorgimento, see F. Della Peruta, 'Il mito del Risorgimento e l'estrema sinistra dall'Unità al 1914', in *Il Risorgimento*, 1–2, 1995, 32–70.

15 A partly different evaluation of that annual celebration is given by I. Porciani, *La festa della nazione. Rappresentazione dello Stato e spazi sociali nell'Italia unita* (Bologna: Il Mulino, 1997), while C. Ghisalberti, 'Lo Statuto

albertino tra mito e realtà', in *Il Risorgimento*, 1–2, 1995, writes of a 'popular veneration' for the Statuto (p. 227). On the other hand, the historians have not paid any attention to the effects inherent in the adoption of the Statuto as the basic law of the new state, especially because its specific features, and the continuity thus established with the Kingdom of Piedmont-Sardinia, greatly diluted the 'national' character of the Kingdom of Italy.

16   The Minister's directive suggested celebrating 8 May (the opening day of the Subalpine Parliament) rather than 4 March. The directive is issued in *Bollettino ufficiale del Ministero della pubblica istruzione*, 1898, 8 (24 febbraio), 317.

17   A. Brofferio, *Storia del Parlamento subalpino iniziatore dell'Unità italiana* (Turin: Belzini Battezzati, 1865). The Minister's quotations are from the directive mentioned in the previous note, and sent to the schools on 23 February, 1898 (just the memorial day of the Paris uprising!) to recommend that pupils attend the Statuto's celebrations.

18   This was the title of a lecture given at the Palazzo Ducale in Urbino, on 4 March 1898, by Manfredi Siotto Pintor, a law professor at the local university.

19   We lack detailed studies on this minor literature, but a few explorations in the many titles mentioned by the *Bibliografia italiana* of that year leave no doubt about their prevailing content.

20   The best example, but by no means the only one, is the early 1890s' harsh response to the uprisings known as the 'fasci siciliani'. Of the vast literature about it see the essays in the collection *I fasci siciliani*, vol. I, *Nuovi contributi a una ricostruzione storica* (Bari: De Donato, 1975).

21   U. Levra, *Il colpo di stato della borghesia. La crisi politica di fine secolo in Italia* (Milan: Feltrinelli, 1974).

22   The moderates' tendency to monopolize even the 'Five Days' for their partisan advantage was evident in the works, for instance, of C. Casati, *Nuove rivelazioni sui fatti di Milano del 1847–48 tratte da documenti inediti* (Milan: Hoepli, 1885): Casati was to be a protagonist of the celebrations organized in Milan by the authorities for the jubilee year.

23   Tobia, *Una patria per gli Italiani*, p. 180; on the Milan celebrations see pp. 152–8.

24   Ibid., p. 179.

25   A report on the demonstration and a listing of the groups attending it may be found in *La Nazione*, 27 and 28 April 1898.

26   A chronicle of the day may be found in *Commemorazione del cinquantesimo anniversario dell'8 agosto 1898* (Bologna: Merlani, 1898), which relates also the speech by the Mayor of Bologna. Recalling the 'calamitous events' of May he warned against the dangers to 'the country's stability', and obviously 'the calamity' he referred to was the citizens' protest rather than the troops firing on innocent bystanders. On the split on commemoration day in Bologna see also M. Baioni, *La 'religione della Patria'. Musei e Istituti del culto risorgimentale (1884–1918)* (Treviso: Pagus, 1995), p. 77.

27   Baioni, for instance, relates the stark 'anti-revolutionary' language of the Historical Exhibition at the Museo del Risorgimento in Treviso: Ibid., p. 75.

28   The *Rivista storica del Risorgimento* was published in Milan, from 1895, by an editorial group that, after prolonged tensions, eventually split up.

29   C. Cattaneo to C. Correnti, 20 November 1851, in Cattaneo, *Epistolario*, Rodolfo Caddeo ed. (Florence: Barbèra, 1953), vol. 3, p. 176.

30   The liberals' feeble interest for the national idea was recently highlighted by Raffaele Romanelli in the above-mentioned Venice conference; his paper has been published in H.-G. Haupt and S. Soldani (eds), *1848. Scene di una rivoluzione europea*, special issue of *Passato e presente*, 46, 1999.

31   Bright contemporary descriptions of 'an 1848 memorial celebration in a town of one thousand souls' in 1898 are in Della Peruta, *Il mito del Risorgimento*, p. 50.

32   G. Salvemini, *Le origini della reazione* (1899), now in idem, *Scritti sul Risorgimento*, P. Pieri and C. Pischedda eds (Milan: Feltrinelli, 1961), p. 26.

33   A quick survey of those years' interpretative innovations may be found in S. Soldani, 'Milleottocentoquarantotto', in *Storia d'Europa*, vol. II, *Il mondo contemporaneo* (Florence: La Nuova Italia, 1980), p. 560.

34   See C. Pavone, *Le idee della Resistenza. Antifascisti e fascisti di fronte alla tradizione del Risorgimento* (1959), now in idem, *Alle origini della Repubblica. Scritti su fascismo, antifascismo e continuità dello Stato* (Turin: Bollati Boringhieri, 1995), pp. 3–69. On this topic see also A. Varni, 'Il secondo Risorgimento', in *Il Risorgimento*, 1–2, 1995, 535–43.

35   B. Croce, 'Non travisare la storia', *Nuova gazzetta del popolo*, 6 November 1947.

36   See E. Rota (ed.), *Il 1848 nella storia italiana ed europea*, 2 vols (Milan: Vallardi, 1948), and Accademia nazionale dei Lincei–Fondazione Alessandro Volta, *Il 1848 nella storia d'Europa* (Rome: 1949).

37   A. Gramsci, *Il Risorgimento* (Turin: Einaudi, 1949), p. 57: 'The liberal movement's success in evoking a liberal catholic force and in pushing even Pius IX to briefly tread on liberalism's own terrain (thus disgregating the catholic ideological and political system and depriving it of self-confidence) was the Risorgimento's masterpiece', because it made possible 'to actually conceive the possibility of a united Italian state'.

38   E. Papa, 'Commemorazioni del 1848', *La civiltà cattolica*, vol. I, 1949, p. 188. The journal's two articles were focused on the notion of papal primacy in Vincenzo Gioberti and in Roberto Taparelli D'Azeglio, a leader of the Piedmontese 'reactionary party'.

39   B. Croce, 'Non travisare la storia'.

40   G. Manacorda, 'Pellegrino Rossi', in *L'Unità*, 19 November 1948.

41   The quotations are from F. Catalano, 'Tendenze moderate e tendenze democratiche nel '48 e nel '49', *Belfagor*, 1949, 651, and C. A. Jemolo, *Chiesa e Stato in Italia negli ultimi cento anni* (Turin: Einaudi, 1948), p. 716. Jemolo had been attacked in the *L'Osservatore romano* of 12 November 1948, no. 264 (P. di Borgo, 'Aspetti religiosi del Risorgimento italiano'), for his lecture at the Lincei Conference, when he had drawn a clear distinction between 'religious spirit' and 'Catholic ideology' in 1848 (Paolo di Borgo was the pseudonym of Egilberto Martire).

42 A. Caracciolo, 'Celebrazioni italiane del 1848', *Società*, V, 1949, no. 1, pp. 125–42, and no. 2, pp. 284–96.

43 'Solemn commemoration of Pellegrino Rossi', in *L'osservatore romano*, 17 November 1948, n. 268.

44 N. Rodolico, 'Pellegrino Rossi', in *L'Osservatore romano*, 14 November 1848, n. 266. On the polemics fuelled by those days' articles and speeches see P. Alatri, 'Rassegna bibliografica di studi e celebrazioni sul '48 italiano', in *Il 1848. Raccolta di saggi e di testimonianze*, Quaderno n. 1 di *Rinascita*, 1948, 127.

45 Caracciolo, 'Celebrazioni', p. 135.

46 For a comment on the conference see ibid.; Caracciolo qualified the papers given by Giuseppe Berti and Gastone Manacorda as 'Marxist'. A brief, positive report was also published in *Rinascita*, 1948, n. 9–10, 360.

47 News about the arguments that erupted during those conferences may be found in Alatri, 'Rassegna', 137 and 139–40.

48 Istituto per la storia del Risorgimento italiano, *Atti e Memorie del XXVII congresso nazionale* (Milan: Cordani, 1948), pp. 21–2 and 534.

49 Ibid., p. 256 (A. Genoino), and p. 534 (P. Pecchiai).

50 Valsecchi spoke of 'a new aulic historiography upside down, that denies what was previously affirmed, and affirms what used to be denied': 'Scienza storica e "revisione" del '48', in ibid., pp. 719–20.

51 See E. Sereni, 'Attualità del Giusti. La cultura toscana del '48 e il significato storico della mezzadria', and D. Cantimori, 'Realtà storica e utopia nel 1848 europeo', in *Il 1848–1849. Conferenze fiorentine* (Florence: Sansoni, 1950), pp. 19–48 and 157–74 (the quote is from p. 171). It is worth noticing that Cantimori defined as 'utopian' the liberal rather than the communist ideas. He argued that liberal ideas had been shipwrecked then, not to take centre-stage ever again, at least in their 'pure' form (ibid., pp. 163–4).

52 See *Il 1848 nell'Italia meridionale*, special issue of *Archivio storico delle Provincie Napoletane* 1950.

53 On agrarian struggles in the South in those years see G. Barone, 'Stato e Mezzogiorno (1943–1960)', in *Storia dell'Italia repubblicana*, vol. I, *La costruzione della democrazia* (Turin: Einaudi, 1994), pp. 319–51. On the early twentieth-century studies see the 1911 remarks by L. Ambrosini, *Borghesia meridionale*, later published in idem, *Cronache del Risorgimento e scritti letterari* (Milan and Rome: La cultura, 1931). He argued that they demonstrated that 'in most of the South the enthusiasm of 1848 was just the culminating event of class divisions and struggles', and he made a suggestion to 'abandon the obtuse and worn-out patriotic mentality' (ibid., p. 77).

54 Tobia, *Una patria*, p. 178.

55 L. Ginzburg, 'La tradizione del Risorgimento', in idem, *Scritti* (Turin: Einaudi, 1964), p. 114.

56 K. Marx and F. Engels, *Manifesto del partito comunista*, translated from the critical edition of the Moscow Marx-Engels-Lenin-Institut, with an Introduction by E. Cantimori Mezzomonti (Rome: Rinascita, 1948).

9
First Performances – Staging Memories of the French February Revolution

Rebecca L. Spang

I do not remember when I first was told that 'France' – or, 'the French' – are obsessed with remembering. Described by Jean-Pierre Rioux as a 'retromania' and by Richard Terdiman as a 'memory crisis', the 'right to recover the past' has become, in many cases, a duty.[1] History, according to Henry Rousso, can no longer serve a therapeutic function in France because it no longer forges a consensus; instead it gives rise to innumerable, often incurable, syndromes.[2] Rousso's analysis of the 'Vichy Syndrome', for instance, shows a cycle of repression yielding to compulsion. Forgetting Vichy, or remembering it – either provokes irresolvable guilt and seems to show a culture condemned to 'act out' what it cannot 'work through'.[3]

This patterned repetition of history, commemoration and memory has been widely taken as symptomatic of a crisis that is national in character. Life in the Hexagon is haunted by the 'Ghost of a Nation Past' in a way that many find distinctively French, even in this decade of widespread *fin-de-siècle* malaise and global *fin-de-millésime* anxiety.[4] Whether prompted by France's loss of great power status, or by the disappearance of the peasantry, or by the still anguished legacies of Vichy, collaboration and the Algerian War, the memory frenzy is often described as a specifically French phenomenon, as inherently and idiosyncratically French as poststructuralism, *pain de campagne* or Pernod. The passing of a specific time must, it seems, also entail the loss of a particular place. Proust's narrator was in search of lost time, but what emerged from his crumb-laden infusion was a place, the town of Combray.

Hypermnesia in contemporary France manifests itself in many forms. Memoirs of the famous and politically active sell well, as do the 'counter-memoirs' that describe them eating forbidden birds and holding contraband opinions.[5] 'Ordinary' people, once obscure, write their memoirs and become media figures overnight: Lucie Aubrac and Emilie Carlès are only two of the most notorious.[6] The remarkably anodyne celebration in 1989 of the French Revolution's bicentennial; the celebratory events in 1990 around the hundredth anniversary of Charles de Gaulle's birth (which fortuitously coincided with the fiftieth anniversary of his radio address of 18 June and the twentieth anniversary of his death); and even the controversy around celebrating 1500 years since the baptism of Clovis – all reveal an unusual concern to make the past into a central feature of the present. No year, it seems, can be a prime number; the present can always be evenly divided by the past. A hundred years of cinema can be easily celebrated, as can 75 years of French *Vogue.* The year 1998 alone saw plans to note the four hundredth anniversary of the Edict of Nantes and the hundredth anniversary of Zola's 'J'Accuse!' in addition to the quinquacentennial of the 'Republic without Terror' (as Laurent Fabius termed the Second Republic of 1848).

It is unsurprising, then, that the remit of French National Heritage has grown phenomenally in the past two decades, building expansively on the successes of 1980's 'Year of Patrimony'. French Heritage now includes *bandes dessinées,* pop music and at least one very deserving swimming pool, as well as the art museums, Loire river valley châteaux and classical theatre troupes it formerly circumscribed.[7] Even something so prima facie passing and ephemeral as the act of eating has been pulled into the heritage vortex, as the Ministry of Culture's ongoing 'culinary patrimony' project has assiduously inventoried the cheeses, preserves, pâtés and other alimentary products of France's regions. Since 1992, this endeavour has been pedagogical as well as enumerative: French schoolchildren now attend classes in which they are instructed in the value of their *patrimoine gastronomique.* If, in the Third Republic, it was Madame Bruno's *Tour de la France par deux enfants* that taught children civic pride and the outlines of national history, today that tour is presided over by the Institut français du goût and teaches children not of the factories of Le Creusot and the mills of Toulouse, but the truffles of Périgord and the spicecakes of Reims.[8]

France is not all bonbons and madeleines. Seven thick volumes edited by Pierre Nora – *Les Lieux de mémoire* (*Realms of Memory*, 1984–92, reissued in 1997) – are the monuments to French mnemonic anxiety probably best known by historians.[9] Conceived as a study of 'the places where the collective heritage of France was crystallized',[10] the project operates with a decidedly fluid understanding of what a 'place' might be. Including buildings (the Eiffel Tower, the Pantheon) and regions (Alsace, the Vendée), as well as individuals (Joan of Arc, Ernest Lavisse), books (Marcel Proust's *Remembrance of Things Past* and Augustin Thierry's *Letters on the History of France*) and activities (visiting famous authors, or the Tour de France bicycle race), it is a study of France 'as a reality that is entirely symbolic'.[11] If France is an imagined community, then this work is a study of what French people (and others) imagine when they lie back and think of France.[12]

Nora's important analysis of the workings of French memory raises two interrelated questions for this paper (which, in turn, notes problems with Nora's formulations). One question concerns the connection of national memories to international contexts, while the other, here discussed first, concerns his very definition of 'history' and 'memory'. As evoked in the introduction to the first volume of *Les Lieux de mémoire*, the real problem facing French memory is that it has tumbled into a historical – and historiographical – abyss. Counterintuitive as it may seem, the production of more and more history actually bespeaks the disappearance of more and more memory. Nora takes it as axiomatic that history and memory are best defined in opposition to each other. He grants that the terms are often used almost interchangeably, but insists that sloppiness of vocabulary hides a more dire truth. 'What we call memory today is not memory but already history. The so-called rekindling of memory is actually its final flicker as it is consumed by history's flame,' he writes, arguing that modern 'memory' has ceased to be social, spontaneously lived or magical.[13] No longer 'rooted' in daily practices or shared beliefs, memory has retreated into the domain of individual psychologies, giving way in the public realm to something much more wilful, deliberate, archival and disenchanted: history.

For Nora, 'true' (or traditional) memory 'lives in the warmth of tradition', but history is cold, staged, artificial and documented.[14] Once the province of professional historians alone – men such as Thierry and Guizot, who contributed so much to the nineteenth-century consolidation of a French 'memory/nation' – the cancerous growth of history has now thoroughly overtaken memory. In the late twentieth century, history 'terrorizes' the last shards of memory. 'The ambition of the historian', Nora ominously claims, 'is not to exalt what actually happened, but to annihilate it.'[15] History, for Nora, is an avenging force ('our substitute for imagination'). Contrived and orchestrated, it is a compulsive activity that attempts futilely to plug the gaps left in society by the passing of time, the coming of modernity and the very practice of history itself. Pierre Nora – the historian – makes history seem, if not an impossible profession, at least a highly undesirable one.

The stated aim of *Les Lieux de mémoire* is to study France as a reality that is 'entirely symbolic', but the project expresses an unmistakable yearning for some lost time when those symbols fit together unproblematically, when a symbolic reality might be as good as any other. Nora's insistence on the difference between history and memory recalls other nostalgia-tinged binaries of French intellectual debate. Like Rousseau's division of artificial urban spectacles from meaningful village festivals, or Lévi-Strauss' distinction of 'engineering' from 'tinkering' (*bricolage*), or Proust's delineation of voluntary and involuntary memory, Nora's account privileges the second, ostensibly more natural, term.[16] Indeed, he gestures quite specifically at Rousseau's villagers and Lévi-Strauss' 'savages' when he refers longingly to 'the kind of inviolate social memory that primitive and archaic societies embodied, and whose secret died with them'.[17]

The failure of French memory is, for Nora, partially a historical problem, one that dates from 'the crisis of the 1930s'. The decade of republicanism's struggles with fascism and communism and of the Great Depression initiated an ongoing process that was further accelerated by the economic boom of the 1950s and 1960s. Yet if it is historically specific, the death of memory is also, for Nora, historiographically driven: 'Historiography begins when history sets itself the task of uncovering that in itself which is not history, of showing itself to be the victim of memory and seeking to free itself from memory's grip.'[18] Nora accuses the 'new social history' of the 1960s and 1970s of encouraging an ironic attitude toward once iconic moments of national history. When historians began to read school manuals, such as Lavisse's history textbooks of the 1890s, not as repositories of basic facts but as tools in the Third Republic's campaign to make peasants into Frenchmen, then 'historiography sows doubt; it runs the blade of a knife between the heartwood of memory and the bark of history'.[19]

For all the pathos, there is something disingenuous about these comments on social history's rereading of Lavisse: in 1962, it was Nora himself who published a study of how Lavisse's editorial activities contributed to building the French nationalism of the Third Republic.[20] Mourning memory, and yet gesturing toward his own, early, not-to-be-forgotten work as a prime instance of the 'iconoclastic and irreverent' historiography that destroyed it, Nora tears down one monument in order to erect a new one. As others have noted, *Les Lieux de mémoire* thereby ends up a memorial itself, its volumes just as much a part of national mythmaking as was Lavisse's *Histoire de France*.[21] The year 1848 emerges from this encyclopedic analysis, however, as a definite mnemonic non-lieu. Despite the collaboration of Maurice Agulhon, France's most respected historian of the Second Republic, the Revolution of 1848 barely figures at all in *Les Lieux de mémoire*.

Between 'the great Revolution' of 1789 and the Commune of 1871, 1848 appears only in so far as it resembles another 'generational' conflict that Nora describes as having no real reason to happen: 1968.[22] A long historiographical tradition supports Nora's evocation of 1848 as an effect with no cause, but even if we were to accept that 1848 in France was an accident we would not be obliged to conclude that it therefore was not a significant site of memory.[23] The simple fact that an event has not been strategically planned in advance does not necessarily imply that it cannot be remembered – just as strategically – in hindsight. (Conspiracy theorists aside, no one thinks that the car crash in which Princess Diana died was premeditated; it is, however, emphatically remembered.)

To read *Les Lieux de mémoire*, it would seem that in the French context, at least, nothing crystallizes around 1848. Yet Daniel Pick has suggested that it was the very experience of 1848 that made 'inheritance' into a crucial issue for nineteenth-century French science and politics and Raymond Aron thought the legacy of 1848 comparable in mnemonic weight to that of the Resistance.[24] Nora, in contrast, ignores the Second Republic in order to privilege the early years of the Third Republic as the key moment for the formation of 'Republican memory'. He insists, as well, on the significant contributions made by the Restoration and July Monarchy to 'national memory,' but 1848's memories qualify as neither 'national' nor 'republican'.[25]

Difficult to fit into the chronological infrastructure of *Les Lieux de mémoire*, the revolution of 1848 also crucially challenges Nora's analytic distinction between history and memory. For it has long been a commonplace that it was the memories of 1789 that moved French people to make history in 1848. According to the historians involved with Lavisse's collaborative *Histoire de France*, the events of 1848 had an ambivalent relation to the past. In the 1840s, the Revolution of 1789 was a source of inspiration – 'the memories that mattered, that thrilled and excited the French people...were memories that took them back to the time of the Revolution and the Empire' – but it was also shrouded in 'legends and memories of a time they barely understood, a time of assignats and guillotines'.[26] Nora (and others) have belittled Lavisse's early twentieth-century history as the epitome of Third Republic positivism, of nationalism passing for historical science, but these accounts of memory's role in the outbreak of mid-century revolution demonstrate a far more nuanced understanding of how history is made. Indeed, they suggest that the omission of 1848 from an inventory of French memory can hardly be accidental. Rather, the revolutionaries of 1848, who *both* revived the songs, language and costumes of 1789 *and* marked significant differences between their regime and the earlier one, demonstrate that history can be made (and become part of people's genuine, even shared, memories) in the act of remembering.

If we accept Nora's memory/history binary, we might argue that what I have just called 'memories' are better termed 'histories', that singing *La Marseillaise*, waving a tricolour flag or dating correspondence 'Year Fifty-Five of the Republican Calendar' were not acts entrenched in 'genuine' memory but the unanticipated side effects of a political culture steeped in revolutionary grandeur. Indeed, this perspective is almost standard in discussions of 1848, which has often been troped as a repeat, an ersatz, in some accounts an outright phony, revolution. This sentiment was most famously expressed in the opening sentences of Marx's *Eighteenth Brumaire of Louis Bonaparte* ('Hegel remarks somewhere that all facts and personages of great importance in world history occur, as it were, twice. He forgot to add: the first time as tragedy, the second as farce'), but it is easy to find other instances of it.[27] For example, in the popular-history series, 'Thirty Days That Made France', the volume dedicated to the February Revolution is entitled *The Republic's First Resurrection*; in Flaubert's *Sentimental Education,* often considered 'the' novel of 1848 in France, one character imitates 'Blanqui, who in turn imitated Robespierre' and another becomes a famous actor thanks to a sequence of interchangeable roles in which he participates in a series of identically scripted revolutions.[28]

Like Marx and Flaubert, Alexis de Tocqueville was drawn to theatrical conceits. Commenting on the events in the Chamber of Deputies on 24 February, he wrote: 'The whole time I had the feeling we had staged a play about the French Revolution, rather than that we were continuing it . . . we tried without success to warm ourselves at the hearth of our fathers' passions; their gestures and attitudes as seen on the stage were imitated, but their enthusiasm could not be copied.'[29] De Tocqueville, who was a member of the July Monarchy Chamber of Deputies and of the Second Republic's Legislative Assembly (and its Constitutional Committee), as well as Minister of Foreign Affairs in 1849–50, was present for many of the 1848 revolution's key moments. Yet even the most passionate descriptions in his *Souvenirs* (*Recollections*) have an odd dissociated quality to them, as if these were not really his own memories or actions that he was recording. De Tocqueville's sense throughout is one of melancholia, despair, emptiness.

Yearning for 1789, when revolution was real and people acted spontaneously, de Tocqueville found 1848 a makeshift stage with second-rate actors. Inspired by the poet-politician Lamartine (whose *History of the Girondins* was one of four major histories of the Great Revolution to be published in 1847–8), the men around him formed political groupings named after those of 1793 and decreed that 'we should all wear the dress of members of the Convention, in particular the white waistcoat with turned-down collar always worn by actors playing Robespierre'.[30] De Tocqueville alternately pities and mocks those who try to imitate the revolution but it is important to note that his attitude toward them did not derive from any personal experience of that earlier revolution. For, like so many participants in 1848, while de Tocqueville had personal memories of the revolution of 1830 (which had brought Louis Philippe to the throne) he had been born too late (1805) to have many of the Great Revolution. Nonetheless, de Tocqueville insisted that what he saw happening around him was a sort of fiction, while what he had read about in books – and doubtless heard about from his parents – was reality. De Tocqueville's critique of 1848 thereby strikingly parallels Nora's understanding of the relationship of history to memory. The February Revolution for de Tocqueville was – like Nora's definition of 'history' – cold, staged, calculated, an attempt to re-create something earlier, older and irretrievably lost.

In the *Recollections*, 1789 and 1848 are related as reality is to stage-play, as meaningful political debate is to idle cultural activity. For the 14 years prior to 1848, however, strict censorship and severe laws against association had meant that political intervention in France had nearly always been obliged to stage itself as something other than what it was.[31] Elections and putative debate occasioned far less excitement than the trials of journalists and the holding of banquets; political cartoons that were easily interpreted (at least by some readers) had to be replaced with increasingly obscure caricatures.[32] De Tocqueville's pet binary of audience and actors had been deliberately blurred by some of the most popular performances of July Monarchy boulevard theatre: Frédérick Lemaître's famously ad-libbed performances as the scoundrel Robert Macaire made a conventionally pious melodrama, *L'Auberge des Adrets*, into a vehicle for political and social commentary.[33] Hoping to capitalize on this success, other playwrights wrote impromptu scenes into their own texts. For example, in *Les Cabinets particuliers* (1832), the plot is repeatedly interrupted by a man in the balcony who says that he is the real-life husband of the starring actress.[34] Since he categorically refuses to allow her to play a love scene with a dashing young actor, he is eventually himself offered the leading male role. Stumbling into the prompter's pit, misreading his lines, singing tunes other than those played by the orchestra, the irate-husband character ('Jacquard, manufacturer of phosphorous matches') was a not uncommon instance of scripted improvisation.

A similar logic informed the era's best-known organized political activities: the reform banquets of 1840 and 1847–8. Only legal because they were nominally private, sociable and friendly functions (read: 'drunken'), banquets slipped through a loophole in the 1834 Law on Association.[35] This law had made governmental approval obligatory for all regularly organized meetings and had imposed harsh fines and jail sentences on anyone who belonged to an unauthorized group, but purely convivial, single-occasion gatherings had been explicitly exempted from the legislation. In order to be legal, reform meetings therefore took the form of dinner parties (hence further intervening in the rhetoric of fat and lean that so structured French political culture in the first half of the nineteenth century). Scripted so as to appear spontaneous – an obligation that required organizers to send 'invitations' to all those attending – the banquets of the July Monarchy were only politically effective because of their avowed distance from official political life.

De Tocqueville's critique of 1848 relies on differentiating copies from originals, farces from dramas and actors from audience in a way that had been, frankly, almost unthinkable in July Monarchy culture. In his *Recollections,* de Tocqueville's insistent and emphatic framing of the events of February 1848 as mere playacting provides a way to control and dismiss them; his *Souvenirs* patrol the frontiers between real history (including his memories of the performance) and something that has been made up, something that is only a fiction. 'A vile tragedy played by a provincial troupe', he wrote, ever faithful to his conceit.[36] But is not a play the thing, to catch the conscience of a king? After all, even in his own memoirs, de Tocqueville could not fully control the relation between reality and representation. In the margins of his manuscript, de Tocqueville remarked that his wife had found the passage beginning 'the whole time I had the feeling we had staged a play' laboured, forced and unpersuasive; in order to make this account of playacting more compelling, he planned to rewrite it and instructed himself to emphasize 'the imitation and the frigidity resulting therefrom'.[37] For all his aspirations to the original, then, it was by *re*vising, *re*writing, and *re*copying those pages that de Tocqueville hoped to bring them to life.

De Tocqueville's theatrical metaphors are pervasive and complex. Their frequency alone offers sufficient reason to note them, but they do more than structure his *Recollections.* They also inform de Tocqueville's understanding of the Old Regime and the Revolution of 1789 – an analysis he only began to formulate in the years following Louis Napoleon's 1851 coup and his own subsequent retirement from political life. Throughout most of de Tocqueville's adult life, eighteenth-century history and the outbreak of the revolution had admittedly been subjects of passionate study and research – for his father. Not Alexis, but Hervé de Tocqueville had written a *Philosophical*

History of the Reign of Louis XV and published a *Survey of the Reign of Louis XVI*.[38] Alexis de Tocqueville, himself, came only indirectly to the study of the Old Regime. In the aftermath of Napoleon III's declaration of the Second Empire, de Tocqueville was struck (as were many others) by the parallels between the events of 1789–1804 and those of 1848–51. In both instances, a revolution had culminated in a republic that then was taken over by a Bonaparte: in order to understand this pattern, de Tocqueville, *fils,* envisioned a study focusing on the First Empire. But he quickly concluded that it would be impossible to comprehend the period of Napoleon's political leadership without first studying the regime under which the young general had won so many impressive victories and turned so many heads. De Tocqueville therefore undertook an analysis of the Directory (1795–9) but this, too, seemed inadequate, for it could not be so easily separated from the remainder of the revolutionary era. By 1852, de Tocqueville's projected study of the First Empire (1804–15) began in 1789; one more step backward in time brought him to write *The Old Regime and the French Revolution* – a book that notoriously has nothing whatsoever to say about the revolution itself.[39] De Tocqueville's route to the Old Regime was a path of regression and a search for pure origins.

To any reader, it is evident that de Tocqueville's account of the Old Regime differs radically from his version of 1848. De Tocqueville, usually credited with the first sociological analysis of the revolution of 1789, wrote a largely narrative memoir of 1848. Full of stirringly described events and bitingly adept character sketches, the *Recollections* has little in common stylistically with *The Old Regime and the French Revolution.* Yet if style, subject matter and even the method and extent of research separate de Tocqueville's Second Republic from his Old Regime, a sense of disengagement from 'real life' pervades them both. Recall, for instance, that de Tocqueville traced the excesses of the Great Revolution to the predominant role played in it by men of letters, lawyers and aristocrats: centralizing absolutism had stripped these men of a meaningful place in Old Regime public life, but it had left them the leisure and learning to busy themselves with debating the errors of government. These men, in de Tocqueville's depiction, could have only the most abstract and literary notions of politics because they had had no real experience of it, and it was this purely theoretical knowledge that proved so dangerous:

When one studies the history of our Revolution, one sees that it was guided by the same spirit that produced so many books of abstractions. One finds the same fondness for general theories, complete legal systems, and exactly symmetrical laws and the same scorn for actual facts. There is the same confidence in grand theories, the same taste for originality, novelty, and ingenuity. . . . It is a terrifying spectacle! For what may be a great talent in a writer can be a horrible vice for a statesman.[40]

The men of 1789 had no more idea of what they were 'really' doing than did the men of 1848 (unlike the drafters of the American Constitution).[41] The *Recollections'* pervasive theatre metaphors, then, are much more than a fruitful conceit suggested by the accident of Lamartine's personal gift for dramatic posturing or by the emptiness of quarante-huitard rhetoric. Rather, they are fundamentally linked to de Tocqueville's broader understanding of the workings of centralization.[42] Already in 1842, he had written that members of 'the public' reacted to world events as if they were in a theatre; the experience of 1848 may have reinforced this sensibility but it did not create it.[43] Theatricality, understood as a sense of disengaged spectatorship, may well be a common feature of modern life, but the revolutionaries of '48 cannot be held responsible for it.[44]

When the centennial of the February Revolution came to be celebrated in 1948, the language of playacting and farce returned again. This time, it was the French Communist Party that protested: the commemoration could hardly be genuine as long as it was orchestrated by 'a banker and a fascist'.[45] Celebrating 100 years of universal suffrage (rather awkwardly, as French women had become members of that 'universe' in 1946) and 99 years of French postage stamps, the centenary was inaugurated with formal ceremonies in February. On the 22nd, Vincent Auriol and Pierre de Gaulle (presidents, respectively, of the French Fourth Republic and of the Paris City Council – 'a banker and a fascist') visited the Place de la Bastille. Auriol laid a wreath on the graves of those who died in the streetfighting of February 1848 (in March 1848, their bodies had been added to those of the Parisians killed in the Three Glorious Days of the July Revolution of 1830). At the Hôtel de Ville, a liberty tree (artificial, according to the Communists) was planted but most other ceremonies had to be curtailed in light of the 15 centimetres of snow that had fallen on

Paris in that 24-hour period. A concert, featuring works by Bee-thoven and Chopin, and a lecture series at the Sorbonne concluded the first weekend's official celebrations which were boycotted by Communist Party deputies and city councillors.

Throughout the spring months, 1848 was further remembered, but it shared a crowded commemorative calendar with the hundredth anniversary of Chateaubriand's death, the three hundredth annivers-ary of the Treaty of Westphalia and other such events. In late April, the Bibliothèque Nationale's display noting that it had been a hun-dred years since the birth of the 'decadent' poet Huysmans gave way to a sizable exhibition about 1848. The most famous item displayed, Delacroix's *Liberty Guiding the People*, dated from the 1830 revolution that had brought Louis Philippe to the throne rather than the later one that had chased him from it, but the exhibition's April opening was timed to coincide almost exactly with the unambiguously happy anniversary of slavery's abolition in the French colonies (definitively decreed on 27 April 1848).[46] Once that had been remembered, though, the commemoration of 1848 was largely complete. The dead of the June Days were cursorily honoured by the Fourth Republic as part of its celebration of 'springtime, work and youth', and the Communist Party noted them in celebrating the hundredth anni-versary of the first French edition of the *Communist Manifesto*.

Writing in 1939, the historian, art historian and Hispanist, Jean Cassou, had asserted that the ideals of 1848 were easily mocked because they had been made official under the Third Republic.[47] Uni-versal manhood suffrage, a free press, accessible education and an official anti-clericalism: so many of 1848's most 'romantic' and idealistic ambitions had been realized since 1875. Yet these accom-plishments seemed saccharine, best suited to school prize award ceremonies; by 1939, the regime's detractors had become more vocal and visible, if not more numerous, than its adherents. Attacked by monarchists and Communists, riddled with corruption, and seem-ingly incapable of dealing with economic or foreign-policy crises, the Third Republic of the 1930s bore only the vaguest resemblance to an embodiment of revolutionary ideals.[48] In a postwar referendum, the French had voted overwhelmingly to end the Third Republic and replace it with a new regime. Once the French Communist Party had been voted down, shouted out and excluded from government, however, the constitution of the new Fourth Republic bore a striking resemblance to that of the Third.[49] Honouring the ideals of 1848 while attempting to distance themselves from the Third Republic that had brought those ideals to fruition, the commemorators of 1948 faced a conundrum: how to conjure the spirit of '48 without also summoning the ghost of 1940 and Vichy? When a historian termed 1848 'a living source – pure, generous, and abundant', the revolution was made to sound suspiciously like a mineral water.[50] When Minister of Education Depreux was reported as saying that 'the Second Republic asked wonderful questions, it is up to the Fourth to answer them', one could not help but wonder what the Third Republic had done.[51]

Edouard Herriot, president of the National Assembly and, at the age of 76, grand old man of the Radical Party, could maintain that 'the Republic's number does not matter' but stirring pronouncements only partially compensated for an underlying uneasiness: if the Republic's number did not matter, then surely the Fourth was as much the product of the discredited Third as of the glorious Second?[52] Albert Camus, writing in the Resistance newspaper, *Combat*, immediately after the Liberation of Paris (August 1944), had stated that 'the old France, the regime of boutiques and legislative banquets, is gone and should not be revived' and there had been widespread, non-partisan support for this position.[53] But banquets, of some form or other, were the most obvious emblem of 1848 and they played a prominent part in the commemorations of 1948. In mid-May, Auriol's calendar was devoted to a recreation of the Mâcon banquet of July 1847. While the original had been not an electioneering but a reforming banquet, and while it was most famous for the thunderstorm that had nearly brought the tentpoles down on Lamartine's head, the iconography of 1948 was almost identical with that of the Third Republic's famous mayors' banquets of 1889 and 1900. (Unsurprisingly, the Communist Party revived the critique made in 1848 by republican radicals: the only thing real about a political banquet was the food.)

Throughout the centenary spring, writers across the political spectrum demonstrated breathtaking ingenuity in explaining 1848's relevance to the world of a hundred years later. Sartre's *Les Temps modernes* intimated that 1848 was most significant as an object lesson in how military dictators came to power and juxtaposed a courtier's tribute to Napoleon III with a letter supporting Charles de

Gaulle.[54] Pierre de Gaulle shared *Les Temps modernes'* fear of a new despotism, but cast the Soviet Union in the villain's role rather than his brother.[55] The Communist Party daily, *L'Humanité*, meanwhile, emphasized that the Fourth Republic was like the July Monarchy in having no independent policies and being the puppet of an international syndicate of 'Jews and capitalists'.[56] Twice in February, *L'Humanité's* front page reproduced Daumier's topical caricatures of one hundred years earlier (including one of Robert Macaire), such that the corruption of the July Monarchy was brought to comment on the extreme inflation in food prices that structured the postwar economy.[57] A writer for *Le Monde* offered an extensive and unexpected analogy: he saw the Soviet Union since 1917 and France of the Restoration and July Monarchy as two comparable instances of an accelerated, state-managed transition to capitalism that had dire consequences for individual liberties and personal freedoms.[58]

A striking variety of morals could be derived from the history of 1848. Yet despite the apparent divergence, there was widespread agreement that matters of foreign policy were paramount. France's colonial legacy was, unsurprisingly, important to this analysis. While the Communist Party saw decolonization as the only logical follow-up to the Second Republic's abolition of slavery, David Rousset pleaded that France's foreign policy should focus rather on slavery's continued existence – in the form of the Soviet gulags.[59] Rousset's argument demonstrates that European politics, even more than colonial questions, bore the brunt of 1948's analogies. Showing themselves all equally good students of Lavisse's *Histoire de la France contemporaine* (with its strong emphasis on military, diplomatic and political histories), Communists, Gaullists, Socialists and neutralists agreed that Louis Philippe's pacifist foreign policy had done much to prepare the way for 1848.[60] According to André Maurois, France under the July Monarchy had not been badly governed but it had been disappointed; accustomed by the Revolution and Empire to years of glory, the French people found Louis Philippe's pacifism dismal and dreary while his minister, Guizot, first tied French foreign policy too closely to Britain and then supported the arch-conservative Metternich in his attacks on the 'liberal' pope, Pius IX.[61] Only the aged Léon Blum, visibly weakened by his years in Vichy's prisons and loudly heckled for his role in negotiating the Blum-Byrnes Agreement with the United States, suggested in his lecture at the

Sorbonne that Louis Philippe's dedication to peace had had anything noble or decent to recommend it.[62] The king, according to Blum, had been motivated by his own memories of the Revolution's wars; having fought at Jemappes, Louis Philippe understood the human costs of glory only too well. Bravely aligning himself with the 'woman's perspective', Blum declared that 'French mothers today' knew Louis Philippe had been right, but in the 1840s 'our fathers' had wanted war. When, in December 1848, those belligerent men elected Louis Bonaparte president of the Second Republic, they were voting for war.[63]

In late winter 1948 – when the Marshall Plan was being ratified by the United States Congress and the Prague coup had made Czechoslovakia into a Soviet satellite – international affairs offered the most compelling interpretative framework for arguments about 1848. Yet debate rarely touched on the question of whether the revolution of that year had been European in nature. Rather, it was exclusively the French revolution of 1848 that was mined for relevant 'lessons': the very handsome *Livre du centenaire* was over 300 pages long, but a mere dozen of those were devoted to Georges Bourgin's discussion of '1848 in Europe'. Even the Peace of Westphalia – the commemoration of which had been funded by the same unanimous vote of the National Assembly that agreed to celebrate the anniversary of 1848 – was remembered not as the end of Europe's Thirty Years War but as the beginning of France's annexation of Alsace.[64] Commemorations were conducted in 'lieux' made distinctively 'French'.

A comment in Vincent Auriol's presidential diary brings together this paper's two themes in a poignant and telling fashion. While in Mâcon for the Lamartine 'Anniversary Banquet', Auriol made what he intended to be a major speech on foreign policy. His intentions fell on largely deaf ears, however, for the speech received far less attention than he had anticipated. 'The press', he wrote, 'dedicates all its pages to Princess Elizabeth – which is very good – and to *faits divers*. But they do not give my speech the place it deserves. Journalists are not interested in foreign affairs and public opinion, of course, follows them. It is all *panem et circenses*. Frightening! When the fate of humanity is at stake.'[65]

Auriol's remarks were based on the distinction of 'real life' from 'spectacle' that also structured Nora's and de Tocqueville's analyses (and that constitutes one of modernity's commonplaces). Yet why did he condone the columns devoted to Princess Elizabeth, whose slate-blue, ottoman-silk coatdress seems an unlikely player in the deciding of humanity's fate? Her dinner at the embassy, her dinner at the Tour d'Argent – were these not just so much bread (for the princess) and circuses (for public opinion)?[66] In Paris to attend the opening of an exhibition celebrating 'Eight Hundred Years of British Life in Paris', Elizabeth was, however, participating in a commemoration, a spectacle staged for a purpose. If the exact significance of 1148 for 'British Life in Paris' was lost on many, if not all, observers (just who, we might well ask, was 'British' in the twelfth century?), few could help but notice that the heir to the British throne had made Paris the site of her first official state visit. Princess Elizabeth's itinerary in Paris, like Auriol's speech in Mâcon, was an intervention in Cold War state spectacle in a way that the local *faits divers* of murder, suicide and men who bit dogs could not be.

Still, such 'diversions' have often played a significant role in French history.[67] In the realm dismissed by Vincent Auriol as entertainment, all sorts of unlikely, hitherto nameless, people may take centre stage. Sufficiently remembered – but who is to judge 'sufficiency'? – a *fait divers* may become a cause célèbre, perhaps even something to be commemorated. Jean Cassou, whose contributions to the historiography of 1848 in France are both among the smartest and the most forgotten, knew this when he wrote that it was by means of the newspaper feuilleton that poverty and misery entered French political life.[68] Cassou's sensitivity to the role played by the newspaper press, feuilleton literature and Daumier's caricatures demonstrates that literature and theatre can be understood by the historian as an engagement with history and not a diversion from it. Commemorations and revolutions, no matter how theatrical and staged they may feel, need not be understood as mere afterthoughts.

Notes

1 J.-P. Rioux, 'La mémoire collective', in J.-P. Rioux and J.-F. Sirinelli (eds), *Pour une histoire culturelle* (Paris: Seuil, 1997), pp. 325–55; R. Terdiman, *Present Past: Modernity and the Memory Crisis* (Ithaca, NY: Cornell University Press, 1993); T. Todorov, 'The abuses of memory', trans. M. Lin Chang, *Common Knowledge*, 5:1 (spring 1996), pp. 6–26.

2   H. Rousso, *The Vichy Syndrome*, trans. A. Goldhammer (Cambridge: Harvard University Press, 1991); E. Conan and H. Rousso, *Vichy, un passé qui ne passe pas* (Paris: Fayard, 1994).

3   S. Freud, 'Recollection, Repetition and Working Through' (1914), in *Collected Papers*, trans. J. Rivière (New York: Basic Books, 1959), vol. 2, pp. 366–75; for some suggestive comments on how historians might make use of these concepts, see D. LaCapra, *Representing the Holocaust: History, Theory, and Trauma* (Ithaca, NY: Cornell University Press, 1994), especially chapters 1–2.

4   S. Englund, 'The ghost of a nation past' (review of P. Nora, ed., *Les Lieux de mémoire*), *Journal of Modern History*, 64 (June 1992), 299–320; F. Hartog, 'Temps et histoire: "Comment écrire l'histoire de France?"', *Annales: Histoire, Sciences Sociales*, 50: 6 (November–December 1995), 1219–36; G. Flynn (ed.), *Remaking the Hexagon: The New France in the New Europe* (Boulder, CO: Westview Press, 1995), part one, 'The weight of history in France today'. R. Gildea's *The Past in French History* (New Haven, CT: Yale University Press, 1994) emphasizes the existence of competing political cultures of memory, but it too focuses exclusively on France. For a critique of the notion that memory and history are particularly Gallic issues (or, even, necessarily national ones), see J. M. Winter, *Sites of Memory, Sites of Mourning* (Cambridge: Cambridge University Press, 1995) which argues for the profound effects of the First World War on *European* culture and memory.

5   P. Péan, *Une jeunesse française: François Mitterrand, 1934–1947* (Paris: Fayard, 1994).

6   L. Aubrac, *Outwitting the Gestapo*, trans. K. Bieber and B. Wing (Lincoln: University of Nebraska Press, 1994); E. Carlès, *A Life of Her Own: A Countrywoman in Twentieth-Century France*, trans. A. Goldberger (New Brunswick, NJ: Rutgers University Press, 1991).

7   D. Looseley, *The Politics of Fun: Cultural Policy and Debate in Contemporary France* (Oxford: Berg, 1995), especially chapters 6, 9, 10.

8   J. Lang, 'La Guerre du goût n'aura pas lieu' and J. Puisais, 'L'Eveil au goût dans les écoles', both in *Revue des deux mondes*, January 1993. Two recent works that do more to mythologize gastronomy than to analyse it are J.-R. Pitte, *Gastronomie française, histoire et géographie d'une passion* (Paris: Fayard, 1991) and P. Ory, 'La Gastronomie', in P. Nora (ed.), *Les Lieux de mémoire* (Paris: Gallimard, 1984–92), part 3, vol. 2, *Les France: Traditions* (1992), pp. 823–53.

9   P. Nora (ed.), *Les Lieux de mémoire* (Paris: Gallimard, 1984–92) now partially available in an English translation, L. Kritzman (ed.), *Realms of Memory: Rethinking the French Past*, trans. A. Goldhammer (New York: Columbia University Press, 1996). References are to the English-language edition unless otherwise noted.

10 P. Nora, introduction to *Realms of Memory*, p. xv.

11 Ibid., p. xxiv.

12 B. Anderson, *Imagined Communities*, revised edn (London: Verso, 1991).

13 P. Nora, 'Between memory and history,' *Realms of Memory*, p. 8.
14 Ibid.
15 Ibid., p. 3. Nora's 'memory/nation' refers to a specific turn-of-the century constellation in which personal and social memories, academic history and nationalism all supported each other 'symbiotically' (p. 5). The post-war weakness of the Third Republic was both the cause of, and an effect of, the collapse of this synthesis.
16 C. Lévi-Strauss, *The Savage Mind* (Chicago: University of Chicago Press, 1966), chapter 1; Terdiman, *Present Past*; C. V. McDonald, *The Proustian Fabric; Associations of Memory* (Lincoln: University of Nebraska Press, 1991); J.-J. Rousseau, *Politics and the Arts. Letter to M. d'Alembert on the Theatre*, ed. and trans. A. Bloom (Ithaca, NY: Cornell University Press, 1968); on the preoccupations shared by these authors, see J. Boon, *From Symbolism to Structuralism: Lévi-Strauss in a Literary Tradition* (New York: Harper & Row, 1972) and *Other Tribes, Other Scribes* (Cambridge: Cambridge University Press, 1982), chapter 7.
17 Nora, *Realms of Memory*, p. 2; for an extended analysis of the ways in which the history/memory binary is complicit with projects of colonialism, see E. Ezra, 'The Identification of Difference' (PhD diss., Cornell University, 1992).
18 Ibid., p. 4.
19 Ibid.; Nora also briefly discusses Lavisse's work in his 'Preface to the English-language edition', p. xix. In a now classic work, E. Weber highlighted the role of mandatory education as well as military service and improved transportation networks in making *Peasants into Frenchmen: The Modernization of Rural France, 1870–1914* (Stanford, CA: Stanford University Press, 1976). His account fits well with Nora's sense of a schematic break between peasant traditions and national history; a more nuanced vision is offered by J. Lehning, *Peasant and French: Cultural Contact in Rural France during the Nineteenth Century* (Cambridge: Cambridge University Press, 1995).
20 His 'Ernest Lavisse: son rôle dans la formation du sentiment national' appeared in the July–September 1962 issue of *La Revue historique* and is one of the two essays by Nora in the first volume of *Lieux de mémoire*.
21 Englund, 'The ghost of a nation past'; L. Valensi, 'Histoire nationale, Histoire monumentale', *Annales*, 50: 6 (November–December 1995), 1271–7.
22 Agulhon wrote the articles on 'The center and the periphery', 'Paris' and 'The Townhall' (*La Mairie*); Nora briefly compares 1848 and 1968 in 'La Génération'.
23 Historians who have treated 1848 as France's 'accidental' revolution include: G. Duveau, *1848, The Making of a Revolution*, trans. Anne Carter (New York: Random House, 1967), pp. 8–9; P. Stearns, *1848: The Revolutionary Tide in Europe* (New York: Norton, 1974), p. 71.
24 D. Pick, *Faces of Degeneration* (Cambridge: Cambridge University Press, 1989), pp. 45–50, 56–9; R. Aron, *Le Figaro*, 4 March 1948, p. 1. Aron also

argued that 1848 was the episode in nineteenth-century history most relevant to twentieth-century life, because both had seen a three-way conflict between liberal democrats, socialists (communists) and Bonapartists (fascists). See his 'The sociologists and the revolution of 1848', chapter 5 of his *Main Currents in Sociological Thought,* trans. R. Howard and H. Weaver (Harmondsworth: Penguin Books, 1968).

25 Nora, 'Présentation', *Les Lieux de mémoire,* vol. 2: 1, *La Nation* (pp. 571, 576 in Quarto edition)

26 E. Lavisse (ed.), *Histoire de la France contemporaine,* vol. 5, S. Charlèty, *La Monarchie de juillet* (Paris: Hachette, 1921), p. 403; ibid., vol. 6, Ch. Seignobos, *La Révolution de 1848 – Le Second Empire* (Paris: Hachette, 1921), p. 17.

27 K. Marx, *The Eighteenth Brumaire of Louis Bonaparte* (New York: International Publishers, 1963), p. 15.

28 H. Guillemin, *La Première résurrection de la République* (Paris: Gallimard, 1967); G. Flaubert, *Sentimental Education,* trans. R. Baldick (Harmondsworth: Penguin, 1964), pp. 177, 301.

29 A. de Tocqueville, *Recollections,* eds J. P. Mayer and A. P. Kerr, trans. G. Lawrence (London: Macdonald, 1970), p. 53.

30 Ibid., p. 100.

31 H. A. C. Collingham, with R. S. Alexander, *The July Monarchy* (London: Longman, 1988), pp. 157–85.

32 J. Cuno, 'Charles Philipon and la Maison Aubert: The Business, Politics and Public of Caricature in Paris, 1820–1840' (PhD diss., Harvard University, 1985); R. J. Goldstein, *Censorship of Political Caricature in Nineteenth-Century France* (Kent, OH: Kent State University Press, 1989); R. Terdiman, *Discourse/Counter-Discourse* (Ithaca, NY: Cornell University Press, 1985).

33 J. McCormick, *Popular Theatres of Nineteenth-Century France* (London: Routledge, 1993), pp. 106–7.

34 Xavier and Duvert, *Les Cabinets particuliers* (Paris: Barba, 1832).

35 See my '"La Fronde des nappes": fat and lean rhetoric in the political banquets of 1847', in Carroll Coates (ed.), *Repression and Expression: Literary and Social Coding in Nineteenth-Century France* (New York: Peter Lang, 1996), pp. 167–81, and *The Invention of the Restaurant: Paris and Modern Gastronomic Culture* (Cambridge: Harvard University Press, 2000).

36 De Tocqueville, *Recollections,* p. 53.

37 Ibid.

38 R. R. Palmer, *The Two Tocquevilles* (Princeton, NJ: Princeton University Press, 1987).

39 Ibid., p. 148.

40 A. de Tocqueville, *L'Ancien régime et la révolution* (Paris: Flammarion, 1988), p. 238.

41 *Recollections,* p. 168.

42 Of the members of the Constituent Assembly, he wrote that some had been deputies or peers under the July Monarchy, but 'all the others...

were complete novices, just as if we had stepped straight out of the Ancien Régime; for our centralization had always kept public life limited to the boundaries of the two Chambers...', *Recollections*, p. 101.

43 A. de Tocqueville,'Lettres sur la situation intérieure', *Oeuvres*, ed. André Jardin (Paris: Gallimard Bibliothèque de la Pléiade, 1991), p. 1109.

44 G. Debord, *Society of the Spectacle* (Detroit, MI: Black & Red, 1983).

45 'Ils avancent la Mi-Carême', *L'Humanité*, 14 February 1948, p. 2.

46 *Le Monde*, 23 April 1948, p. 8. On 28 April 1998 (p. 17), *Le Monde* reprinted its 28 April 1948 (p. 4) tribute to Victor Schoelcher, the reformer who had argued most vigorously for abolition.

47 J. Cassou, *Quarante-huit* (Paris: Gallimard, 1939), p. 6.

48 P. Bernard and H. Dubieuf, *The Decline of the Third Republic*, trans. Anthony Forster (Cambridge: Cambridge University Press, 1985).

49 M. Larkin, *France since the Popular Front* (Oxford: Clarendon, 1988), chapter 8.

50 '...notre source vivante, pure, abondante, généreuse', Jean Cassou, 'Préface', in Charles Moulin (ed.), *1848, le Livre du centenaire* (Paris: Atlas, 1948), p. xi.

51 'La Quatrième République n'oublie pas ce qu'il doit à la Deuxième', *Le Figaro*, 25 February 1948.

52 *Le Populaire de Paris*, 23 February 1948, p. 1.

53 A. Camus, *Combat*, 24 August 1944, quoted in Tony Judt, *Past Imperfect* (Berkeley: University of California Press, 1992), p. 33.

54 *Les Temps modernes*, 3: 27 (1947–8), pp. 1141–50.

55 Speech reported in *Le Figaro*, 24 February 1948, p. 2.

56 J. Bruhat, 'La Monarchie de Juillet: le règne des Rothschilds et consorts', *L'Humanité*, 17 February 1948, p. 2; 'Les Leçons de 1848', *L'Humanité*, 21 February 1948, p. 3; 'Quand les ennemis de la démocratie célèbrent l'anniversaire de la Seconde République', *L'Humanité*, 23 February 1948, p. 2.

57 *L'Humanité*, 17 February 1948, 22–23 February 1948.

58 G. Hourdin, 'Ce qui reste de la révolution de 1848', *Le Monde*, 1 April 1948, p. 3.

59 R. Roure, 'L'Esclavage', *Le Monde*, 29 April 1948, p. 1; Judt, *Past imperfect*, pp. 113–15; Todorov, pp. 19–20.

60 According to Charlèty, after the Egyptian debacle of 1840: 'France had been humiliated and the King was to blame', pp. 294–5; 'in 1848,... Guizot appeared to be the aged Metternich's successor... and the French people's discontent was sharpened by anger and embarassment', pp. 371–2. Marx taught a similar lesson: 'Glory brings no profit!... the France of the Bourse Jews had inscribed on her banner. Her foreign policy was therefore lost in a series of mortifications to French national feeling', Karl Marx, *The Class Struggles in France* (New York: International Publishers, 1964), p. 37.

61 A. Maurois, 'Les Leçons de 1848', *Les Nouvelles littéraires*, 26 February 1948, pp. 1–2; Guizot was similarly reproached in the PCF's analysis, see 'Les Leçons de 1848', *L'Humanité*, 21 February 1948.

62   R. Kuisel, *Seducing the French* (Berkeley: University of California Press, 1993).
63   L. Nadeau, 'L'Anniversaire de la Révolution de 1848', *France illustration*, 6 March 1948, pp. 230–1, includes extracts from Blum's lecture and photographs of the hall.
64   *Le Monde*, 27 April 1948, p. 4; the 1648 'reuniting'(!) of Alsace with France was hailed as a 'masterpiece of Old-Regime politics', *Le Monde*, 26 May 1948, p. 3.
65   V. Auriol, *Journal du septennat*, (eds) E. Mouret and J.-P. Azéma (Paris: Armand Colin, 1974), vol. 2, pp. 229–30.
66   For Elizabeth's wardrobe and schedule of activities during her visit, see *Le Monde*, 13–18 May 1948, *passim*; *The Times*, 13–17 May 1948, *passim*; *L'Humanité*, 13–14 May 1948.
67   S. Maza, *Private Lives and Public Affairs* (Berkeley: University of California Press, 1993); Jacques Revel and A. Farge, *The Rules of Rebellion: Child Abduction in Paris in 1750* (Cambridge: Polity, 1991).
68   Cassou, *Quarante-huit*, pp. 10–28; J. Cassou, *Le Quarante-huitard* (Paris: Presses universitaires de France, 1948), pp. 16–22.

10

'Nationality Separates, Liberty Unites'? The Historical Commemoration of 1848/49 in Baden, a European Frontier Region*

Jan Merk

I

'To the devil with nationality at all, for with it the classical expression "to divide and to reign" has come into being. Nationality separates, liberty unites, that is how it has been always', wrote the poet Georg Herwegh in a March 1863 letter to Ludmilla Assing reflecting on the revolutionary years 1848/49.[1] Herwegh himself had failed to support the first revolt in Baden in the spring of 1848 leading the 'German democratic legion' from Paris via Strasbourg to the Rhine. The leader of the rebellion, Friedrich Hecker, had hesitated to accept foreign help for the fight for liberty and for the creation of a republic in Baden on the assumption that the people would be against it. Herwegh, with his legion consisting predominantly of German craftsmen as well as of republicans of other nations, had crossed the Rhine too late. Hecker's fighters had already been defeated by the military of Baden and Hessia, and Herwegh's legion had to flee from Württembergian troops over the border to Switzerland.[2] In the frontier region of France–Baden–Switzerland the attempt at cooperation between the republicans across the borders had especially failed.

* Translated by Anita Zelasny.

The location of Baden (bordering France and Switzerland), the social structure of the duchy (dominated by the middle classes of the small urban centres) and its democratic tradition (reaching back to the early-modern period) help to explain the strength of its liberal and democratic movements during the years before the Revolution. In the German Federation, Baden, with its constitution of 1818 and the much observed debates in the parliament, was seen as the model liberal *land*. However, in contrast with its neighbouring countries, France and Switzerland, the duchy also had a repressive nature. Writings that were censored in Baden could be printed in Alsace or in the north-west of Switzerland and then smuggled across the border. Craftsmen from Baden, as well as students, traders and farmers, became interested in politics during their training in Switzerland and France. In November 1847 when victory for the democratic cantons in the Swiss Civil War seemed certain, the 'Tagsatzung', as the parliament was then called, received many supportive letters from Baden. They emphasized the transnational importance of the Swiss Civil War. One letter, signed by 227 people, stated that it was 'a fight for the liberty of all, for light and truth; a fight in the name of civilisation and the eternal right of man. For in this connection stands humanity that every piece of land which is conquered on the holy soil of liberty, belongs to all, it is a benefit for all.'[3]

There were in fact stationings of republican troops in France and Switzerland during the revolutionary years, such as August Willich's corps of republicans from Belfort, or the legion of German craftsmen and republican refugees from Switzerland led by Johann Philipp Becker. But what many revolutionists had hoped for, namely official political and military support from republican France and democratic Switzerland for the third revolt in the early summer of 1849 in Baden, failed to materialize. The cooperation of republicans across borders was limited to appeals in newspapers, the collection of money, the purchase of arms, the influx of voluntary fighters and the possibility of an escape route after the repression of the revolution in Baden.[4]

Even less successful than border-crossing activities during the revolution was the forming of common traditions after it. The experiences of 1848/49 had been too diverse, and the future too took individual countries down different paths. Switzerland had adopted a democratic federal constitution. A federal republic replaced the old loose

confederation. Now, consolidation and reconciliation with the conservative counties was on the agenda. In foreign policy the Swiss
Republic needed to hold on to the policy of neutrality to maintain
her position in a Europe determined by newly strengthened monarchies. The federal republic now also took a harder line concerning
the republican refugees, which forced them, despite the threat of
persecution, to return to their home-countries or to emigrate to the
United States.[5] In the Swiss home policy the experience of 1848
strengthened the creation of a myth of the free and independent
nation.[6] In Alsace the revolutionary events of 1848/49 had been
overshadowed by events in the capital Paris. After the suppression of
the June revolt and Louis-Napoleon's election as President, Alsace
revived its bonapartist tradition. Furthermore, the following decades
were burdened by growing power conflict between France and Germany. In comparison to the 'Grand Revolution' in 1789,[7] 1848 had
only a minor impact on the collective memory.

In the German Länder the democratic, republican movement had
suffered a serious defeat. 'A revolution is a tragedy', wrote Heinrich
Heine, warning those who saw the revolution in a romantic light,
'but an even greater tragedy is an unsuccessful revolution.'[8] On this,
the historian Reinhard Rürup commented: 'However great the tragedy of an "unsuccessful" revolution really is, does not only depend
on the counter-revolution but also on the formation of a political
legacy.'[9] The legacy of the 'German Revolution' is fractured and lacking in continuity. Even in Baden the memory of 1848/49 was to a
great extent determined by changing historical interpretations of the
revolution which reflected the various political regimes in Germany.

II

As early as 1851, Ludwig Häusser, a historian from Heidelberg, presented his 'Memoirs of the History of the Revolution in Baden'.[10]
From a liberal perspective and with his research based on extensive
use of documents, he condemned the attitudes of the princely ruled
Länder, as well as the policy of the extreme left during the revolution. His work was a seal on the image of the revolution as a failure.
In the following decades, until the end of the empire in 1918, memoirs above all have been published. In academic historiography, the
memory of the revolution was repressed,[11] and in the archives of the

land Baden at Karlsruhe for instance, many letters of justification
and grounds for certain jurisdictions concerning participants of the
revolution were confiscated from the files of investigation.[12] It seems
that the government of the duchy tried to prevent the future recon-
struction of a more differentiated image of the political motives of
numerous litigants of the insurrections.

Most historical accounts of the revolution in Baden and Germany
aimed 'to convey to the German people the feeling of their political
immaturity, of their incompetence to responsibly shape their own
fate.'[13] From the very beginning 1848 had been called the 'confused
year'. The German national assembly had been presented as an end-
lessly litigating 'Parliament of Professors', lacking the instinct for
power and the capacity for coordination. The violent tactics of the
radicals were denounced.

Scorn and derision about these would-be revolutionaries were not
long in coming. The revolution was played down. A more thorough
consideration of, for instance, the campaign to implement the basic
rights in 1849 did not materialize – a campaign that was fought especially in the German south-west by the masses organized in political
clubs, who had, in the deserted militia of Baden, a useful instrument
of power.

When the example of 1848 was used in German history, it was as
a forerunner to the unification of the Reich in 1871. Heinrich von
Treitschke did not call 1848/49 the 'German Revolution'; instead he
applied this term to 1866 when Prussia defeated Austria and the
Länder in the south-west: a revolution that had been managed
through the army, from above.[14] Seen through this perspective any
further claims of 1848/49 beyond the 'well-meant drive for unification' were seen as a degenerative influence, a deviation from
Germany's distinct historical path.[15] As an explanation for this aberration on the frontier region of Baden, foreign influence was blamed.
A 1903 history book for primary schools writes about the 'revolutionary movement that flowed over from France in the spring of
1848'.[16] Hagenmeyer, a vicar from Baden, after having honoured the
aims to gain civic liberty and a national union which were in his
opinion clearly justified, evaluated the revolutionary years thus:

These aims which happened to be connected from the beginning
with the ideas of the first French revolution, namely 'Liberty,

Equality and Brotherhood' were doomed because of this fact. The practical implementation was also doomed because these ideas were based on the revolutionary principle of the people's sovereignty.[17]

At another point he emphasized the importance of the 'foreign adventurers'.[18] Friedrich von Weech, archivist at Karlsruhe, in his 'History of Baden' disparagingly characterized the 'motley crew of Foreign Legions which had gathered in the capital much to the terror of the people of Karlsruhe'.[19] In the fact of a lack of thorough research on the topic, a distinction was assumed between Badeners and republicans who came from abroad to support the revolts. Dove, a historian from Freiburg, wrote: 'One has to ask for the reasons for such an event so totally alien to the German history,'[20] illustrating his lack of understanding and fixation with the authoritarian state.

The repression of the revolution as a research topic in historical science, the trifling with it in the current historical descriptions, as well as the partial attempt to construct an image of history that suggests a linear development from the so-called 'War of Independence' in 1813/14 against Napoleon via the endeavours for unification in 1848/49 up to the founding of the German Reich in 1870/71 have all had a serious influence on historical consciousness in Baden. Nevertheless, in Baden there remained among many families and circles of friends specific memories of their own participation in the revolution: the experience of the repressive policy of occupation after the defeat of the revolution, of trials of investigation, of fines and jail, of death sentences and forced emigration. A widely known lullaby – the lyrics are by Ludwig Pfau – is a proof of both the bitterness and hope these people felt. In this song we hear about the Prussian soldier, who had killed a father and had thereby made the family poor and brought a deathly hush all over Baden. At the same time, the song tells us, liberty will one day undoubtedly rise again, and then the Prussian soldier will lie in the same grave as the father from Baden.[21]

Rarely were there public gestures of solidarity with the defeated revolutionaries in the first years after 1849. At Freiburg, young women laid flowers on the graves of three republicans who had been put before a firing squad, although this was forbidden.[22] At Lörrach, some women who were well disposed towards the republic wore demonstrative mourning on the holiday celebrating the victory of the Prussian troops over the revolution.[23] And, occasionally, there were demonstrations of support for Friedrich Hecker, the hero of the revolution, who had fast become a mythical figure.[24] The partial survival of the memory of 1848/49 can moreover be illustrated by the fact that, in several places in Baden, people endeavoured to erect monuments to the victims of the revolution. In September 1874, 25 years after the revolution, the unveiling of a monument in Mannheim that celebrated five republicans who had been put before a firing squad turned into a rally that was noticed all over Germany. When shortly afterwards in Rastatt people wanted to erect a statue for their 19 local victims, the state refused the licence. The money that had been collected in Germany and the United States had then to be used for a statue of the poet Hans Jakob Christoph von Grimmelshausen at the small town Renchen. It was only twenty years later that the erection of a monument was permitted, on condition that the inscription would only contain the names of the dead.[25] In the village of Rümmingen the inscription on the gravestone honouring the republican Friedrich Neff also had to be removed by order of the authorities.[26] These examples show that monuments were first erected due to private initiative. For example, at Dossenbach in spring 1870 a circle of supporters of Johann Georg Uehlin, a revolutionary from Schopfheim, were able to establish a memorial stone. It was to remember the ten freedom fighters who had been killed in action and had belonged to the German democratic legion of Georg Herwegh.[27]

However, in contrast to these occasional attempts to form a positive tradition of revolution, the official historical image which glorified the German state (founded in 1871) turned out to be more effective by far. In 1898/99, fifty years after the revolution, the view of the earlier mentioned vicar Hagenmeyer corresponded with the common opinion that there was no reason 'to celebrate an anniversary of this revolution; for it had mostly originated from muddy waters, taking sometimes a rather nasty turn and finding a rather pathetic end.'[28] Above all the Social Democrats saw themselves as the direct historical heirs of the revolutionaries.[29] On 18 March 1898, the anniversary of the 'Revolt on the Barricades' in Berlin provoked a heated debate in the German Reichstag about the revolution. August Bebel, leader of the Social Democrats, unreservedly supported the revolution as a positive tradition.[30] Many liberals thought the defeat of the rebellions more important – rebellions which were in their eyes uncontrollable, dangerous and violent.

An exception, especially in southern Germany, was the left-wing Liberal Party who had split from the national-liberals. In 1873 democrats from Frankfurt and members of the people's party from Württemberg, Baden and Hessia celebrated the twenty-fifth anniversary of the parliament in Frankfurt's Paulskirche – with critical remarks concerning the then indecisive representatives of the people. In March 1898 members of the people's party organized a celebration for the fiftieth anniversary of the revolution at Frankfurt.[31] But their view of German history remained in the minority. A contemporary noted the attitude of Marcus Pflüger, one of the leading members of the left-wing liberal 'Freisinn' in the parliament of Baden, towards the revolution:

> Even at the end of the nineties, when in parliament . . . the heated talk harked back to the time of the revolt in Baden, the parliament was every time witness to the same strange spectacle. The venerable President by seniority Marcus Pflüger packed his files together and silently left the room. He, who had been seriously fighting in 1848, could not bear it, when the revolution in Baden was praised to the skies by the social-democrats, while the centre and the conservatives condemned it as the lowest crime.[32]

Pflüger held an address in March 1898 at a well-attended local ceremony at Lörrach organized by the 'Freisinn'. On the one hand he emphasized the 'total justification' of the rebellions 'because of multiple badly ruling governments and unfulfilled promises'; on the other hand he stressed the links in the drive for unification between 1848/49 and 1870/71.[33] Beside the small group of these left-wing liberals, the social democrats were the ones who made the more lasting efforts in the fight for the legacy of the revolution, to structure and strengthen a tradition which reached back to 1848/49. In 1893 Wilhelm Blos, representative of the social democrats in the Reichstag, in his voluminous history of the 'German Revolution' sharply attacked the tendency of contemporary historiography 'to rearrange world history into a glorification of the reigning system at any one time'.[34] He wanted to prove in his publications 'that the movement of the people in 1848 had pursued totally different aims than those that had been realized in Bismarck's military and bureaucratic state.'[35] Surviving for decades, the social democrats organized commemorations of 1848 at various places. At a commemoration ceremony in the south-western part of Baden in 1898 Swiss representatives of the social democrats from Basle were among the participants.[36]

III

After the end of the empire one part of the tradition of 1848/49 again became relevant to other political parties. The constitution of the Reich, which had been adopted by the Paulskirche at Frankfurt, became, not only for its catalogue of constitutional rights, one model for the constitution of the Weimar Republic. Besides the constitutional law debates, the main point of reference in politics was now the German Empire of 1871. The celebration of the seventy-fifth anniversary of 1848/49 in the Paulskirche at Frankfurt, with the social-democratic president of the German Empire Friedrich Ebert attending, was passed over. A deeper historical consciousness, i.e. what the revolution of 1848/49 could have meant for the newly founded democratic state, was submerged. Already at the turn of the century a contemporary from Baden had judged:

> Frequently the younger generation of our contemporaries has only a very poor and imperfect knowledge of the revolution in the years 1848 and 1849. Many of them, as I have myself been often convinced of, do not know much more than what they have heard in the various stories and anecdotes their parents and grandparents have told them.[37]

In the 1920s a series of historians and journalists in Baden attempted to bring a more positive history of the revolutionary years 1848/49 to a broader public. In 1920, the historian Friedrich Lautenschlager, who worked in the university library at Heidelberg, published a collection of documents on the revolution in Baden.[38] His central topic was the fight of the liberal middle classes for 'emancipation from being treated like children by a police state coined after Metternich's, that hinders any liberal development in economy and law, and in the constitutional life of the counties and the whole nation'.[39] Agitation in the agrarian sector, as well as the formation of an organized labour movement, were taken into account when selecting the documents, and the 'neighbouring political influence of France and Switzerland'[40] were positively assessed for the progress of the liberal movement in Baden. However, the focal point was the constitution of the National Assembly at Frankfurt. Lautenschlager offered with this selection of documents a much broader, and from a liberal viewpoint surprisingly restrained, image of the revolution.

At the end of the 1920s, the journalist Johannes Böser went even further when he published a small regional history of 1848.[41] He presented the rebels' demand for freedom to be more important than the desire even for unity: 'The German wanted to be free as a human being and as a citizen. He wanted to be able to think and talk freely, and he wanted to be responsible for his own fate.'[42] Böser saw in the tradition of these civic rights and liberties a lesson for his own times:

> When the German people after the fall of the empire, had to shape their own fate and rebuild the state in a time of need, the task of the National assembly at Weimar led naturally back to the work of the parliament at Frankfurt. Back to the civic rights of the German people, that had once.... been established in the Paulskirche at Frankfurt. Bismarck had in 1867 and in 1871 put aside the most valuable pieces. Now in the year 1919 the whole of the 'civic rights of the German people' became the basis for the constitution of the German republic. Finally after seventy years the legislative achievement of the Paulskirche had become what its creators had once hoped for. It had become the 'Magna Carta' of the German people.[43]

In another regional-historical study, this one dealing with the 1849 revolt, particular associations of revolutionaries over the border in France and Switzerland were for the first time taken into consideration. The study even suggested analogies with the ideal of the brotherhood of peoples in 1848 and the 'League of Nations', which had been founded in 1920.[44]

Similarly, in Switzerland new research papers appeared in the 1920s, for example the account by Paul Siegfried concerning Basle's attitude during the three revolts in Baden in 1848/49. However, the author endeavoured above all from a national point of view to justify the reserve of the government at Basle and the Swiss policy of neutrality.[45] Not so the Swiss historian Werner Näf. In his 1929 volume concerning 'Switzerland in the German revolution'[46] he emphasized that the Swiss–German relationship had not been at that time a 'political interaction', 'no common actions or a common fate . . . . The connection was a spiritual one.'[47] He then showed, in two chapters entitled 'Democracy' and 'Ideal of Humanity to a citizen of the world', the concrete links and mutual influences. Thereby, he invalidated the thesis of the special historical path of Germany and he brought out the connection of the German liberal and democratic movement with Western European political developments.

However, all these studies had only a minor impact on the unstable Weimar Republic, burdened with political and economic crises. In Baden it was also difficult to restore the submerged tradition of democratic self-confidence. The seminal study of the German revolution by Veit Valentin, considered a standard work on the subject even today because of the huge amount of material it covers and its discussion of political-, social- and cultural-historical issues, came too late to make a greater impact. In the 1920s he had, with several studies on the democratic movement in 1848 and the idea of the League of Nations, attempted to help form a democratic tradition in the new German republic. But when in 1930/31 he published his two-volume 'History of the German revolution in 1848/49' there was not enough time for a free evaluation of his work before the National Socialists came to power.[48]

IV

During the era of National Socialism accounts of the revolution of 1848/49 were based on the interpretations published at the time of the Empire. One example is the 'German history on the Upper Rhine' by Alfred Rapp, which saw multiple editions.[49] The chapter concerning the nineteenth century is titled 'Fatherland Germany', and the decades before the revolution are described as 'Confessions to German unity'. Following the historical view of the National Socialists, Rapp gave more attention to the post-1815 People's Movement than to 1848. However, Rapp did not present a new piece of research, but made only ideologically based reinterpretations and re-evaluations. His anti-liberalism became apparent when he stated that farmers and craftsmen in Baden were in no way participants of the liberal movement. They would only have met with the liberals in their opposition to Metternich's small states system and in the fight against economic and social need. The main goal of the People's Movement in the Upper Rhine would have been Germany's national unity. Anti-intellectualism and anti-parliamentarism became apparent when the debates of the liberal ruling classes in Baden with their high percentage of professors, officials or lawyers in the Land-tag – and later in the German national assembly – were thus pictured, as if they had been in contrast to the so-called true wishes and needs of the people. Anti-semitism was also expressed, when the anti-Jewish riots in the spring of 1848 were judged as an integral part of the extensive People's Movement. Once again 1848 was interpreted as a 'tragic year', a 'year of aberration'.[50] The farmers and craftsmen of Baden were regarded as people who had been seduced, who had followed negative influences from other European countries. Rapp aimed to 'show, how foreign ideas cast a spell over a real people's movement'.[51] Again it was emphasized that the impulse to revolt came from outside:

> The revolution of 1848 is a European event, its origin is to be found in Paris, and the French February Revolution is the mother of the German movement in March. At the Upper Rhine, as in the rest of Germany, this movement did not begin out of a self-willed resolution, no, it was a foreign impulse; from the beginning this Internationalism will be the Achilles heel of the German Revolution of 1848.[52]

The negative influence of German refugees from Strasbourg and in Switzerland was stressed, and their success was considered to be 'the misuse of the true national determination' of the people for republican aims.[53] The 1849 rebellion in favour of civic rights and a constitution was therefore in Rapp's eyes 'the fall of the People's Movement in the Upper Rhine into the abyss of international revolution'.[54] This image was spread not only through Rapp's interpretation, but also through a series of other studies. This was an image which portrayed the revolution as a 'People's Movement' which had been misled and had gone too far.[55]

V

The centenary of the revolution of 1848 was celebrated in a Europe devastated by the Second World War and the catastrophe of National Socialism. It was celebrated in an occupied Germany. For the first time there were large exhibitions to remember the revolution and official ceremonies. In May 1948 an internationally observed celebration of the centenary was held in the restored Paulskirche at Frankfurt.[56] Likewise, at Freiburg, the capital of the southern part of Baden which belonged to the French occupied zone, a ceremony was organized to remember the revolution.[57] Historians, publicists and politicians picked up earlier attempts to form a democratic tradition. Theodor Heuss, who later became President of the FRG, emphasized in his reflections about the legacy of 1848 that in Germany 'the evaluation of the history of the revolution was soon confused by those who had fought in it'.[58] With insight he sketched the future idea of a unified Germany within a unified Europe. He gave prominence to the 'intention of the nation to shape its own state democratically', which he called the 'core of the order' from 1848 to the descendants of 1948.[59]

In July 1948 the Public Education Division of the French Military Government at Baden-Baden organized an extensive exhibition on the revolution in south-west Germany in 1848/49 which set out to demonstrate the integration with the European movement for freedom particularly in the frontier region of Baden, France and Switzerland[60] – in contrast to the historical prejudices which had been spread in Germany and France that the Germans were incapable of democracy. The exhibition catalogue emphasizes in the preface that 'the revolution of 1848 has been celebrated in France in a dignified way':

> There, the revolution has prompted a series of studies and interesting academic papers. Unfortunately it was not the same in Germany ... German nationalism has seen to it that the German people had no knowledge of the facts which could remind them of its hundred-year-old fight for freedom.[61]

The French perspective emphasized just as strongly the tradition of the movement for liberty as it sharply attacked, in the light of the war of 1870/71 and the two world wars, the excessive nationalism of many representatives in the national assembly at Frankfurt. 'Blind in their nationalistic illusion, they closed their minds to the insight, that only liberty is capable of making unity real; without liberty unity is simply slavery.'[62] In Germany in 1948 the tense relationship between the desire for political freedom and the desire for national unity was again highly topical. The ceremonies celebrating 1848 in the western occupied zones and the recalling of the ideal of the con-stitution of 1849 contributed to discussions for the Constitution of the Federal Republic of Germany, and the political formula 'liberty before unity' was slowly becoming acceptable during the Cold War years. However, this discussion apart, the interest in 1848/49 quickly retreated into the background.

The intensive research in the German Democratic Republic has to be mentioned here, not so much in relation to the history of the revolution in Baden, but rather in other territories like Saxony or Berlin. The emergence of the worker's movement is the theme that runs through the whole of this research. It was the subject of large exhibitions in 1948 and also of popular publications. Political ideas narrowed the focus of interpretations on this subject and centred on the thesis of a bourgeois 'betrayal' of the revolution. Thus a closed conception of the world was conveyed to the people which could be used by the political leaders of the GDR as a historical-political justi-fication of their own system. Yet political ideas changed between 1949 and 1989. Numerous accurate studies from the 1950s (and also from the late 1970s) were dedicated to the social history of the revolution, a field of research that had long been neglected by the historiography of the Federal Republic of Germany which had con-fined itself to the history of the Paulskirche and of liberalism.[63] Thus, the divided nature of historical traditions in the different milieus of the empire was continued in the two German postwar states.

This only changed in the 1960s and 1970s, a time of social and political upheaval in the FRG. When Gustav Heinemann in 1969, at that time social-democratic President of the Federal Republic, came to visit Baden-Württemberg for the first time he criticized the wide-spread conservative view of 1848 which was based on the perspective of the victors over the revolutionaries. In opposition, he insisted on the movement's democratic tradition. In 1970, he suggested that Germany should look out for those men in its history 'who have lived and fought for the idea of creating in Germany a life and order based on moral and political self-responsibility'.[64] He wanted to do justice to these men. This prompted competitions in schools, exhibitions and research work. At Rastatt in 1974 Heinemann was able to open 'The Memorial of the Movements for Freedom in German History', Rastatt being a place which had played a special role as the republicans' last bastion in the final phase of the revolution in 1848/49.[65] Heinemann understood the memory of the forgotten movements for freedom, especially the memory of the revolution in 1848/49, as a political contribution to the forming of a political identity in the Federal Republic.

The reinvestment in the historical ideal of 1848/49 found concrete political expression in the civic movements of the 1970s. Particularly in the South of Baden, conservative farmers, liberal lawyers and teachers as well as left-wing groups of students came together to fight against ecological damage. In their demonstrations and meetings, in discussions, addresses and songs, they referred again and again to the deeply rooted democratic traditions of Baden.[66] Here the memory of 1848/49 contributed also to the transborder protest against nuclear power stations at Wyhl in Baden, at Fessenheim in Alsace and at Augst in Switzerland.[67]

After the long propagated thesis of the German 'Sonderweg' a more open, European perspective became obvious in historical research. The immense works on nineteenth-century German history from Langewiesche and Siemann up to Nipperdey and Wehler which were published in the 1980s all stress the complexity of the problems and levels of action in 1848/49. The failure of the revolution is in their view not a German 'special' case but rather the rule in Europe at that time. If there was something specially German about it, it was the long after-effect, the permanent weakening of liberalism.[68]

VI

This concise chronological overview shows that there was in Baden, as well as in the whole of Germany, no unified forming of traditions. It also shows that the memory of 1848/49 was fragmented and in the different political systems highly instrumentalized. Ernst Schulin has very critically pointed out in how biased a way historiography, particularly the official historiography in Germany, has dealt with the topic of the revolution over a long period of time.[69]

In two respects the commemoration of 1848 in the European frontier region of Baden was dependent on the formation of traditions in Germany. On the one hand it was inevitable that some would emphasize the moderate parliamentary path of the Paulskirche and others the more radical path of the people's rebellions. But specifically in Baden, which had been the scene of both developments, it is possible not to polarize the argument but to see that these paths were mutually dependent. On the other hand the commemoration was bound to consider the 'German Sonderweg' in the perspective of democratic development in Europe as a whole. For the formation of traditions in Baden in particular there were, beside the efforts at a clear disassociation, repeated attempts to establish a common history with the neighbouring countries of France and Switzerland. However, the national historiography in Germany, which was over a long period of time very much focused on Prussia, offered no room for the specific memories of the revolutionary years or for the special conditions of the revolution in Baden.

What obviously distinguishes the European frontier region of Baden from other German regions, is the political culture that developed there, with the strong roots of the liberal and democratic movement existing in Baden even before 1848 – and later on as well. The political self-confidence of the citizens remained distinctive, which connected the political culture of Baden with France, but above all with Switzerland.[70] That was one of the reasons why the revolution in Baden in 1849, after the defeated rebellions of 1848, was for a short time successful: although the German republic did not exist, there was a republic within Germany – though restricted to this one *land*, Baden, and restricted to the period of seven weeks. As early as 1849 Friedrich Engels mocked this humble claim:

The highest ideal of the citizen and farmer in Baden has always been the small, bourgeois-agrarian republic (as in Switzerland). A small range of actions for a small humble people, the state not more than a somewhat larger community...; a small, stable industry supported by manual labour, which causes a likewise stable and sleepy condition of society: less riches, less poverty, only middle-class and mediocrity;...no active participation in history, no foreign policy, only small domestic gossip and small squabbles in the families; no important industry, no trains, no world-trade, no social confrontations between millionaires and proletarians, but a quiet, comfortable life blessed and honourable, in the small non-historic modesty of content souls – that is the unruffled Arcadia, which exists in the biggest part of Switzerland. Years ago the citizens and farmers in Baden have gone into raptures about the installation of all this at their home.[71]

Engels had hereby underestimated the drive for independence and self-determination in these small territories. Another revolutionary, Karl Heinzen, had to admit as early as 1847:

Switzerland does not correspond to the political ideal; but of all countries in Europe she stands highest, for she is a republic. The Swiss are their own rulers and hold their destiny in their own hands . . . this advantage causes it, that in Europe they alone are able to look political critique in the eye without blushing.[72]

But Baden was not Switzerland: at least on one point there was a serious difference – its membership of the German federation. This fact made it possible for the grand duke to call in intervention troops from other members of the federation, above all from Prussia, to help put an end to the revolution.[73]

The traditions of a communal democracy that reach even farther back than 1848 have proven, beside direct influences from Switzerland and France, the existence of Baden's distinct political culture. This is a phenomenon of the history of structures and mentalities, a phenomenon of the 'longue durée'. This political culture had influence on the revolution as well as on the formation of its traditions in Baden. In the collective memory positive recollections of 1848/49 and democratic self-confidence were more strongly embedded, and in the families on a local and on a regional level. In his recollections of the revolution, Veit Valentin had already drawn a gradient between north and south, a contrast between those regions which were strongly and those which were more weakly affected by the revolution. The attempt to reanimate the traditions of 1848/49 in a large part of Germany looked in his eyes like 'an act of romantic desperation by the historically educated';[74] only in Frankfurt and in the south-west of Germany did he see a living memory of the revolution among the people.

VII

The 150th anniversary of the revolution in 1998 was commemorated in a central German exhibition with the motto 'Aufbruch zur Freiheit' (Departure for Liberty) in Frankfurt am Main.[75] The parliamentary approach of the Paulskirche was at its focus while the great exhibition of the *land* Baden-Württemberg at Karlsruhe emphasized the three popular revolts.[76] Despite these ongoing differences it needs to be stated that the anniversary year 1998 is marked by an extraordinary agreement, one never before achieved in Germany, about the historical status of the revolution of 1848/49. Concerning its status in the political consciousness, however, the years of repression and contempt have left their mark up to the present. The German Bundestag thus decided to celebrate the jubilee with a ceremony of its own, after having been criticized very strongly by the public. It is this strong public interest which is evident in the fact that both of the mentioned central exhibitions were very successful. Each had more than 100 000 visitors.

Particularly south-west Germany and Baden saw hundreds of local events with a remarkable level of public participation.[77] A 'celebration of liberty' in Offenburg with about 100 000 visitors in September 1997, 150 years after the declaration of the 'Demands of the people', marked the starting-point for this celebration marathon. Until now it has been rare that democratic gains have been celebrated so widely by the German public. This was a celebration 'with freedom cake and Hecker's hat, the Communist party and Wolfgang Schäuble' as the weekly *Die Zeit* described this 'excessive people's party' with ironic distance – and respect at the same time.[78] Research projects, symposia, reviews were part of these undertakings. After the end of the Cold War, with its ideological usage of history and the fight over its legacy, even the more problematic aspects of the revolution can be worked in a more unprejudiced way. An exhibition at Buchen in the North of Baden dealt with the anti-Jewish riots of spring 1848.[79] Moreover, a tri-national exhibition project in Lörrach, Liestal and Mulhouse presented the hopes and disappointments of the revolutionaries in the transborder fight for freedom in a comparative perspective.[80] The now more complex image of the revolution had a distinct focus in 1998: Europe and the memory of the European-wide liberal and democratic movement was crystallizing

as a central topic in many ceremonies and publications.[81] It seems –
to take up once again Georg Herwegh's saying – that also in the
European frontier region of Baden – if only in memory of 1848/49 –
after 150 years 'nationality no longer separates but liberty unites'.

Notes

1   M. Herwegh (ed.), *Briefe von und an Georg Herwegh. 1848* (Paris-Leipzig-
    Munich: 1896), p. 364.
2   [E. Herwegh], *Zur Geschichte der deutschen demokratischen Legion aus Paris.
    Von einer Hochverraeterin.* Grünberg 1849. Compare among others I. Fell-
    rath, G. Herwegh and E. Herwegh, 'Vive la République', in S. Freitag (ed.),
    Die Achtundvierziger. Lebensbilder aus der deutschen Revolution 1848/49
    (Munich: 1998), pp. 33–44.
3   Address from Lörrach on 23 November 1847 in W. Näf, *Die Schweiz in der
    deutschen Revolution. Ein Kapitel schweizerisch-deutscher Beziehungen in den
    Jahren 1847–1849* (Frauenfeld-Leipzig: 1929), pp. 129–30, at p. 130.
4   A general view can be found in the catalogue of the exhibition '*National-
    ität trennt, Freiheit verbindet/Séparés par la nationalité, unis par la liberté*',
    ed. Haus der Geschichte Baden-Württemberg, Dichtermuseum Herwegh-
    Archiv Liestal, Musée Historique Mulhouse and Museum am Burghof
    Lörrach (Stuttgart: 1998).
5   Compare, on the refugee policy in the frontier region France–Baden–
    Switzerland, M. Leuenberger, *Frei und gleich . . . und fremd. Flüchtlinge im
    Baselbiet zwischen 1830 und 1860* (Liestal: 1996).
6   Compare among others F. de Capitani and G. German (eds), *Auf dem Weg
    zu einer schweizerischen Identität 1848–1914. Probleme-Errungenschaften-
    Mißerfolge* (Freiburg: 1987); P. Sarasin, 'Sich an 1848 erinnern. Einige
    unsystematische Überlegungen am Beispiel der Schweiz', in C. Jansen
    and T. Mergel (eds), *Die Revolutionen von 1848/49. Erfahrung-Verarbeitung-
    Deutung* (Göttingen: 1998), pp. 268–78.
7   Compare D. Mollenhauer, 'Nur eine Imitation? 1848/49 in Frankreich',
    in I. Götz von Olenhusen (ed.), *1848/49 in Europa und der Mythos der Fran-
    zösischen Revolution* (Göttingen: 1998), pp. 19–38, and the article by
    R. Spang in this book.
8   Heinrich Heine, quoted from R. Rürup, *Deutschland im 19. Jahrhundert
    1815–1871* (Göttingen: 1984), p. 196.
9   Ibid., p. 197.
10 L. Häusser, *Denkwürdigkeiten zur Geschichte der badischen Revolution*
    (Heidelberg: 1851).
11 F. Baumgart, *Die verdrängte Revolution. Darstellung und Bewertung der
    Revolution von 1848 in der deutschen Geschichtsschreibung vor dem ersten
    Weltkrieg* (Düsseldorf: 1976).
12 Personal information of Kurt Hochstuhl, Badisches Generallandesarchiv
    Karlsruhe.

13 R. Rürup, *Deutschland*, p. 179.

14 A general view is given by M. Hettling, 'Nachmärz und Kaiserreich', in C. Dipper and U. Speck (eds), *1848. Revolution in Deutschland* (Frankfurt am Main/Leipzig: 1998), pp. 11–24.

15 K. Brunner, *Kurzer Abriß der badischen Geschichte für Schulen bearbeitet* (Karlsruhe: 1903), p. 52.

16 Ibid.

17 K. Hagenmeyer, *Die Revolutionsjahre 1848/49* (Karlsruhe: 1899), p. 4.

18 Ibid., p. 103.

19 Ibid., p. 574.

20 A. Dove, *Großherzog Friedrich von Baden als Landesherr und deutscher Fürst* (Heidelberg: 1902), p. 19.

21 Reprint in F. X. Vollmer, *Vormärz und Revolution in Baden* (Frankfurt/Berlin/Munich 1979), pp. 179–80.

22 Ibid., p. 186.

23 T. Scholz, *Revolutionäre... Der Aufstand des Jahres 1849 und seine Folgen im Markgräflerland* (Müllheim: 1926), p. 112.

24 R. Muhs, 'Heckermythos und Revolutionsforschung', *Zeitschrift für die Geschichte des Oberrheins*, 134 (1986), 422–41, at p. 427.

25 W. Blos, *Badische Revolutionsgeschichten aus den Jahren 1848 und 1849* (Mannheim: 1910), pp. 138–42. First investigations on the 'Lieux de mémoire' (Pierre Nora) of the 1848/49 revolution in Baden have been undertaken on the occasion of the 150th anniversary, e.g. Arbeitsgemeinschaft hauptamtlicher Archivare im Städtetag Baden-Württemberg (ed.), *Revolution im Südwesten. Stätten der Demokratiebewegung 1848/49 in Baden-Württemberg* (Karlsruhe: 1997); J. Dresch, 'Das Ringen um das Gedenken an die badische Revolution', ed. Badischen Landesmuseum Karlsruhe, *1848/49. Revolution der deutschen Demokraten in Baden* [Ausstellungskatalog] (Baden-Baden: 1998), pp. 484–6 with descriptions of exhibits pp. 486–92. From the same author there exists also an overview of the anti-revolutionary monuments in Baden, which cannot be dealt with in more detail here, J. Dresch, *Die Monumente des preußischen Triumphs*, ibid., pp. 456–9.

26 Vollmer, *Vormärz*, p. 187.

27 Compare the short comment and other examples in J. Merk, M. Moehring and H. Bürgel (eds), *Lörrach 1848/49. Essays – Biographien – Dokumente – Projekte* (Lörrach: 1998), at p. 11.

28 K. Hagenmeyer, *Die Revolutionsjahre*, Preface.

29 Compare the thought-provoking study concerning the formation of traditions in the national liberal, social democratic and catholic milieu by T. Mergel, 'Sozialmoralische Milieus und Revolutionsgeschichts schreibung. Zum Bild der Revolution von 1848/49 in den Subgesellschaften des deutschen Kaiserreichs', in C. Jansen and T. Mergel, *Die Revolutionen*, pp. 247–67.

30 Stenographische Berichte über die Verhandlungen des Deutschen Reichstags. IX. Legislaturperiode V. Session 2. Band (Berlin: 1898), pp. 1581–1615.

31 M. Hettling, see above n. 14, pp. 19–20; compare *Die Frankfurter März-Feier zum Gedächtnisse des Jahres 1848. Abgehalten in Frankfurt a. M. am 26. und 27. März 1898* (Frankfurt am Main: 1898).

32 A. Fendrich, *Die badische Bewegung der Jahre 1848/49* (Frankfurt: 1924), pp. 43–4.

33 Parts of Pflüger's speech were published in H. Pflüger, 'Die Revolution von 1848 im Markgräfler Land mit alten Familienerinnerungen', *Eckhart – Jahrbuch für das Badner Land* (Freiburg: 1965), pp. 36–51.

34 W. Blos, *Die Deutsche Revolution. Geschichte der Deutschen Bewegung von 1848 und 1849* (Stuttgart: 1893), p. 1.

35 Ibid.

36 H. Bernnat, *125 Jahre Arbeiterbewegung im Dreiländereck* (Lörrach: 1993), pp. 57–8.

37 K. Hagenmeyer, see above n. 17, Preface. Likewise nearly 30 years later T. Scholz, see above n. 23, p. 3.

38 F. Lautenschlager (ed.), *Volksstaat und Einherrschaft. Dokumente aus der badischen Revolution 1848/49* (Konstanz: 1920).

39 Ibid., p. 11.

40 Ibid., p. 18.

41 J. Böser: *Vor 80 Jahren. Ein heimatgeschichtlicher Rückblick auf die Sturm-jahre 1848/49* (Lörrach: [1929]).

42 Ibid., p. 3.

43 Ibid., p. 14.

44 T. Scholz, *Revolutionäre*, 360.

45 P. Siegfried, 'Basel und der erste badische Aufstand im April 1848', in *Gesellschaft zur Beförderung des Guten und Gemeinnützigen* (ed.), *104. Neujahrsblatt* (Basel: 1926); P. Siegfried, 'Basel während des zweiten und dritten badischen Aufstandes 1848/49', in *Gesellschaft zur Beförderung des Guten und Gemeinnützigen* (ed.), *106. Neujahrsblatt* (Basel: 1928).

46 W. Näf, *Die Schweiz*, pp. 5–6.

47 Ibid., pp. 5–6.

48 Compare V. Valentin, *Geschichte der deutschen Revolution von 1848/49*, 2 vols (Frankfurt am Main: 1930/31; reprinted in 1970 and 1998). Bio-graphic information and short comments on his other studies on the topic in B. Faulenbach, 'Veit Valentin', in R. vom Bruch and R. A. Müller (eds), *Historiker-Lexikon. Von der Antike bis zum 20. Jahrhundert* (Munich: 1991), pp. 326–8.

49 A. Rapp, *Deutsche Geschichte am Oberrhein*, 4th edn (Karlsruhe: 1937).

50 Ibid., p. 274.

51 Ibid., p. 287.

52 Ibid., p. 275.

53 Ibid., p. 280.

54 Ibid., p. 277.

55 Compare the short article by M. Vogt, 'Weimar und die NS-Zeit', in C. Dipper and U. Speck, *1848*, pp. 25–34.

56 *1848–1948. Jahrhundertfeier der ersten deutschen Nationalversammlung in der Paulskirche Frankfurt am Main* (Frankfurt am Main: 1948).

57 Compare *Badische Zeitung*, 27 April 1948 and *Das neue Baden*, 30 April 1948.

58 T. Heuss, *1848. Werk und Erbe* (Stuttgart: 1948; reprint 1998), p. 160.

59 Ibid., p. 167.

60 *La Révolution de 1848–1849 dans l'Allemagne du Sud-Ouest/Die Revolution 1848–1849 in Südwestdeutschland. Kurhaus Baden-Baden Juli 1948* [Ausstellungskatalog] (Offenburg/Mainz: 1948).

61 R. Schmittlein, Preface, in ibid., pp. 9–13, at p. 9.

62 Ibid., p. 12.

63 On the various phases of research on the revolution and on the changing standards of interpretation laid down by the politics in the GDR, compare E. Wolfrum, 'Bundesrepublik Deutschland und DDR', in C. Dipper and U. Speck (eds), 1848, pp. 35–49.

64 The president dedicated three great speeches to the topic. Compare G. W. Heinemann, *Allen Bürgern verpflichtet. Reden des Bundespräsidenten 1969–1974*, pp. 23–9 (Stuttgart: 1969), pp. 30–5 (Bremen: 1970) and pp. 36–44 (Rastatt: 1974).

65 Bundesarchiv Außenstelle Rastatt (ed.), *Erinnerungsstätte für die Freiheitsbewegungen in der deutschen Geschichte. Katalog der ständigen Ausstellung*, (Koblenz: 1984).

66 Compare, for example, H. Haumann (ed.), *Vom Hotzenwald bis Wyhl. Demokratische Traditionen in Baden* (Cologne: 1977). On the difficulty of historians contributing with their work to the formation of democratic traditions while keeping up the academic distance, compare Rudolf Muhs' critique on some of the publications from the 1970s 'Hecker mythos'.

67 A. Muschg, *Von Herwegh bis Kaiseraugst. Wie halten wir es als Demokraten mit unserer Freiheit? Mit ausgewählten politischen Gedichten von Georg Herwegh* (Zürich: 1975).

68 Compare, for example, D. Langewiesche, *Europa zwischen Restauration und Revolution 1815–1849*, 2nd edn (Munich: 1989); idem, 'Die deutsche Revolution 1848/49 und die vorrevolutionäre Gesellschaft', Part I in *Archiv für Sozialgeschichte*, 21 (1981), 458–98, and Part II in *Archiv für Sozialgeschichte*, 31 (1991), 331–443; W. Siemann, *Die deutsche Revolution von 1848/49* (Frankfurt am Main: 1985); T. Nipperdey, *Deutsche Geschichte 1800–1866* (Munich: 1983); H.-U. Wehler, *Deutsche Gesellschaftsgeschichte*, vol. 2, *Von der Reformära bis zur industriellen und politischen 'Deutschen Doppelrevolution' 1815–1848/49*, (Munich: 1987).

69 E. Schulin, 'Die deutschen Historiker und die Revolution von 1848/49', Address at the University of Freiburg, 12 February 1998.

70 On the political culture of Baden compare among others H. Fenske, *Der liberale Südwesten. Freiheitliche und demokratische Traditionen in Baden und Württemberg* (Stuttgart: 1981), and the thought-provoking, not uncontroversial piece of work by P. Nolte, *Gemeindebürgertum und Liberalismus in Baden 1800–1850* (Göttingen: 1994). On the influence of France, I. G. von Olenhusen, '1848/49 in Baden. Traum und Trauma der Französischen Revolution', in I. Götz von Olenhusen (ed.), *1848/49*, pp. 81–113. Especially concerning the situation in the frontier region France–Baden–Switzerland,

J. Merk, B. Bruant and M. Leuenberger, 'Der Schauplatz: Die Regio 1798–1848', in *Nationalität trennt, Freiheit verbindet*, pp. 24–49.

71 F. Engels, *Die deutsche Reichsverfassungskampagne*, ed. R. Dublek (Berlin, 1969), p. 63.

72 K. Heinzen, *Teutsche Revolution* (Bern: 1847), quoted after W. Näf, *Die Schweiz*.

73 The latest accounts on the revolution in Baden now stress very strongly the often neglected revolutionary year 1849, compare among others A. G. Frei and K. Hochstuhl, *Wegbereiter der Demokratie. Die badische Revolution 1848/49 – Der Traum von der Freiheit* (Karlsruhe: 1997), and W. von Hippel, *Revolution im deutschen Südwesten. Das Großherzogtum Baden 1848/49* (Stuttgart: 1998).

74 Quoted after M. Vogt, 'Weimar', p. 29.

75 Compare L. Gall (ed.), *1848. Aufbruch zur Freiheit. Eine Ausstellung des Deutschen Historischen Museums und der Schirn Kunsthalle Frankfurt zum 150jährigen Jubiläum der Revolution von 1848/49* (Frankfurt am Main: 1998).

76 Compare the exhibition catalogue *1848/49. Revolution der deutschen Demokraten in Baden*. When Lothar Gall, the director of the exhibition at Frankfurt, judged the revolt under Hecker as a sort of carnival procession (*Badische Zeitung*, 6 March 1998) he provoked heated discussions in Baden-Württemberg. The opposite opinion was presented by F. Vortisch, 'Die Aufstände in Baden – 150 Jahre in der Kontroverse', in J. Merk, M. Moehring and H. Bürgel (eds), *Lörrach*, pp. 6–16. Likewise did Karl Moersch take stock at the official ceremony in the Landtag of Baden-Württemberg, that a successful change of the political conditions in 1848/49 could have only been reached by force, due to the uncompromising attitude of the most powerful German princes, K. Moersch, 'Der Traum vom freien Volksstaat', Address in the Landtag of Baden-Württemberg 17 June 1998.

77 Compare Badisches Landesmuseum Karlsruhe (ed.), *Baden-Württemberg feiert die Revolution 1848/49. Veranstaltungen in den Jahren 1997–1999*, 1st edn (Lahr: 1997), and Haus der Geschichte Baden-Württemberg (ed.), *Baden-Württemberg feiert die Revolution 1848/49. Veranstaltungen April 1998 – Dezember 1999*, 2nd edn (Stuttgart: 1998).

78 B. Erenz, 'Ja, er lebet noch!', *Die Zeit*, 19 September 1997.

79 Compare the exhibition catalogue Haus der Geschichte Baden-Württemberg, *Heute ist Freiheit. Bauernkrieg im Odenwald* (Stuttgart: 1998).

80 Compare the exhibition catalogue *Nationalität trennt, Freiheit verbindet*.

81 Compare among others D. Dowe, H.-G. Haupt and D. Langewiesche (eds), *Europa 1848. Revolution und Reform* (Bonn: 1998); D. Langewiesche (ed.), *Internationale Aspekte und Verbindungen in der Revolution 1848/49* (Karlsruhe: 1998); I. Götz von Olenhusen (ed.), *1848/49 in Europa*. At the meeting of the German historians in 1998, organized at Frankfurt near the Paulskirche, Dieter Langewiesche pointed out how fruitful the evaluation of local studies and exhibition catalogues of the anniversary year can be for the formation of historical traditions but also for academic historiography.

Part V
Conclusion

11

How European Was the Revolution of 1848/49?*

Reinhart Koselleck

Those who ask whether the revolution of 1848/49 was a European event are immediately faced with the objection that there was not one revolution but many. Strictly speaking this cannot be denied, for the centres of unrest were spread across the whole of Europe and resulted in a number of different revolutions. Upheavals occurred at a regional, territorial and national scale, but much of Europe, especially in its remoter parts, was little affected and whole regions remained altogether untouched by the turmoil. This becomes clearer when we look at the margins of Europe.

Spain, which had been plagued by civil wars ever since the Napoleonic invasion of 1808, remained relatively quiet. So did Scandinavia and Great Britain, Ireland being too exhausted by hunger and emigration to risk anything like the uprising of 1798. The civil war which had led to the separation of Belgium from the Netherlands had already been brought to an end, but a constitution was introduced in The Hague no earlier than 1848. It was the large and geographically continuous central part of Europe which was affected by revolution: from Denmark to Sicily, from France and Holland to Posen on the eastern borders of the German Federation and farther into Hungary and Transylvania. True, it was not a revolution of Europe, for Europe was not a politically active entity. But it was a European revolution. The hegemonial powers, whose strength differed widely, were involved together. Their pentarchy remained intact and

---

* Translated from the German by Johannes Haubold.

continued to function smoothly despite minor constitutional changes. In the end they backed the reaction in the course of which the old system of legitimacy was rehabilitated in 1848–50. Only the *coup d'état* of Napoleon III changed the familiar picture, leaving France with a dictatorship which was first bloody, then benign. It remained a provocative exception among the European monarchies.

The overall political system, then, which had been in place since 1815 and which never ceased to affect directly or indirectly the domestic affairs of the single countries, remained unchanged. To use the political jargon of the time, there was a sliding scale from the rather liberal west to the conservative German Federation and the reactionary Russia which subtly and variously affected all constitutional life in Europe. In this respect too the uprisings, which in France, in the area of the former German Empire – by then the German Federation – in Italy and in eastern Europe escalated into full-scale revolutions, had in common their overall European character.

First of all, the revolutionaries faced a number of shared social and economic challenges. As yet there were only a few industrialized regions with high population density, as for instance parts of Belgium, northern France, the area around Lyons, northern Italy, Saxony, the Ruhr region and Berlin, Bohemia and upper Silesia; but they were already under pressure from British competition which was technically more advanced in the production of coal and steel. Symptoms of the crisis were already converging; the gradual transition from manufacture to industrial production caused similar problems throughout Europe. There was no single answer to the secular alternative of unregulated production and trade on the one hand and the highly regulated modes of production that had been part and parcel of the feudal system on the other. Neither the bourgeoisie and its entrepreneurs nor the craftsmen and workers in their various regions reacted uniformly and univocally, nor indeed did the governments. Nowhere could economic progress be reconciled with social interests; and yet it was precisely this combination of disparate factors which was both revolutionary and European at the same time.

Secondly, similar things can be said about the inhabitants of rural areas who still formed the major part – 70 to 80 per cent – of the overall population. Despite regional differences, overpopulation was a widespread problem. In times of crop failure, and especially before the revolution, this situation led to devastating outbreaks of famine.

Rural workers were hoping in vain for help and work in the as yet pre-industrial cities. The further east we go, the more we see farmers and farmworkers suffering from the burdens imposed on them by the feudal system. Feudal taxes which were levied on persons or their belongings by no means only benefited the state. They still went into the pockets of the landowners who continued to act as a ruling class between the state and the mass of its subjects. The whole of middle, southern and eastern Europe suffered from this pre-modern leftover, and the driving force behind the rural revolutions was to abolish it. Here too we can speak of a generally European phenomenon, although the legal inequalities attacked by the revolutionaries differed widely from one region to another. The fact that the rural populations were largely successful in their plight helps to explain their more and more conservative mentality after 1848, approaching the position of the rural population of France after 1800, who went so far as to back a man like Napoleon III. We have found another generally European phenomenon.

Thirdly, and perhaps most importantly, the revolutionary fight for constitutional reform was also generally European. It was led by liberal intellectuals and entrepreneurs, and thanks to the democratic support of bourgeois and sub-bourgeois masses it started off being hugely successful. The political system of almost every country changed from a bureaucratic or neofeudal structure to a constitutional one with varying degrees of parliamentary elements added. Ministries were replaced everywhere, sometimes even monarchs (e.g. in Vienna, Munich and Turin); but nowhere apart from France did the monarchy itself disappear. All courts and courtly households continued to function – if sometimes in exile. One visible outcome of the revolutionary changes was that the economically leading bourgeoisie was integrated into a society still dominated by the aristocracy. In the area of the German Customs Union the Belgian constitution functioned as a model, and at one remove there was the model of the idealized British constitution. Nowhere in Europe was the result of the revolution anything more than a graded suffrage of the sort that already existed in Britain. It privileged wealth or education or both at the same time.

There is a fourth way in which the revolution of 1848–9 was a European event – and that is in its national fragmentation. This was to prove fatal for its success. In the years 1848 and 1849, European structures also emerged at the social, economic and constitutional levels. But in the immediate context of political action these structures continued to be subject to regional, territorial or national fragmentation. There was neither a liberal nor a democratic international movement which could have acted across the borders, let alone an international organization of socialist workers. Their manifestos may have reached an international audience, but their activities remained within the confines of the state. Indeed, revolutionary activity above all was conceived of as national, in Denmark, Germany and Bohemia as much as in Hungary, Poland and Italy. As a result, the revolutionaries' political intentions came to exclude each other, and the success of the revolution in one part of Europe blocked and annulled its success elsewhere. Since none of the postulated national boundaries were generally acceptable, the revolutionaries fought among themselves. If their political manifestos had an international appeal, their actions were decidedly national in character – as was their failure. Nowhere did the nation-states emerge which the revolutionaries postulated on the model of France. France had taken the first revolutionary step in 1789 when it had already been consolidated by the monarchy. It was the perfect nation-state, but for the time being it remained the unattainable ideal.

In their lack of success as much as in their rise we can see the shared European structures of these revolutions. For it is precisely their national character which led them to undermine each other. There was no institution which could have coordinated the national movements at an international level, in fact quite the contrary. The most fundamental reason for the violent end to all revolutionary protest is probably to be sought here, while its partial success in other fields such as social, economic and constitutional innovation was appropriated and confirmed by 'reactionary forces' after 1849.

But the revolutions of 1848/49 did not only have certain structures and conflicts in common which can rightly be called European. The shared elements go further than that; indeed they go so far that the sum of the single revolutions may – with due caution – also be defined as an overarching European revolution. If Europe was not politically active as a whole, it was certainly affected as a whole. Europe is the point of reference without which the various revolutionary processes cannot be understood. Already before 1848, road-building, railways and telegraphs provided an unbroken network of communication which helped to link the single uprisings like a system of communicating tubes.

What was most innovative about this revolutionary nexus, however, was the fact that the centres of discontent which generated upheavals and escalated into revolutions appeared spontaneously throughout Europe. To be sure, they all had their own causes which were aggravated and articulated within regional, territorial or national contexts. But in all these places, revolution was both spontaneous and genuine. I have argued already that these revolts were characterized by a number of shared European elements. For the first time, then, the revolutions of 1848/49 deserve the name of a great European revolution. As I hope to show, it was also to be the last time.

When we turn to the French Revolution, differences with that of 1848 become readily apparent. The uprising started in Paris from where it spread through France and finally the whole of Europe. As its name indicates to the present day – and rightly so – it was a French revolution which later went out with its armies in order to revolutionize the neighbouring countries and conquer them under the leadership of Napoleon. There was no good intrinsic reason for dissolving the Holy Roman Empire around 1800 and turning it into French satellite states or provinces from Lübeck to Rome. Here the causes for the revolution lay outside the Empire, in Paris first and foremost. The traditional structures of the Empire and the fact that it had been unable to defend itself for some time simply made it possible for them to be effective. The redistribution of political, social and economic power and the processes of secularization and mediatization that it involved were negotiated between Paris and St Petersburg. The new order only broke down when Napoleon also wanted to conquer Russia herself. It is obvious in what ways this revolution differs from that of 1848. In 1848 the revolt springs up directly and spontaneously in many different places. The February revolution in Paris had at most given the signal for the other uprisings, but it was not their cause, to employ this useful distinction first made by Thucydides.

The system of the five hegemonial powers which was established in 1815 remained intact, providing the larger political framework to the events of 1848. Likewise, the single revolutionary events were equally distributed over the major political spaces of Europe which these five powers never failed to influence and police. By contrast with the events that led up to the French Revolution of 1789, which was entirely an internal French affair, those that resulted in the revolution of 1848 took place all over Europe.

The July revolution of 1830 stands somewhere in the middle. It doubtless started in Paris from where the Bourbons were chased away. But its dramatic spread to the east already had intrinsic reasons which can no longer be fully accounted for by what had happened in Paris. The Dutch kingdom fell apart. Belgium was created as a new state with new borders, a process which also involved changes to the western border of the German Federation. In some German federal states the old feudal constitutions were reformed, culminating in the first ever violent expulsion of a German potentate, the Duke of Braunschweig (later in life he was to help Karl Marx with printing costs). Finally, there was the Polish uprising and its brutal suppression. All these dramatic events point to the fact that the seed of the French Revolution had put down roots and was ready to shoot up anywhere in Europe. Not surprisingly, we see the growth of various genuine centres of revolutionary activity in the time that follows. By the 1840s they had already put Europe in a situation of general crisis. In the *north* any liberalization of the Danish constitution involved the question of whether or not Schleswig could be included and Holstein excluded. The aim was to create a unified Danish nation-state without any obligations to the German Federation of which Holstein was a part. As long as Holstein remained with Denmark, Danish involvement with the German Federation was constitutionally inevitable. Civil war and external war – depending on the varying legal status of those involved – were bound to break out and did in fact do so in 1848.

In *Prussia* the *Vereinigter Landtag* (Representational Assembly) had its first meeting in 1847. This institution saw its task in preparing for the much debated constitution which was indeed introduced in the following year. The osmotic borders of the *German Federation* – like those of the old Empire – created problems throughout middle, eastern and southern Europe, problems which partly affected the German Federation, partly the hegemonial powers Prussia and Austria with their possessions outside the Federation. There were uprisings in *Galicia* which were directed against Polish landowners. They were suppressed in 1846, with the additional effect of Austria annexing Cracow. Slavonic minorities threateningly raised their voice in *Bohemia* and *Hungary*, demanding more than merely corporate participation.

These minorities could turn into majorities, depending on the degree of autonomy that was demanded and the geographical boundaries envisaged. We get a similar picture in *Italy* where the traditional dynastic rule of the Bourbons and the Habsburgs was now seen, in the light of nationalism, purely as foreign suppression. There were a number of revolts, and the new pope Pius IX, too, seemed to be aiming for a national and liberal Italy.

Not surprisingly, then, the revolution of 1848 first broke out in southern Italy, in *Palermo* and *Naples*, where constitutions were forced onto the ruling monarchy. From there it spread to France. A trial run for the European revolution had already taken place a year earlier when under the suspicious eyes of all the hegemonial powers civil war broke out in *Switzerland*. It lead to the formation of a constitutional federation. Just as Belgium in 1830 had signalled constitutional change from the north-western corner of the German Federation, there was a new challenge from the south-west in 1847. The signs for change in Europe became clearer and more frequent.

It was not just the shared social and economic challenges of the incipient industrialization and the end of 'feudal rule' which created the problems that – despite differences between town and countryside – were characteristic throughout Europe. Everyone everywhere demanded political and constitutional participation along with a reform of the legislation and the executive, and this shared longing for reform created analogous conflicts in all countries. At the very least, all revolutionary movements of 1848 shared the aim of introducing civil rights and a graded suffrage as a basis for political emancipation and for the formation of political associations and parties – the latter as a first step toward exerting some influence on the newly created parliaments. True, there continued to exist the old scale from west to east as regards the success of liberal policies. Then as before it reached from Great Britain (without Ireland), Belgium and Prussia (including the Customs Union inside the German Federation) to Austria and Russia (France under Napoleon III was the first country to break the pattern). But despite the persistence of the traditional picture, we are now in a position to say that the various uprisings did come into being as one European revolution.

The national movements ended in complete failure. Under the circumstances they could only have been realized as democratic revolutions in the name of a sovereign people. But the European hegemonial powers prevented this from happening in 1849. They intervened at all major trouble spots directly or indirectly, thus safeguarding their interests against any notion of national self-determination. As far as this point was concerned there was agreement in every capital from London to St Petersburg.

However, the revolution of 1848 cannot only be said to be the first European revolution; it was also the last of its kind. For all the civil wars and revolutions which took place in Europe after the middle of the century were confined to single countries or states. No revolution went beyond the political borders that had already existed when it broke out or were created or redrawn in its course. All the later troubles, riots and revolutions remained on a national scale, and they were eventually recast in terms of democratic nationalism. What is more, all the civil wars and revolutions that took place after 1848 were in a political sense the consequences of inter-state wars. Constitutions were not changed any more except as a result of a lost or won war. This can easily be shown by a diachronic overview.

It is not difficult to see a link between the Russian defeat in the *Crimean War* and the waves of liberalization that followed. The abolition of serfdom in 1861 was brought about by the defeat as was the more radical Polish attempt – the last one for the time being – to achieve independence from Russia. When it broke down in 1863 it brought to an end any liberal concessions the Russians had made in the past. Russia suffered her next defeat in the *Japanese War* of 1905. Within the same year a revolution broke out which led to the formation of the first imperial Duma. Finally, the third defeat against Austria-Hungary and Germany in the *First World War* resulted in the February revolution and – with German help – the October revolution of 1917, which in turn was followed by a sequence of bloody civil wars. Their questionable results have been reversed in an equally questionable manner only recently with the end of the Cold War.

The Balkan states, too, came into being in the course of nationalistic wars. These so-called Balkan wars resulted in characteristically artificial borders, which the shrinking Ottoman empire could do nothing but accept. The hegemonial powers were either involved directly or oversaw the process from a distance. The nationally ambiguous and osmotic western, northern, eastern and southern borders of the German Federation were abolished in a similar fashion during the so-called 'wars of unification'. In legal terms, the conflicts of

1864 and 1866 were still civil wars, for the Danish king, who was try-
ing to extend his nation state via Schleswig into Holstein, was both
in terms of state law and in terms of international law as the duke of
Holstein a member of the German Federation; hence the Federation's
right to intervene on the grounds that he had breached the constitution. *De facto*, however, the war was an external one which resulted
in a clear if unjust border – unjust in the national sense – in northern
Schleswig.

The same is true for the war between *Prussia* and *Austria* of 1866.
From the point of view of federal law it was a civil war, fought in the
interest of a reformation of the federal constitution. In reality, however, it was led entirely as a war between two states and as such
resulted in a characteristically sudden and mild peace. Particularly
when compared to the American Civil War, which lasted four years,
this was a 'civilized' not a 'civil' war. Again it was only the consequences of the war which had a revolutionary effect. For the first
time the Customs Union, which was dominated by Prussia, elected a
parliament. The chamber was by no means pro-Prussian. And yet, it
was to become the forerunner of the Prussian-dominated Second
Empire which separated from the Austro-Hungarian monarchy. In
Austria itself the questions which had not been solved in 1849 posed
themselves afresh in 1866. The result was the Austro-Hungarian federation, a political structure with a strong monarchical and minister-
ial head but two parliaments in two countries. This constitution
remained in place for another 50 years until it foundered because it
had failed to integrate the Slavonic peoples into its federal system.

The end of the Austro-Hungarian monarchy led to the creation of
a series of new constitutions with concomitant civil wars, especially
in the remaining core states of Austria and Hungary. Once again, the
revolutionary processes involved came as a direct consequence of the
lost world war. Thanks to the treaties of Paris the successor states
Romania, Poland, Czechoslovakia and *Yugoslavia* could see themselves
as being on the winning side. But having inherited the difficulties of
their multinational predecessor, they were unable to solve them any
more than the double monarchy had done. The problems were particularly glaring in *Czechoslovakia* and *Yugoslavia*, but none of the
new countries managed to see the members of its large national
minorities as belonging to the new nation and sharing its rights.
There was no country where those who had not been equals could be

made equals by way of national democracy. The new nation-states carried the burden they had inherited from the Austrian-Hungarian monarchy without coming any closer to solving the problems. Any revolutionary changes in their constitution resulted from extreme external shocks, especially those of the years 1938 to 1945. The decisive factors were foreign intervention, military defeat and military victory, or any combination of the three. Nowhere was it possible to find internal solutions which would have been specific to one state. Finally, the socialist constitutions, as much as their gruesome German forerunners, were all – apart from Tito's Yugoslavia – imposed by the Bolshevik victors.

A similar picture emerges when we look at southern and western Europe. *Italy* was united and the existing foreign dynasties abolished by revolutions and civil wars in the wake of Mazzini and Garibaldi. The Papal States, too, were destroyed in this way. The breakthrough, however, came with war. Only in alliance with Napoleon III (1859) or Prussia (1866) could the Savoys who had formerly been unsuccessful bring about the dynastic reparcelling of the land which resulted in a constitution for the newly unified state. This development reached its climax with the expulsion of the French troops from Rome in 1870, which came as a direct result of the French defeat at Sedan earlier in the same year. Again we see wars between states bringing about revolutionary changes in constitution.

When the Italian monarchy was turned into a republic in 1946, it too came as a reaction to the defeat against the western powers – a war, that is, not a revolution.

Finally, every single one of the revolutionary changes in constitution which *Germany* and *France* underwent in turn were the result of victory and defeat in the bloody wars they fought against each other. The fall of Napoleon III which was caused by Prussia generated the Third Republic, and the sack of Paris created the situation in which the uprising of the Commune could be drowned in streams of blood. The German revolution of 1918 is almost a mirror image of France in 1871. Again it led to the creation of a republic and a series of civil wars merely as a consequence of the military defeat. Without war no revolution. The tables were turned yet another time in 1940 and again in 1944/5. The Third republic became the state of Vichy which was conquered soon after and gave way to the Fourth Republic. As for the German side, a democratic and a socialist constitution were imposed after the end of the German Reich. All this is entirely the work of military defeats. Here again, both Germany and France testify to the principle: without war no revolution. Indeed, we can go so far as to say that it was the wars, and nothing else, which generated the civil wars, the acts of civic violence and the terror that set in motion and went hand in hand with each revolutionary change in constitution.

These examples may suffice to illustrate the unique character of the revolution of 1848 as a European event. There is nothing like it either before or after. Only toward the middle of the last century did the numerous genuinely independent revolutionary processes that were set off in the single countries converge to form a unique and grand nexus of events. This nexus can indeed be called a European revolution – if not a revolution of Europe. For despite common economic, social and political challenges and conflicts, every single one of the riots, upheavals, civil wars and constitutional reforms played their specific role in the context of the countries in which they occurred. But they did so all at the same time, in parallel fashion and in reaction to one another, so that single factors which may appear to be independent can only be judged properly within their European context. The revolution of 1848 was brought to an end by the intervention of the five hegemonial powers. Prussia and Austria became active as soon as they had suppressed their own revolutions. Russia in the east used military force; England and France in the west resorted to political threats. The rules of foreign policy which had been drawn up in 1815 were rehabilitated. They were to last until the Great War.

What has been said last is not aimed at resuscitating the theoretically absurd quarrel over the question of whether it was primarily external or internal political factors that contributed towards a change in constitution or a war. Both aspects may carry different weight in different circumstances, but they are nevertheless in constant interaction with one another – that is to say, as long as there are states with relatively unlimited sovereignty which hold up the distinction between internal and external affairs. As long as this was the case, it can hardly be surprising that the civil wars and revolutions since 1849 were also primarily limited to the territory of the single states.

We can now formulate a basic scheme of events for the last 200 years. The French Revolution stood at the beginning. In its name and in its wake there came 23 years of war, with consequences for the whole of Europe which were certainly revolutionary. In the middle of the nineteenth century we find something like a balance between spontaneous and genuine civil wars and inter-state wars. Civil wars and revolutions spread over almost all the countries and states of central Europe, each in their context and all at once. Where the revolutions resulted in war – as for example in Denmark, Italy and Hungary – they were brought to an end by the prevailing powers and with the conventional means of diplomacy or warfare. For the time being the *status quo ante* had been reaffirmed with gunshots, and yet the European revolution remained the primary context of events, a revolution which in its intensity and cumulative character was to remain *sui generis*.

After the European revolution of 1848, more and more states more or less successfully took shape as nation-states. As a result, violent constitutional *coups d'état*, civil wars and revolutions could only come about in the aftermath of inter-state wars. This does not say much about the social or economic conditions of the events in question, for they could lie far beyond the reach of a single state. But it is clear that the larger political and international constellation remained stable enough so that only shifts in the power-relations between the states could open a path to internal change; they were the catastrophes of our century.

As for the later development, we might add that after 1918 the Bolshevistic and fascistic coups, as well as their fascistoid and otherwise violent varieties, have led to another almost pan-European constellation. The fascistic regimes of southern and eastern Europe can still be seen as a result of the defeats or victories of 1918; the same is true for the gradual and semi-legal changes that were made to the German constitution under the National Socialists from 1933 to the beginning of the war. At the same time, however, these developments defy a unilinear explanation. They rather produced a new type of constitutional change which was linked with certain states and peoples who in turn developed revolutionary activity beyond mere revolutionary rhetoric. From Moscow to Madrid they all shared a national and social motivation to varying degrees. The Spanish Civil War, as well as standing in the ancient tradition of inner-Iberian conflict, was at the same time a civil war and an international war with three intervening foreign powers – Italy, Germany and the USSR – which had the half-hearted support of the two western powers. It thus becomes a symbol for the newly emerged phase of transition. Since then the boundaries between war and civil war have been blurred, and the end of the Second World War has done nothing to change this trend. A single glance at the border regions of Europe and beyond them to the rest of the globe reminds us daily of the fatal truth of this point.

In 1939 Germany started leading its war against Poland which later escalated into the Second World War with the methods of a brutal civil war. Having been defined as subhuman, the enemy was terrorized, killed and wiped out on a grand scale. This was aimed first of all against the Jews. The Slavonic peoples were to follow.

Since then our heuristic distinction between a war that brings about a revolution and a revolution that results in a war has lost much of its analytic force. Throughout the last decade civil wars have once more been unleashed in the remoter parts of Europe with the illusionary aim of creating democratically homogeneous nation-states. They are gruesome civil wars which masquerade as wars of state foundation, to be seen in the states which succeeded the former Yugoslavia as well as in those states which have sprung from the former Soviet federation of the USSR.

Europe on the other hand is for the first time building federal structures in an attempt to contain and channel the national democratic forces which have so far led to civil wars and wars. From a historical point of view it is the Europe which in 1848/49 for the first and last time started off and underwent a shared revolution. All subsequent revolutions were the result of nationalistic inter-state wars. Perhaps this is a good reason for reminding ourselves of the common aims and conflicts of the revolution of 1848.

Index

Diana, Princess of Wales, 168
Dossenbach, 190
Dresden, 58, 69, 75 f
Dufour, Henri, 60
Dupont, Pierre, 86, 88, 93, 95, 97

Ebert, Friedrich, 192
economic developments, 9, 36 f,
    46, 55, 62, 88, 107 f, 114–16,
    149, 157, 167, 192, 194 f,
    210 f, 215
Edict of Nantes, 165
Egypt, 93
Einaudi, Luigi, 154
Elizabeth, Queen of Great Britain,
    178 f
Engels, Friedrich, 14, 133 f, 157, 159,
    175, 199 f
England, *see* Great Britain
ethnicity, 13, 37, 57, 64, 96, 108,
    110 f, 114, 117, 119, 127
Europe, concepts of, 5 f, 7–17, 20 f,
    88 f, 93–6
European Democratic Committee,
    see democrats
European integration, 12, 20, 21,
    145 f, 196, 201 f
exile, 8, 16, 77, 87, 187, 195, 211

Fabius, Laurent, 21, 165
fascism, 145, 153 f, 167, 174, 220;
    see also Germany, national
    socialism; Spain, Civil War
Ferrari, Giuseppe, 153
Fessenheim, 198
Festeau, Louis, 94 f
feudalism, 9, 211, 215; *see also*
    corvée
Fichte, Johann Gottlieb, 108
Flaubert, Gustave, 55, 170
Florence, 144, 150
France, 8–10, 14–18, 21, 32–5, 38 f,
    44–6, 54, 65, 67, 75, 85–105,
    109, 112 f, 116, 144, 164–79,
    185–8, 193, 196, 198 f, 201,
    209–12, 215, 218 f

Ancien Régime, 173
July Monarchy, *see* France,
    Revolution of 1830
Resistance, 168, 176; *see also* Vichy
Revolution of 1789, 8 f, 13, 18 f, 32,
    34, 41, 52–4, 59, 62, 91–6, 100,
    165, 169–74, 188 f, 212 f, 219 f
Revolution of 1830, 8, 32, 50, 53,
    95, 100, 169 f, 174–8, 214
Francophilism, 32
Frankfurt, 14, 66, 72, 76, 85, 191,
    200 f; *see also* Frankfurt
    Parliament
Frankfurt Parliament, 8, 12, 14–16,
    19 f, 56, 59, 66, 85, 95, 98, 106,
    112, 116–18, 125, 127–30, 135,
    191–3, 196 f, 199, 201
Franz Joseph I, Emperor of Austria, 57
Freiburg (Breisgau), 189, 196
Freiburg (CH), 60
Freiligrath, Ferdinand, 8
Freytag, Gustav, 58
Frič, Josef Václav, 130
Friedrich Wilhelm IV, King of
    Prussia, 33 f
Friedrich, Grand Duke of Baden,
    106, 200
Fröbel, Julius, 16, 111

Gagern, Friedrich von, 114
Gagern, Heinrich von, 114
Galicia, 13, 214
Garibaldi, Giuseppe, 150, 153 f, 218
Gasperi, Alcide de, 157
Gaulle, Charles de, 165, 176 f
Gaulle, Pierre de, 174, 177
Gaullism, *see* Gaulle, Charles de
gender, 10, 17, 40, 46, 51, 64–78, 90,
    174, 189 f
generational conflict, 168;
    see also 1968
Genoux, Claude, 95
Germany, 5, 8 f, 16, 18 f, 31–3, 38 f,
    44–6, 53, 57–9, 75, 77, 85–8, 94 f,
    106–19, 125, 127, 135, 151, 157,
    185–202, 210, 212–16, 220 f